BIG BOOK OF BOXES
LE GRAND LIVRE DES BOÎTES
DAS GROSSE BUCH DER VERPACKUNGEN

BIG BOOK OF BOXES
LE GRAND LIVRE DES BOÎTES
DAS GROSSE BUCH DER VERPACKUNGEN

evergreen

© 2009 EVERGREEN GmbH, Köln

Publisher: Paco Asensio

Editorial coordination: Anja Llorella Oriol

Illustrations and texts: Thais Caballero

Text editing: Cristian Campos

Translations and proof-reading: Cillero & de Motta

Graphic design and layout: Emma Termes Parera

Printed in Spain

ISBN 978-3-8365-1713-3

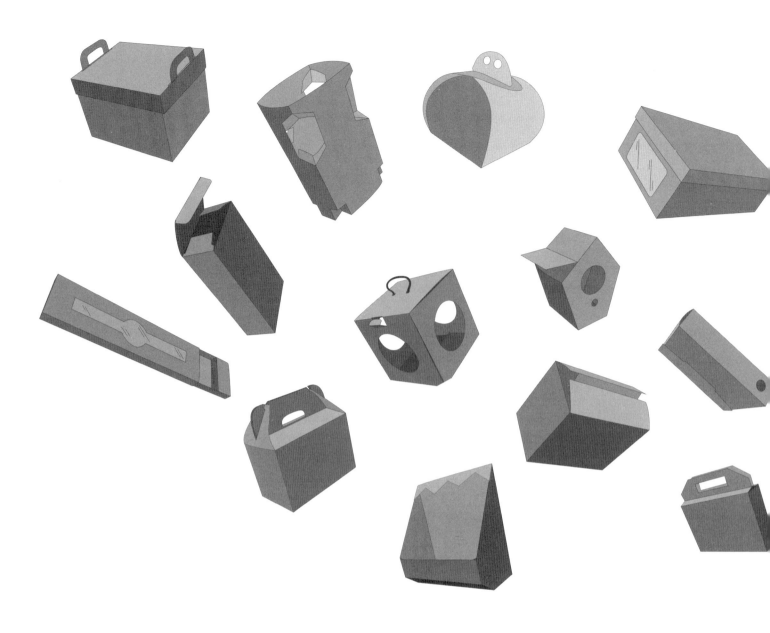

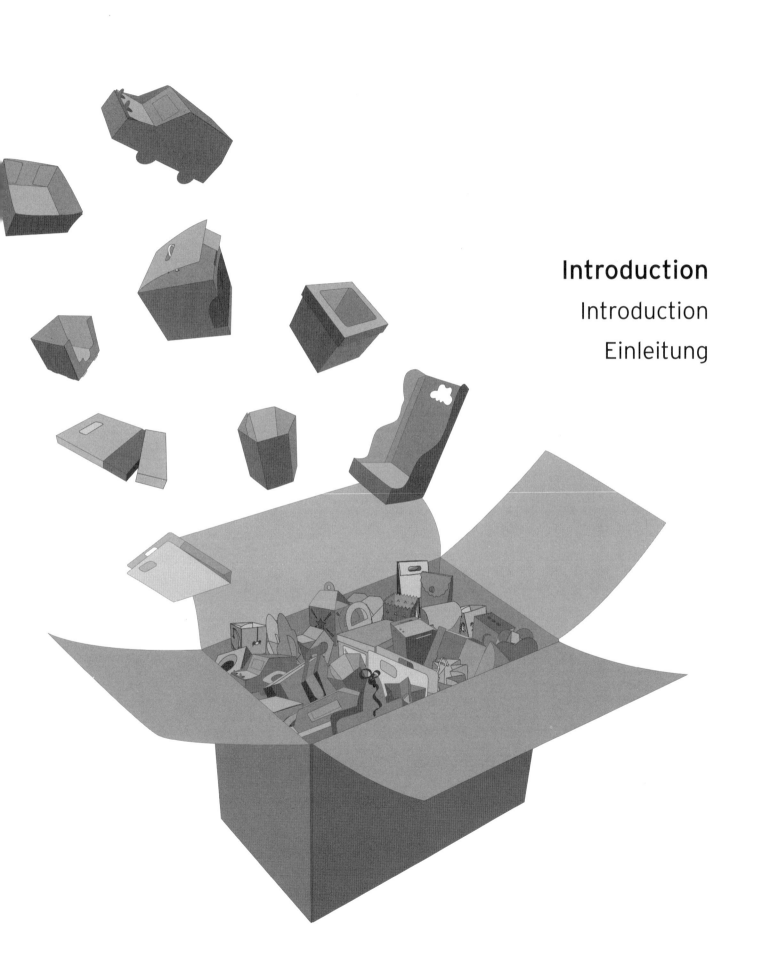

Introduction

Introduction

Einleitung

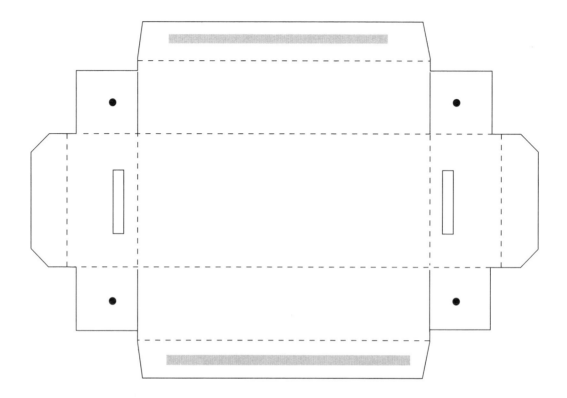

Dot of glue: put adhesive • Point de colle : mettre de la colle •
Leimpunkt: Kleber auftragen

– – – Discontinued lines: fold here • Lignes discontinues : plier ici •
Gestrichelte Linien: Hier falten

——— Continuous lines: cut here • Lignes continues : couper ici •
Durchgezogene Linien: Hier schneiden

● (·) Black dot: use adhesive tape • (·) Point noir : utiliser les bandes
adhésives • (·) Schwarzer Punkt: Klebeband verwenden

✳ (*) Asterisk: sticking elements tape, string, staples, etc.
(*) Astérisque : eléments d'union spéciaux : rubans, cordes, agrafes…
(*) Stern: Besondere Verbindungselemente: Bänder, Seile, Klemmen…

Everyone knows the problem: over the years, objects and mementoes pile up to the extent that in the end there are only two solutions: throw out or sort out. This book has thrown itself wholeheartedly behind the second alternative, offering the reader not only practical, but also creative and original ideas on how to maintain order in the office or home on a sustainable basis. Alongside boxes, crates, folders, box-files, shelves, pen-and-pencil holders and magazine racks, there are suggestions for unusual containers suitable for Christmas, Easter or other festive occasions.

Each packaging idea comes with detailed instructions, showing where to fold, cut and glue, along with a perspective drawing informing the reader what the finished article should look like. All the instructions can be copied from the book, enlarged or reduced as required, or they can be printed out from the accompanying CD.

All the plans and models are intended to be reproduced without difficulty, but of course, depending on inclination and purpose, they can be adapted as the reader sees fit, by, for example, using coloured, patterned, marbled or textured paper, or varying the weight of the paper or cardboard. Many of the packages illustrated here need no adhesive, but are simply folded together and held in place by a tape or ribbon. This variant is not just particularly pleasant when it comes to putting the item together, but also extremely creative, giving each box a personal touch. All that needs to be kept in mind is that different thicknesses of material may require modifications to the pattern.

This reference and pattern book offers readers 300 attractive packaging solutions, with snappy ideas either to bring additional order into their lives, or for creating all kinds of individual models for gift occasions of all kinds.

Chacun connaît bien le même problème. Au fil du temps, objets et souvenirs divers s'accumulent tant et si bien qu'il ne reste plus que deux solutions : les jeter ou les trier. Cet ouvrage opte clairement pour la seconde alternative et propose au lecteur des idées non seulement pratiques, mais aussi ingénieuses et originales, afin de mettre durablement de l'ordre au bureau comme à la maison. A côté des boîtes, caisses, classeurs, dossiers, pots à crayons et porte-revues sont présentés d'insolites coffrets et écrins pour Noël, Pâques ou autres occasions de fêtes.

Chaque emballage est accompagné d'une description détaillée, indiquant les lignes de pliure et de découpage ainsi que les collures, et d'un croquis en perspective, pour que le lecteur se fasse une idée du résultat final. Toutes les instructions peuvent être soit photocopiées et leur format agrandi ou réduit à volonté, soit imprimées à partir du CD.

Tous les schémas et modèles sont conçus en vue d'un assemblage facile, mais ils peuvent être modifiés, selon l'utilisation qui va en être faite, et être fabriqués à base de papier en couleur, d'imprimés ou de textures spéciales, ou bien encore d'un grammage différent de carton ou de papier. De nombreux emballages proposés ici ne sont pas collés, mais ajustés et fermés d'un ruban. Cette variante ne facilite pas seulement l'assemblage, mais stimule la créativité en conférant à chaque boîte une note personnelle. Il suffit seulement de veiller à ce que, en cas de modification, les modèles soient bien adaptés au nouveau grammage du carton.

Cet ouvrage de référence, riche en illustrations, offre au lecteur 300 possibilités séduisantes d'emballages, qu'il s'agisse de remettre de l'ordre dans sa vie avec astuce ou de créer des modèles uniques de cadeaux de toutes sortes.

Jeder kennt das Problem, dass sich im Laufe der Zeit Gegenstände und Erinnerungsstücke derart anhäufen, dass sich nur zwei Lösungsmöglichkeiten anbieten: wegwerfen oder sortieren. Dieses Buch hat sich eindeutig für die zweite Alternative entschieden und bietet dem Leser nicht nur praktische, sondern auch kreative und originelle Ideen, wie man nachhaltig Ordnung im Büro, aber auch zu Hause halten kann. Neben Kisten, Kästen, Archivmappen, Stehordnern, Ablagen, Stiftebechern und Zeitungsständern werden ausgefallene Boxen und Schachteln für Weihnachten, Ostern oder sonstige festliche Anlässe vorgestellt.

Jeder Behälter wird mit einer detaillierten Anleitung, die die Falz- und Schnittlinien, aber auch die Klebestellen aufzeigt, und einer perspektivischen Zeichnung dargestellt, damit der Leser weiß, wie der Gegenstand nach seiner Herstellung aussehen soll. Alle Anleitungen lassen sich entweder aus dem Buch kopieren und beliebig vergrößern oder verkleinern, oder aber mit Hilfe der CD nach Wunsch ausdrucken.

Alle Vorlagen und Modelle sind für den einfachen Nachbau gedacht, lassen sich aber natürlich je nach Absicht in jeder Hinsicht verändern, indem man beispielsweise farbige, mit Mustern bedruckte oder speziell marmorierte und texturierte Papiere verwendet oder die Grammatur des Kartons bzw. Papiers variiert. Eine ganze Reihe der hier abgebildeten Behälter wird nicht geklebt, sondern zusammengesteckt und mit einem Band verschlossen. Diese Variante ist nicht nur eine besonders angenehme, was den Zusammenbau betrifft, sondern auch eine äußerst kreative, verleiht sie doch jeder Box eine persönliche Note. Man muss lediglich beachten, dass die Vorlagen bei Modifikationen in den Kartonstärken angepasst werden müssen.

Dieses Nachschlage- und Vorlagenbuch bietet dem Leser 300 attraktive Verpackungslösungen, sei es um mit pfiffigen Ideen zusätzliche Ordnung in sein Leben zu bringen oder um besonders individuelle Modelle für Geschenkanlässe jeder Art zu kreieren.

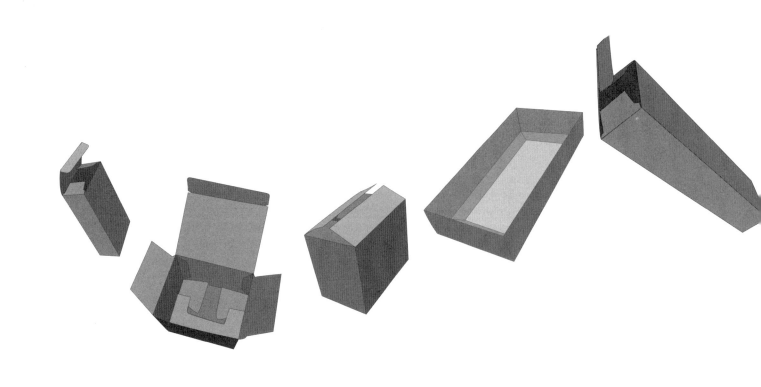

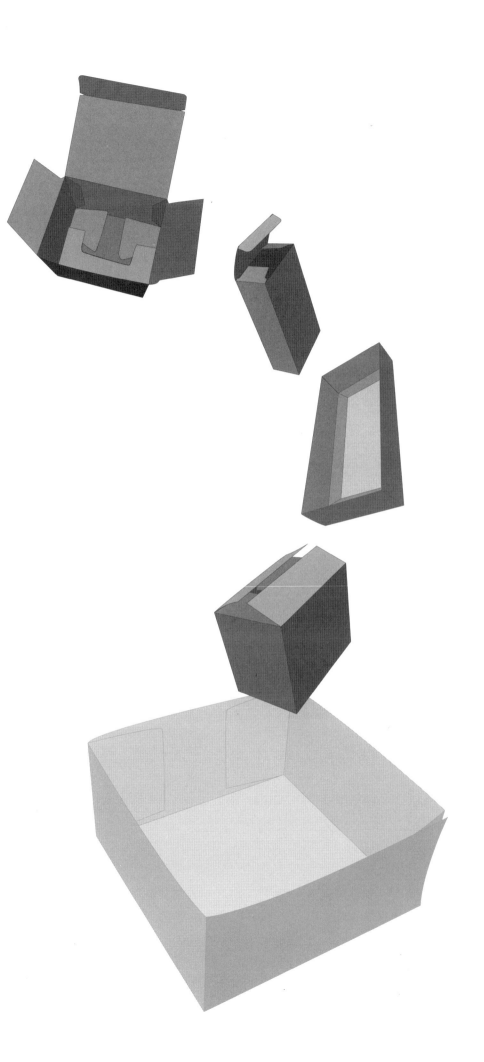

Basic models

Modèles de base

Grundmodelle

Modelos básicos

Modelli base

Modelos básicos

Basismodellen

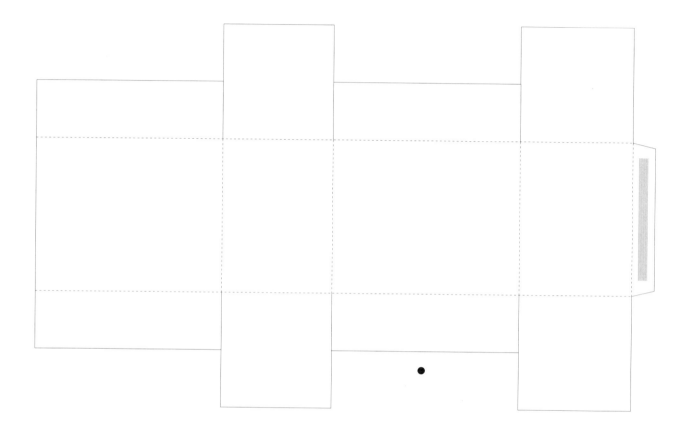

Basic box with flaps · Carton d'emballage · Box mit Laschen · Caja básica con solapas · Scatola base con alette · Caixa básica com abas · Basisdoos met flappen

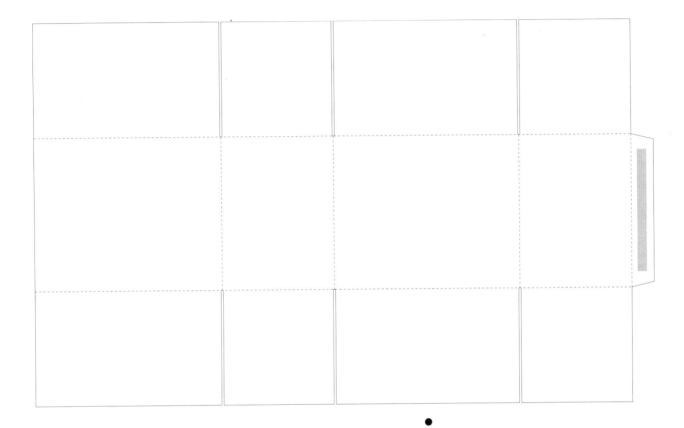

Basic box with superimposed flaps · Carton d'emballage avec languettes superposées · Box mit überlappenden Laschen · Caja básica con solapas superpuestas · Scatola base con alette sovrapposte · Caixa básica com abas sobrepostas · Basisdoos met over elkaar sluitende flappen

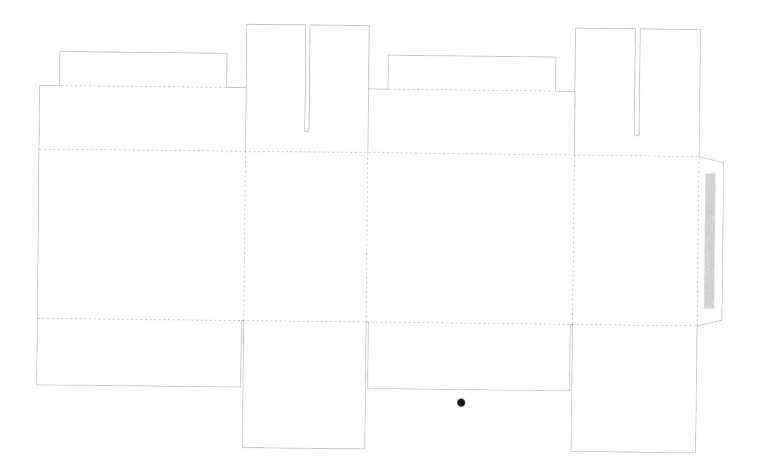

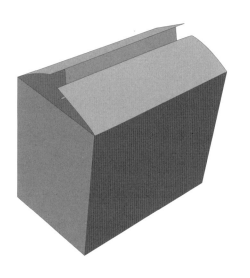

Basic box with flap and divided main closure • Carton d'emballage avec languettes et séparation centrale • Box mit Lasche und unterteilendem Verschluss in der Mitte • Caja básica con solapa y cierre central separador • Scatola base con aletta e chiusura centrale divisoria • Caixa básica com aba e fecho central separador • Basisdoos met flappen en scheidingssluiting in het midden

Basic box with inverted flaps • Carton d'emballage avec languettes inversées • Schachtel mit versetzten Laschen • Caja básica con solapas invertidas • Scatola base con alette invertite • Caixa básica com abas invertidas • Basisdoos met tweezijdige flappen

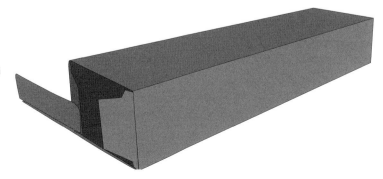

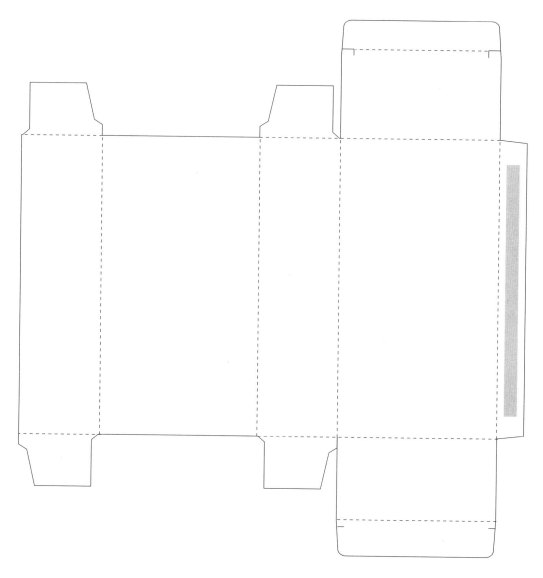

Basic box with joining flaps · Carton d'emballage avec languettes
alignées · Box mit gegenüberliegenden Laschen · Caja básica con solapas
alineadas · Scatola base con alette allineate · Caixa básica com abas
alinhadas · Basisdoos met flappen

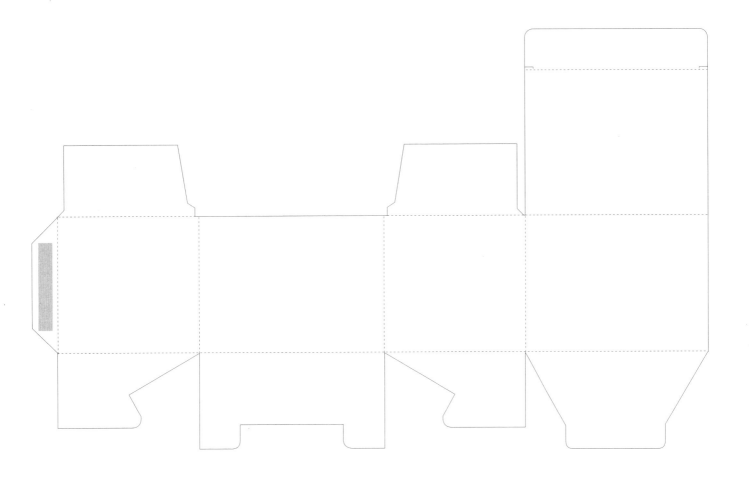

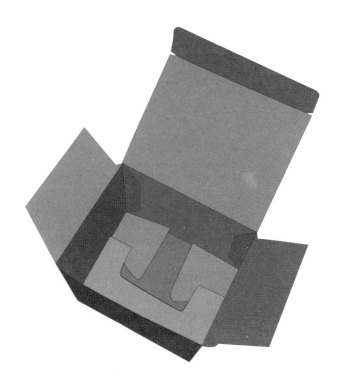

Basic box with T-shaped closure • Carton d'emballage avec fermeture en T • Box mit T-Verschluss • Caja básica con cierre en T • Scatola base con chiusura a T • Caixa básica com fecho em T • Basisdoos met T-sluiting

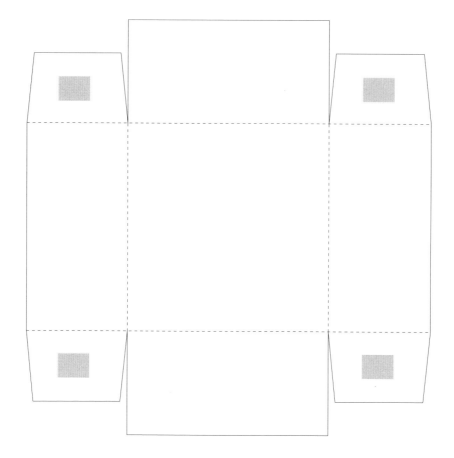

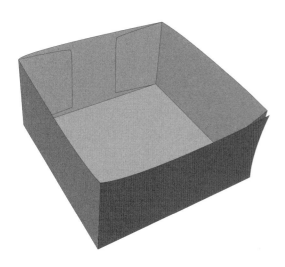

Basic tray • Caisse • Ablage • Bandeja básica • Vaschetta base • Bandeja básica • Basisbakje

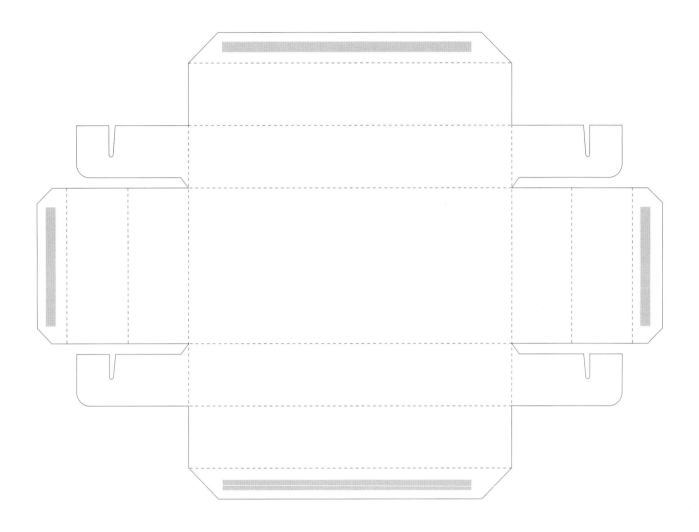

Basic tray with strap closure • Carton avec languettes de
fermeture • Box mit Einstecklaschen • Caja básica con cierre
de tiras • Scatola base con chiusura a legacci • Caixa básica
com fecho de tiras • Basisdoos met lipsluiting

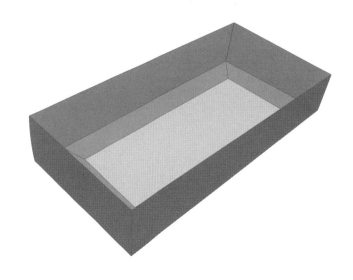

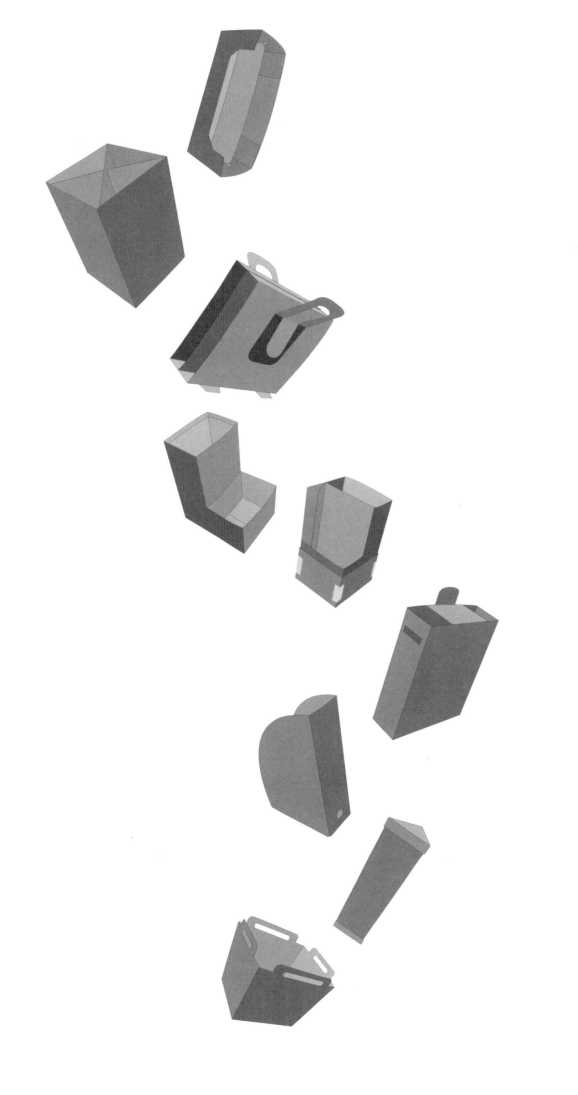

Boxes for the office

Boîtes pour le bureau

Boxen fürs Büro

Cajas para la oficina

Scatole per l'ufficio

Caixas para o escritório

Dozen voor kantoor

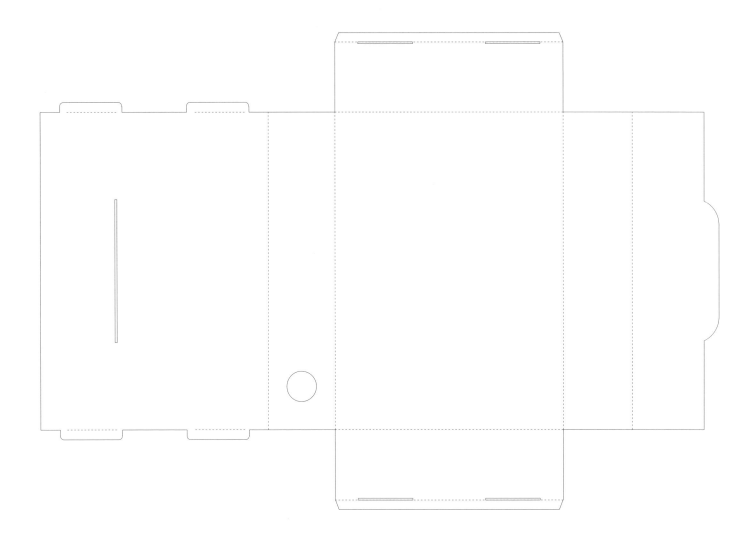

Self-assembly file with envelope closure • Boîte archives dépliable avec fermeture façon enveloppe • Ordner mit Umschlagverschluss zum Zusammenstecken • Archivador automontable con cierre de sobre • Scatola archivio automontante con chiusura a busta • Arquivador automontável com fecho de envelope • Zelfbouw archiefmap met envelopsluiting

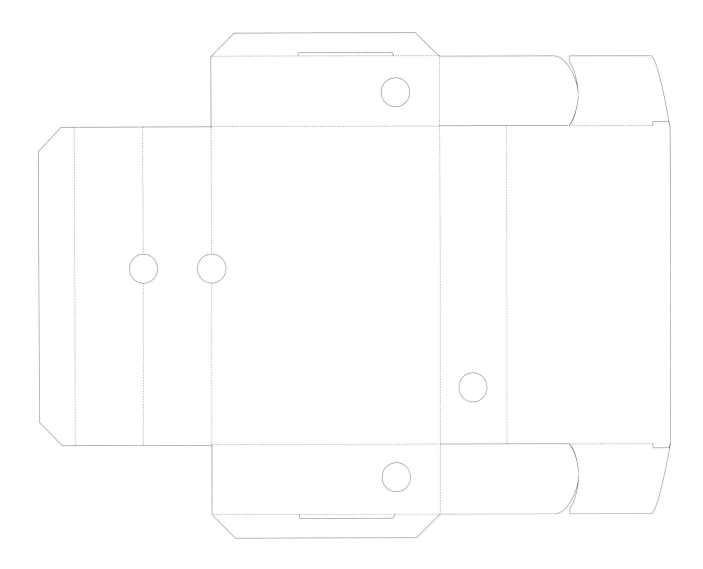

Self-assembly file box with window and flap closure • Boîte archives dépliable avec fenêtre et fermeture à rabat • Archivbox mit Fenster und Laschenverschluss zum Zusammenstecken • Caja archivadora automontable con ventana y cierre de solapa • Scatola archivio automontante con finestrella e chiusura ad aletta • Caixa arquivadora automontável com janela e fecho de aba • Zelfbouw archiefdoos met venster en flapsluiting

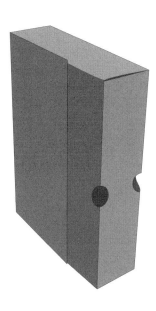

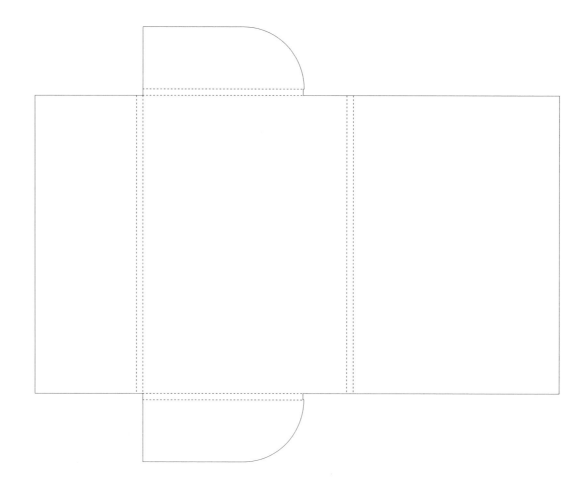

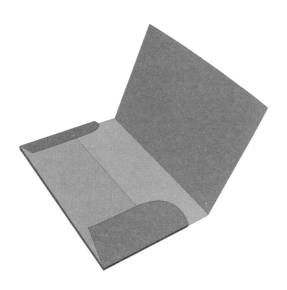

Self-assembly document-holder folder • Chemise
porte-documents dépliable • Dokumentenmappe zum
Zusammenstecken • Carpeta portadocumentos automontable •
Cartella portadocumenti automontante • Pasta porta-documentos
automontável • Zelfbouw schrijf- en dossiermap

Self-assembly document-holder with biased sides and die cut handle · Porte-documents dépliable avec rebords partiels et poignée évidée · Dokumentenmappe zum Zusammenstecken mit verkürzten Seitenteilen und ausgestanztem Griff · Portadocumentos automontable con laterales parciales y asa troquelada · Portadocumenti automontante con bordi parziali e maniglia fustellata · Porta-documentos automontável com laterais parciais e asa cunhada · Zelfbouw dossiermappen met zijflappen en gestanste handgreep

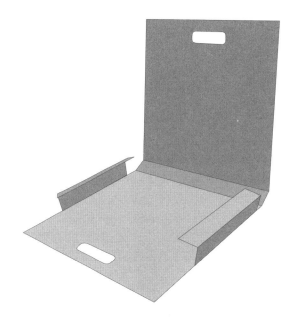

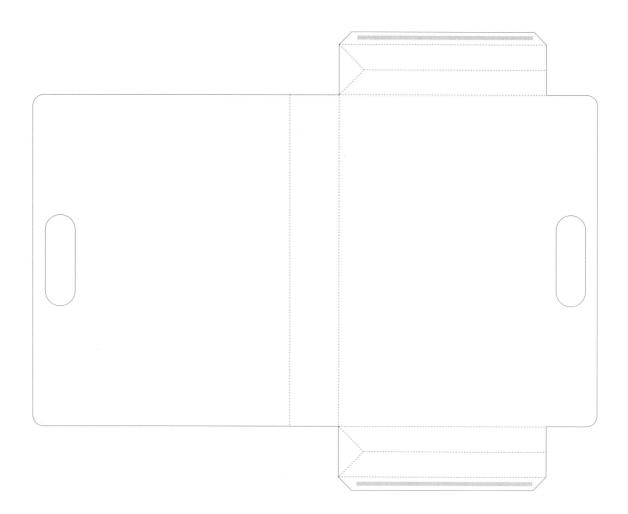

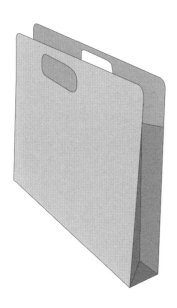

Document-holder with gusseted sides and die cut handle • Porte-documents avec soufflés latéraux et poignée évidée • Dokumentenmappe mit Seitenfalten und ausgestanztem Griff • Portadocumentos con fuelles laterales y asa troquelada • Portadocumenti con soffietti laterali e maniglia fustellata • Porta-documentos com foles laterais e asa cunhada • Dossiermappen met zijvouwen en gestanste handgreep

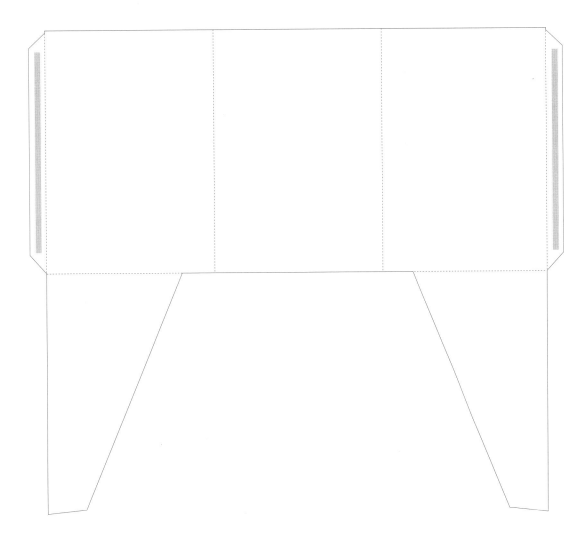

File with double side pockets • Chemise classeur avec double poche latérale • Dokumentenmappe mit seitlichen Einstecklaschen • Carpeta archivadora con bolsillos dobles laterales • Cartella archivio con doppie lunette laterali • Pasta arquivadora com bolsas duplas laterais • Archiefmap met dubbele zijvakjes

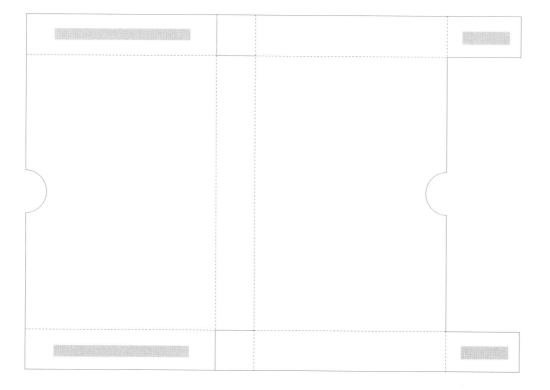

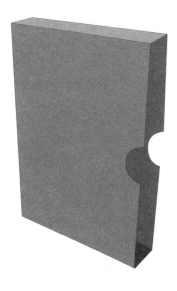

Book cover • Couverture de livre • Buchhülle • Funda para libro • Astuccio per libro • Capa para livro • Hoes voor boek

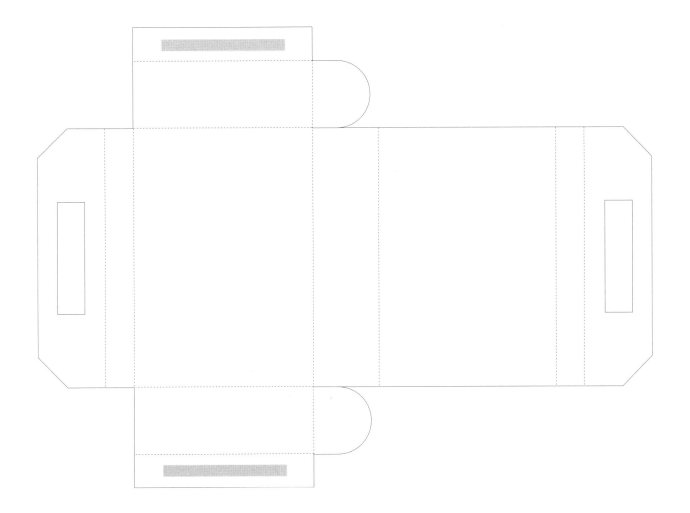

Fixed width self-assembly briefcase • Malette dépliable à poignée fixe • Handkoffer zum Zusammenstecken • Maletín automontable de ancho fijo • Valigetta automontante a larghezza fissa • Pasta automontável de largura fixa • Zelfbouw aktetas met een vaste breedte

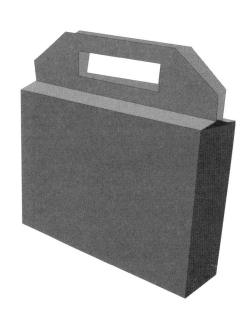

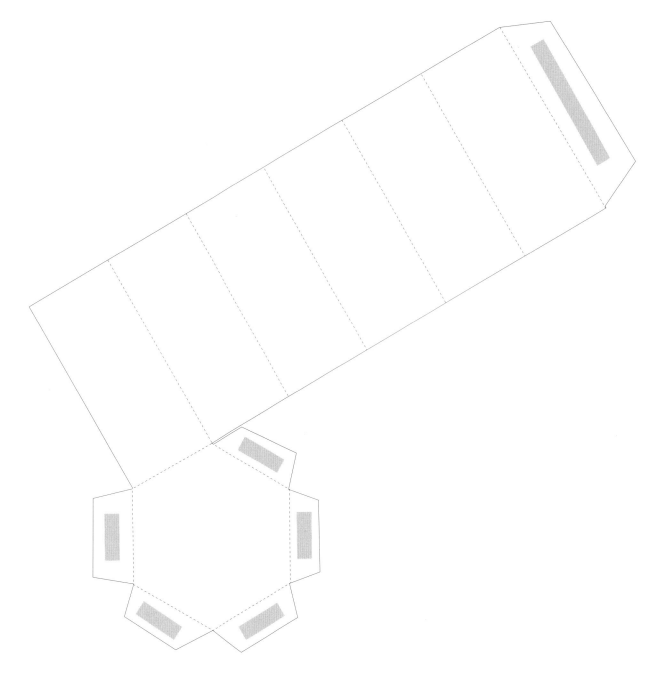

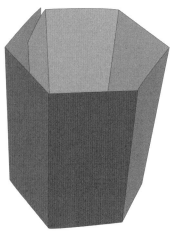

Hexagonal-based pencil holder • Pot à crayon à base hexagonale • Sechseckiger Stiftebecher • Cubilete para lápices, de base hexagonal • Portamatite a base esagonale • Estojo para lápis de base hexagonal • Zeshoekig potloodbakje

**Wall-mounted document holder box with gusseted
sides** • Boîte porte-documents à suspendre, avec soufflé •
Hängende Dokumentenmappe mit Seitenfalten • Caja colgante
portadocumentos, con fuelle • Scatola portadocumenti sospesa
con soffietto • Caixa de pendurar porta-documentos com
fole • Hangdoos dossiermappen, met vouwflap

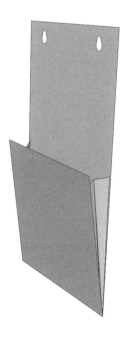

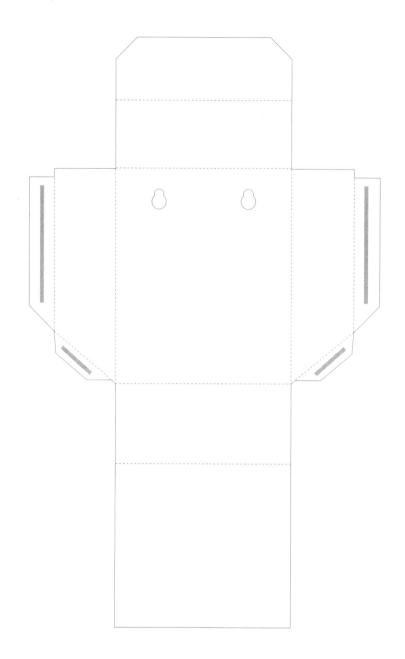

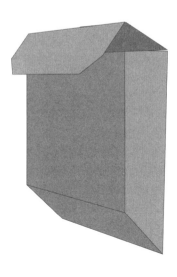

Wall-mounted document holder with lid • Boîte porte-documents à suspendre, avec rabat supérieur • Hängende Aktenbox mit Deckel • Caja colgante portadocumentos, con tapa • Scatola portadocumenti sospesa con coperchio • Caixa de pendurar porta-documentos com tampa • Doos voor dossiermappen om aan de wand te hangen, met deksel

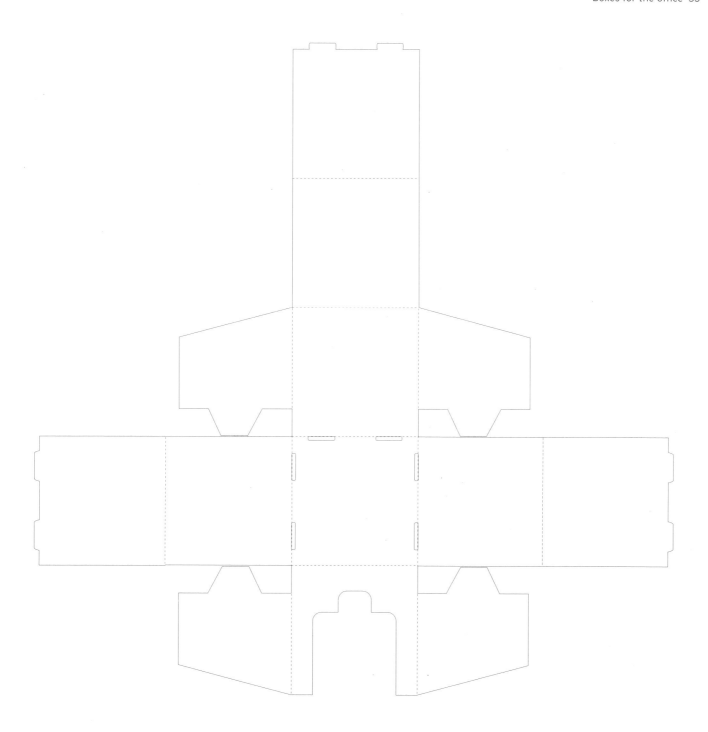

Box for Post-it notes with die cut front dispenser • Boîtes à bloc-notes avec orifice de distribution à l'avant • Notizzettelbox mit ausgestanztem Spenderteil • Caja para tacos de notas, con troquel dispensador frontal • Scatola per foglietti notes con dispenser frontale • Caixa para bloco de notas com cunha dispensadora frontal • Doos voor post-its, met opening aan de voorzijde

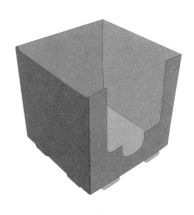

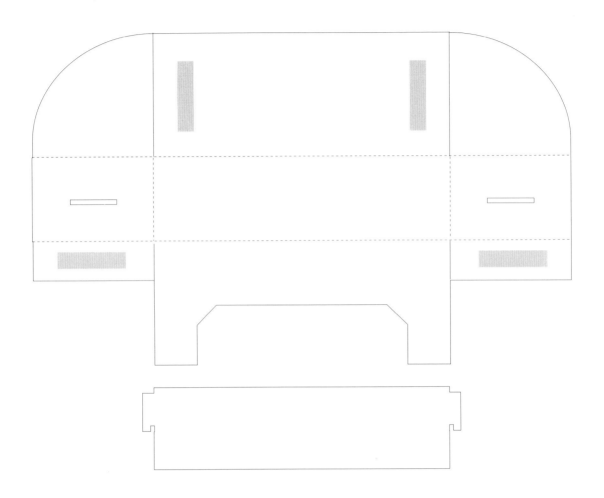

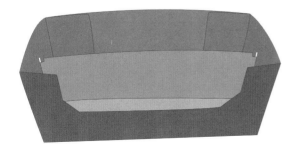

Two-compartment mail box • Porte-courrier à deux compartiments • Briefbox mit zwei Fächern • Caja para correspondencia, con dos compartimentos • Portacorrispondenza a due scomparti • Caixa para correspondência com dois compartimentos • Doos voor correspondentie, met twee vakken

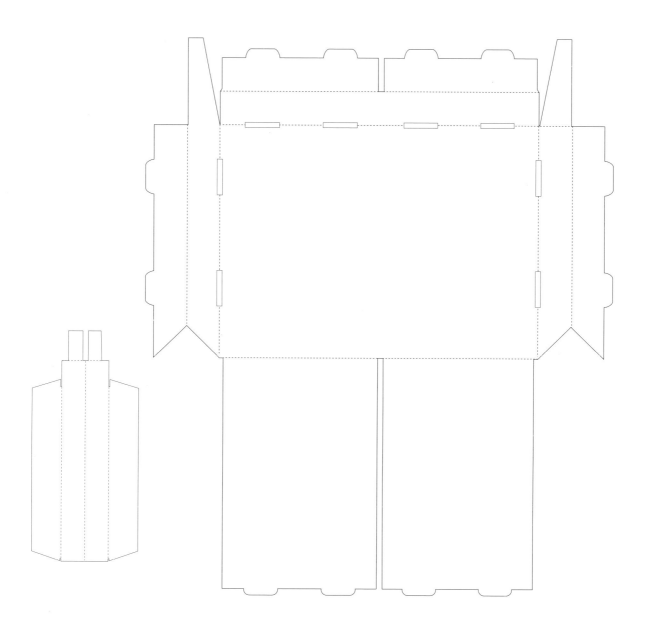

Two-compartment paper tray • Porte-papier à deux compartiments • Papierablage mit zwei Fächern • Bandeja para papel, con dos compartimentos • Vaschetta per documenti a due scomparti • Bandeja para papel com dois compartimentos • Opbergdoos voor papier, met twee vakken

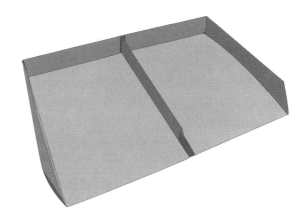

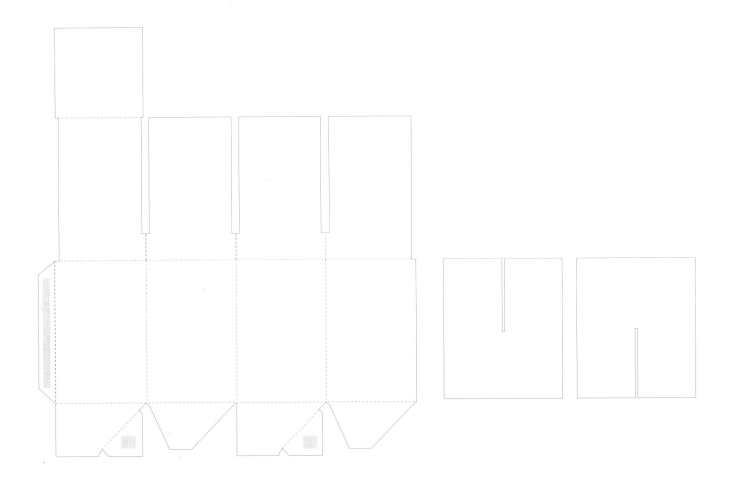

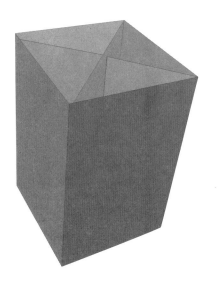

Pencil holder with interior triangular compartments · Pot à crayon avec compartiments intérieurs triangulaires · Stiftebecher mit dreieckigen Innenfächern · Cubilete para lápices, con compartimentos interiores triangulares · Portamatite con scomparti interni triangolari · Estojo para lápis com compartimentos interiores triangulares · Bakje voor potloden, met driehoekige binnenvakjes

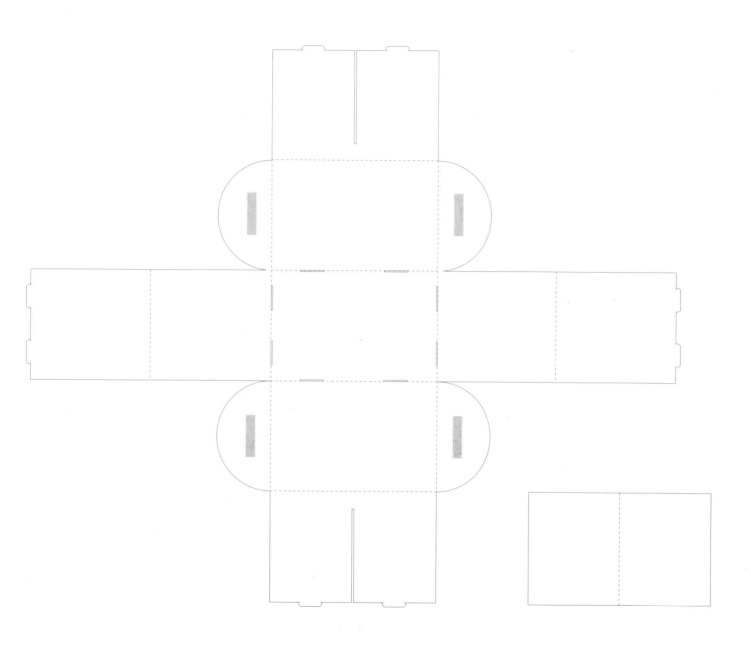

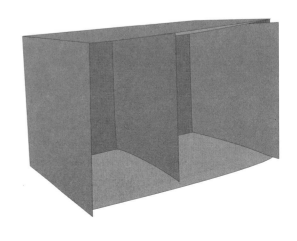

CD box with divider • Porte-CD avec séparateur • CD-Box mit
Unterteilung • Caja para CD con separador • Scatola per CD
con divisorio • Caixa para CD's com separador • Doos voor cd's,
met twee vakken

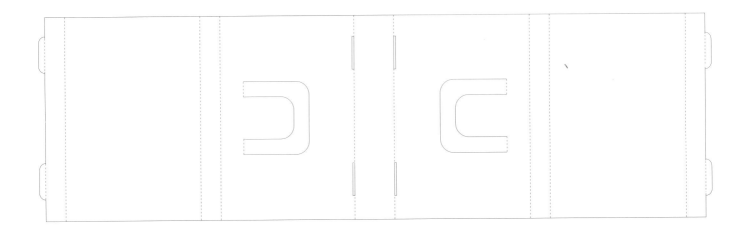

Box for two books with normal spine and handle • Malette pour deux livres, avec tranche commune et poignée • Handkoffer mit Griff für zwei Bücher • Maletín para dos libros, con lomo común y asa • Valigetta per due libri con dorso comune e maniglia • Capa para dois livros com lombada normal e asa • Aktetas voor twee boeken, met gewone rug en hengsel

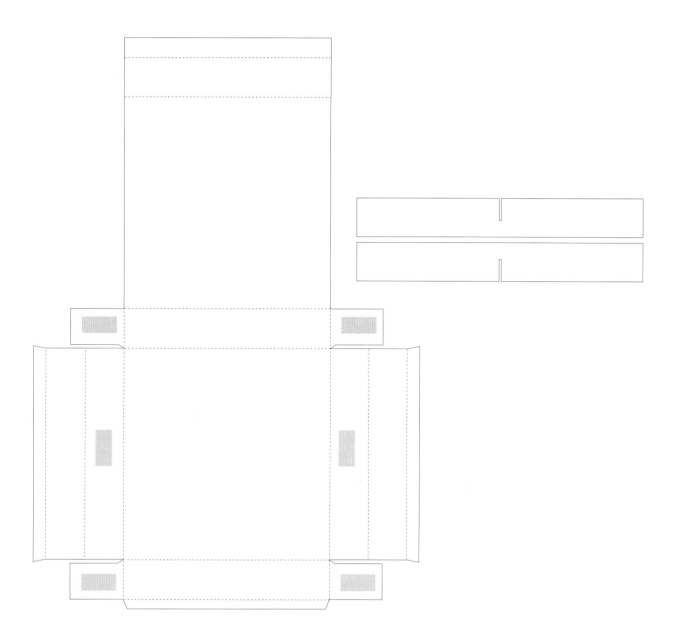

Four-compartment box for storing writing material with lift up lid and button closure • Coffret quatre compartiments pour fourniture de bureau, avec couvercle à bascule et fermeture clic clac • Schachtel mit vier Fächern, Klappdeckel und Klickverschluss für Schreibutensilien • Caja de cuatro compartimentos para material de escritorio, con tapa basculante y cierre clic • Scatola per cancelleria a quattro scomparti, con coperchio basculante e chiusura a bottone • Caixa de quatro compartimentos para material de escritório, com tampa móvel e fecho clic • Doos met vier vakken voor schrijfmateriaal, met kanteldeksel en kliksluiting

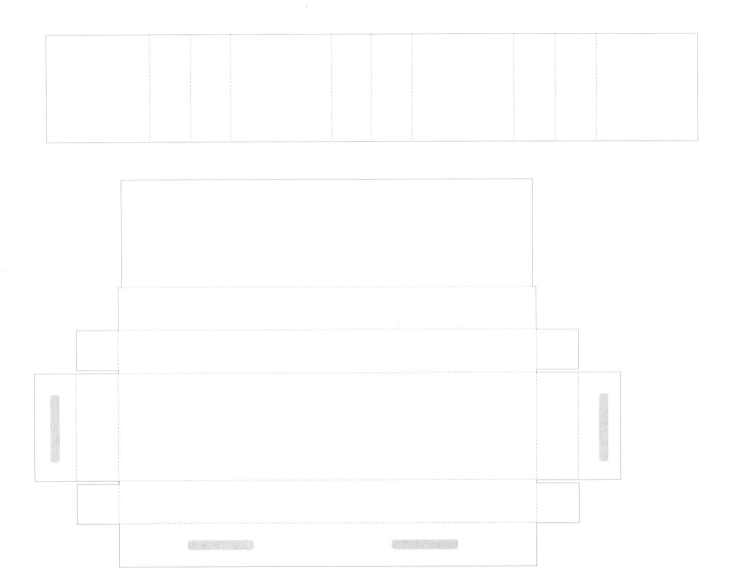

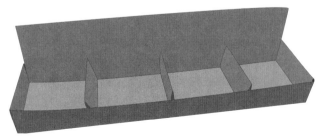

Desk box with four compartments • Plateau de rangement avec quatre compartiments • Schreibtischablage mit vier Fächern • Caja de sobremesa con cuatro compartimentos • Vaschetta portacorrispondenza con quattro dispenser • Caixa de secretária com quatro compartimentos • Bakje voor op tafel met sorteervakjes

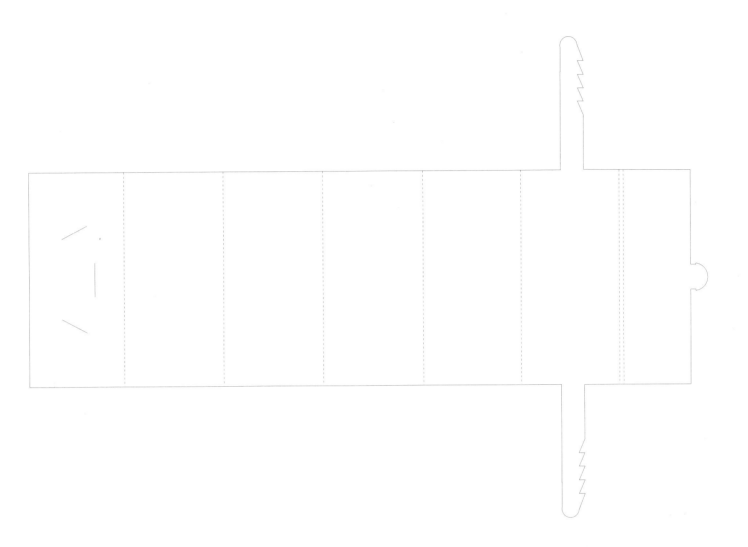

Invoice folder with accordion gusset • Chemise classeur
pour factures, avec soufflé accordéon • Rechnungsordner mit
Seitenfalten • Carpeta clasificadora para facturas, con fuelle
de acordeón • Cartella per archiviazione fatture, con soffietto
a fisarmonica • Pasta classificadora para facturas, com fole de
acordeão • Sorteermap voor facturen, met harmonicavouw

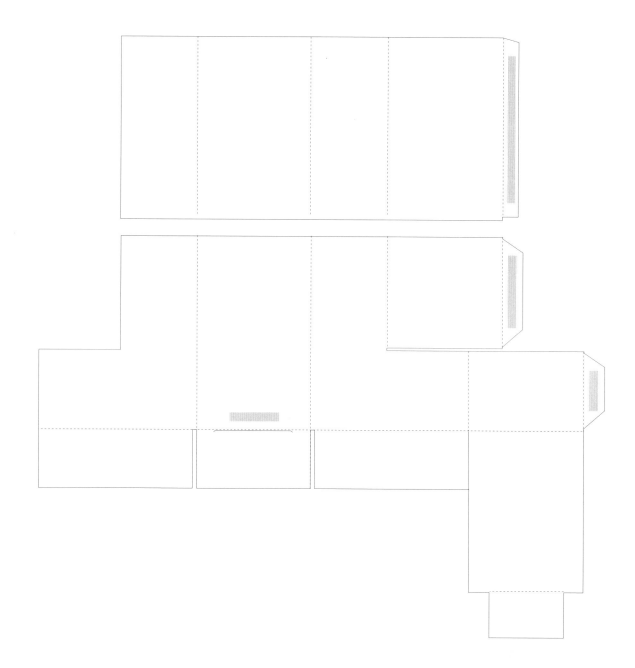

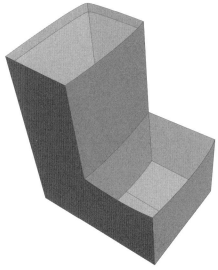

**Pencil and paperclip holder. Model 1 with reinforced
sides** • Pot à crayon pour stylos et trombones. Modèle 1 avec
intérieur renforcé • Becher für Stifte und Büroklammern.
Modell 1 mit Innenverstärkung • Cubilete para lápices y clips.
Modelo 1 con interior reforzado • Portamatite e clip. Modello 1
con interno rinforzato • Estojo para lápis e clips. Modelo 1 com
interior reforçado • Bakje voor potloden en paperclips. Model 1
met versterkte binnenkant

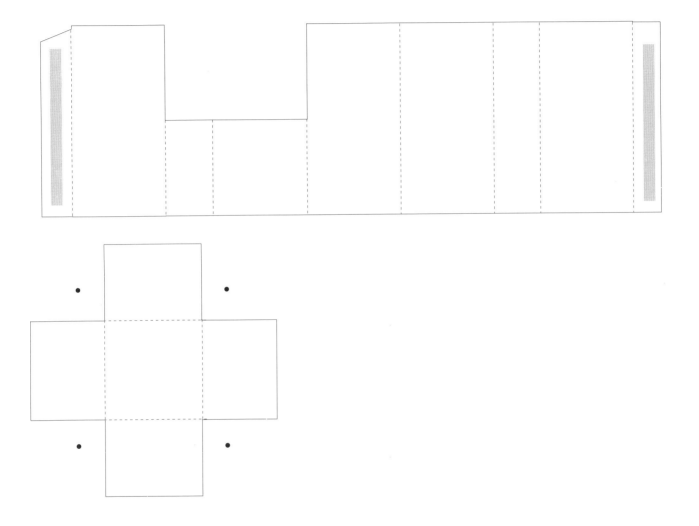

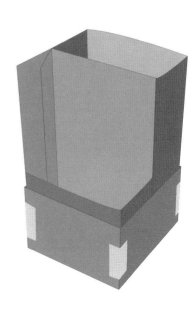

Pencil and paperclip holder. Model 2 • Pot à crayon pour stylos et trombones. Modèle 2 • Becher für Stifte und Büroklammern. Modell 2 • Cubilete para lápices y clips. Modelo 2 • Portamatite e portaclip. Modello 2 • Estojo para lápis e clips. Modelo 2 • Bakje voor potloden en paperclips. Model 2

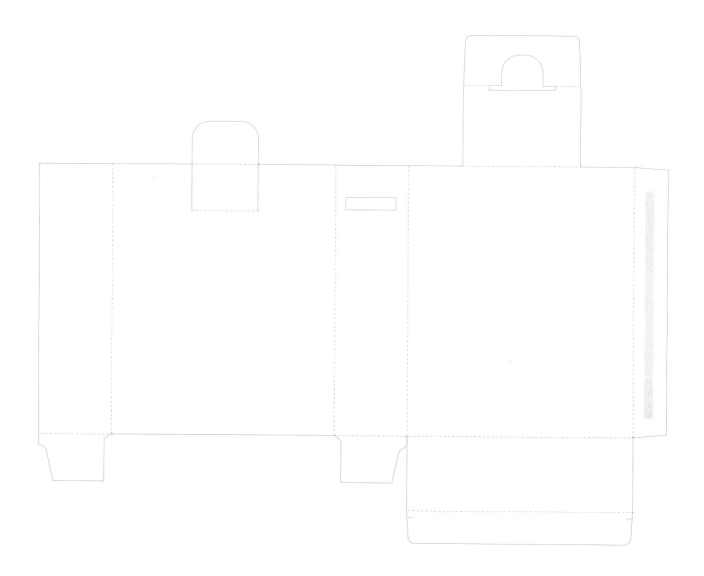

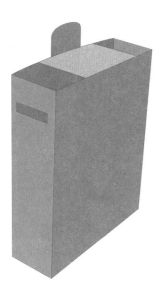

Tape dispenser box with die cut side • Dérouleur de ruban avec orifice latéral • Spenderbox für Schleifenband mit seitlicher Ausstanzung • Caja dispensadora de cintas, con troquel lateral • Scatola porta nastro, con dispenser laterale • Caixa dispensadora de cintas, com cunha lateral • Tapehouder, met opening aan de zijkant

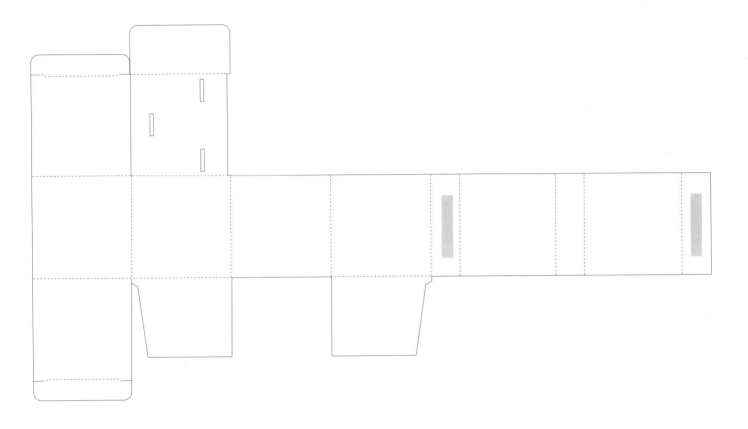

Tape dispenser box with upper window and sections •
Dérouleur de ruban avec ouverture supérieure
et compartiments de rangement • Spenderbox
für Schleifenband mit Fächern und Fenster
oben • Caja dispensadora de cintas, con ventana
superior y compartimentos • Scatola porta nastro,
con apertura superiore e scompartimenti • Caixa
dispensadora de cintas, com janela superior e
compartimentos • Tapehouder, met openingen aan
de bovenkant

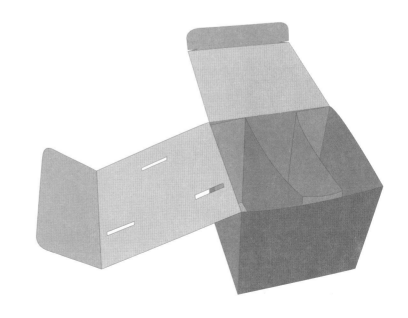

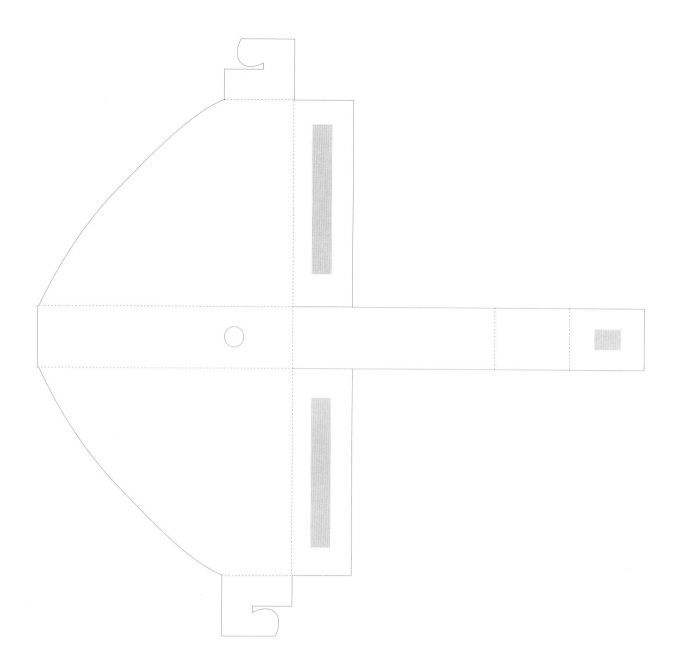

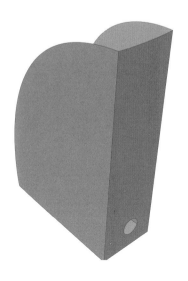

Magazine holder. Model 1 • Porte-revues. Modèle 1 •
Zeitschriftenordner. Modell 1 • Archivador de revistas.
Modelo 1 • Portariviste. Modello 1 • Arquivador de revistas.
Modelo 1 • Archiefdoos voor tijdschriften. Model 1

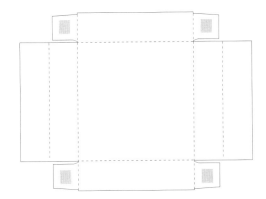

Accordion box with sleeves for three CDs • Boîte accordéon avec étui pour trois CD • Schachtel mit Ziehharmonikahülle für drei CDs • Caja acordeón con funda para tres CD • Scatola a fisarmonica con astuccio per tre CD • Caixa acordeão com capa para três CD's • Harmonicadoos met bodem voor drie cd's

A

Pencil tray with sleeve and interior divider. Part 1 · Etui à crayons coulissant avec intercalaire intérieur. Partie 1 · Stifteetui mit Schuber und Innenunterteilung. Teil 1 · Estuche para lápices con separador interior y faja. Parte 1 · Astuccio con fascetta e divisorio interno. Parte 1 · Estojo para lápis com separador interior e faixa. Parte 1 · Potloodbakje met hoes en vakken. Deel 1

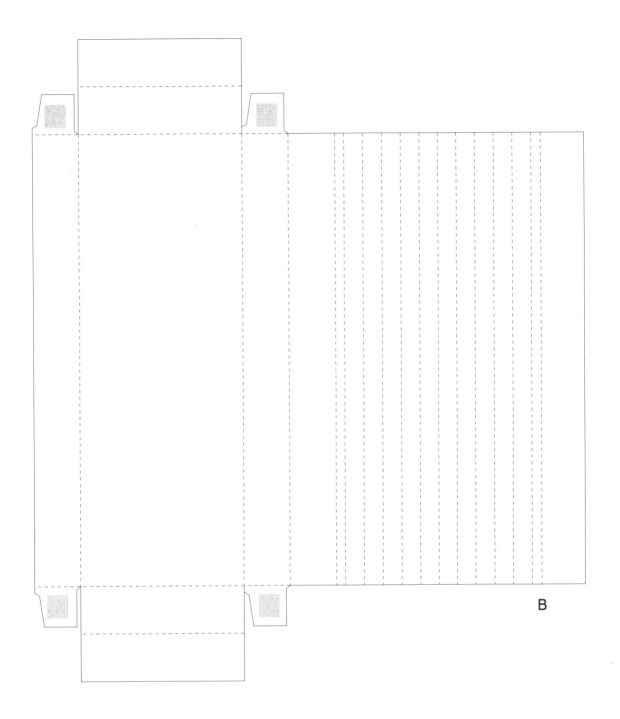

Pencil tray with sleeve and interior divider. Part 2 • Etui à crayons coulissant avec intercalaire intérieur. Partie 2 • Stifteetui mit Schuber und Innenunterteilung. Teil 2 • Estuche para lápices con separador interior y faja. Parte 2 • Astuccio con fascetta e divisorio interno. Parte 2 • Estojo para lápis com separador interior e faixa. Parte 2 • Potloodbakje met hoes en vakken. Deel 2

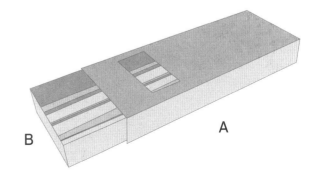

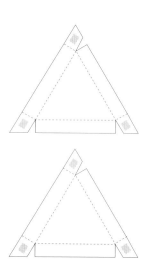

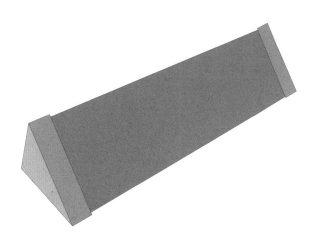

Triangular box for storing plans • Boîte triangulaire pour ranger les plans • Dreieckige Box zum Aufbewahren von Plänen • Caja triangular para almacenar planos • Scatola triangolare per archiviazione di planimetrie • Caixa triangular para armazenagem de projectos • Driehoekige doos voor het opbergen van kaarten

Tray for writing paper • Plateau pour papier à lettre • Ablage
für Briefpapier • Bandeja para papel de carta • Vassoio per
carta da lettere • Bandeja para papel de carta • Bakje voor
briefpapier

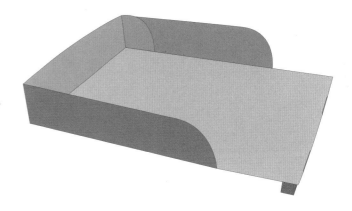

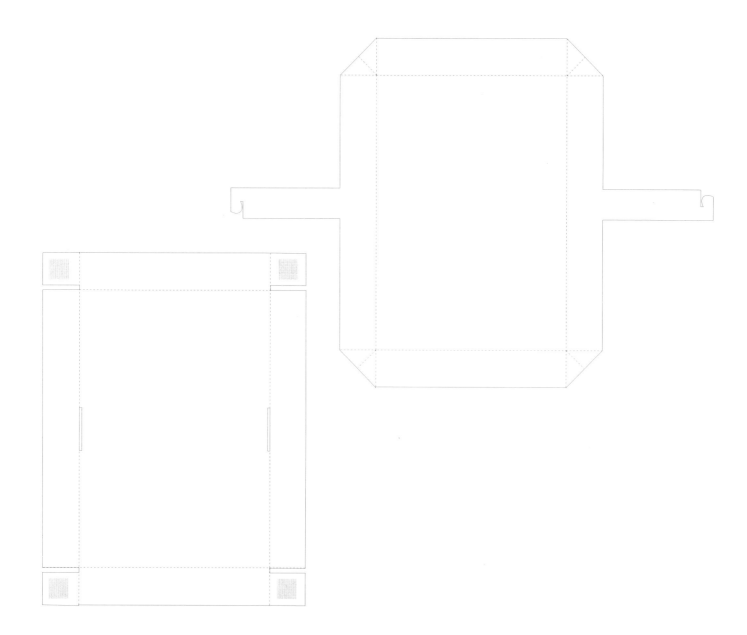

Box for sheets with exterior tape closure • Boîte pour planche de dessin, avec languettes extérieures de fermeture • Box für Klarsichthüllen mit Streifenverschluss außen • Caja para láminas con cierre de bandas exteriores • Scatola per lucidi, con nastri di chiusura esterni • Caixa para quadros, com fecho de bandas exteriores • Doos voor sheets, met bandsluiting aan de buitenkant

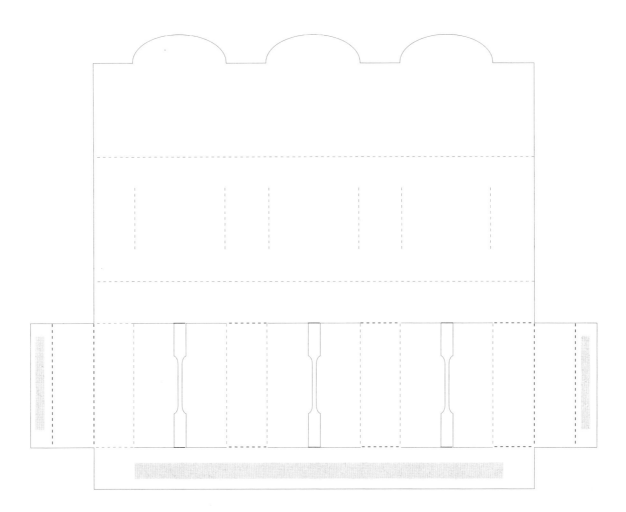

Desk dispenser box for office material • Plateau de rangement pour fourniture de bureau • Schachtel für Büromaterial mit drei Fächern • Caja dispensadora de sobremesa para material de oficina • Scatola portaoggetti da scrivania • Caixa dispensadora de secretária para material de escritório • Sorteerdoos voor op tafel voor kantoormateriaal

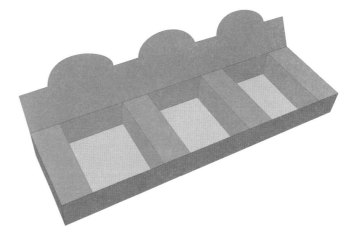

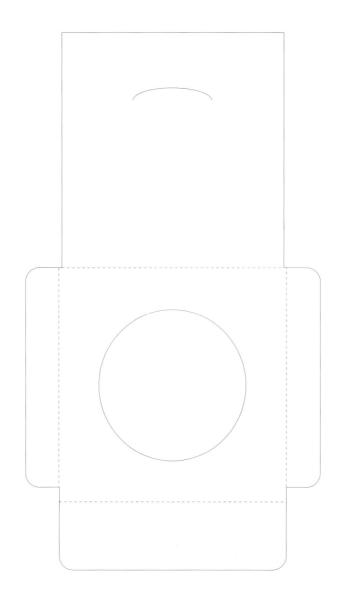

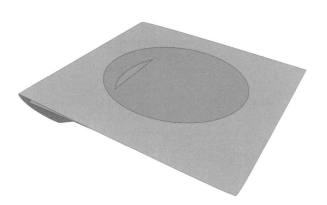

Basic CD sleeve • Enveloppe classique pour CD • Einfache CD-Hülle • Sobre básico para CD • Bustina base per CD • Envelope básico para CD • Hoesje voor cd

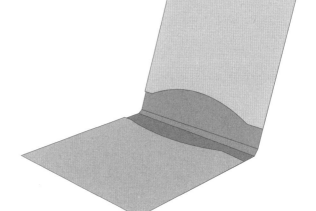

Sleeve for two CDs • Enveloppe pour deux CD • Hülle für zwei
CDs • Sobre para dos CD • Bustina per due CD • Envelope para
dois CD's • Hoes voor twee cd's

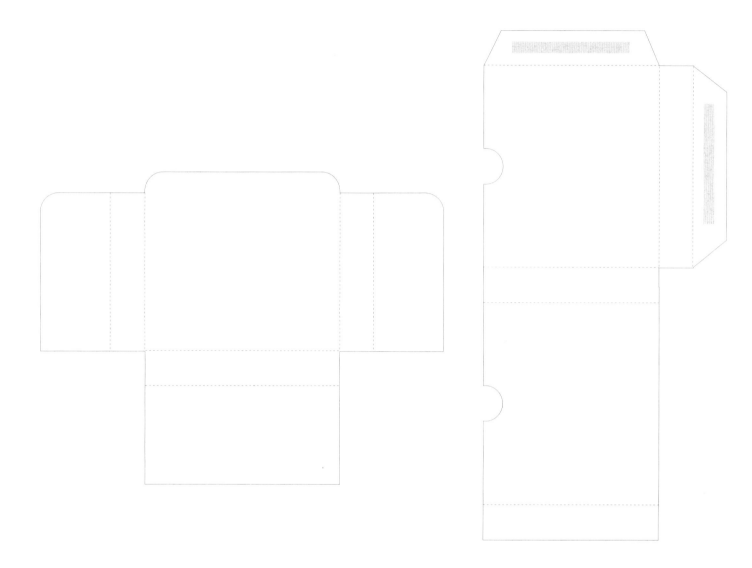

Box for three CDs with sleeve • Boîte pour trois CD avec étui • Schuber für drei CDs • Caja para tres CD con faja • Bustina per tre CD con aletta • Caixa para três CD's com faixa • Doos voor drie cd's, met hoes

×3

Wall-mounted dispenser box with three vertical folders • Boîte verticale à suspendre au mur contenant trois dossiers • Wandablage mit drei Fächern • Caja dispensadora de pared colgante con tres carpetas vertical • Scatola a parete sospesa, verticale con tre cartelle • Caixa dispensadora vertical de pendurar na parede com três pastas • Opbergsysteem voor aan de wand met drie vakken

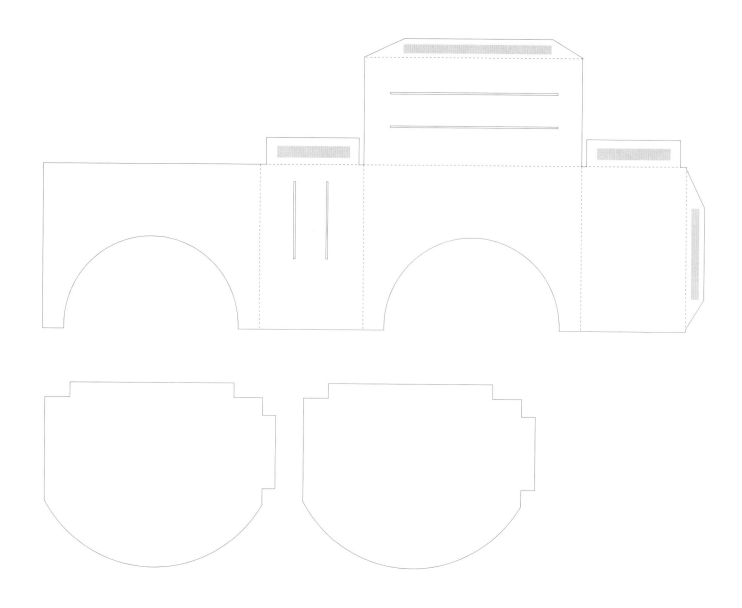

File box with three compartments and removable folders.
Part 1 • Boîte archives à trois compartiments et dossiers séparables. Partie 1 • Archivbox mit drei Fächern und herausnehmbaren Mappen. Teil 1 • Caja archivadora con tres compartimentos y carpetas extraíbles. Parte 1 • Scatola per archiviazione a tre scomparti con cartelle estraibili. Parte 1 • Caixa arquivadora com três compartimentos e pastas extraíveis. Parte 1 • Archiefdoos met drie vakken en uitneembare dossiermappen. Deel 1

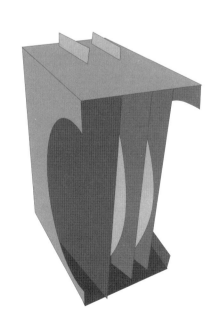

File box with three compartments and removable folders.
Part 2 • Boîte archives à trois compartiments et dossiers
séparables. Partie 2 • Archivbox mit drei Fächern und
herausnehmbaren Mappen. Teil 2 • Caja archivadora con
tres compartimentos y carpetas extraíbles. Parte 2 • Scatola
per archiviazione a tre scomparti con cartelle estraibili.
Parte 2 • Caixa arquivadora com três compartimentos e
pastas extraíveis. Parte 2 • Archiefdoos met drie vakken
en uitneembare dossiermappen. Deel 2

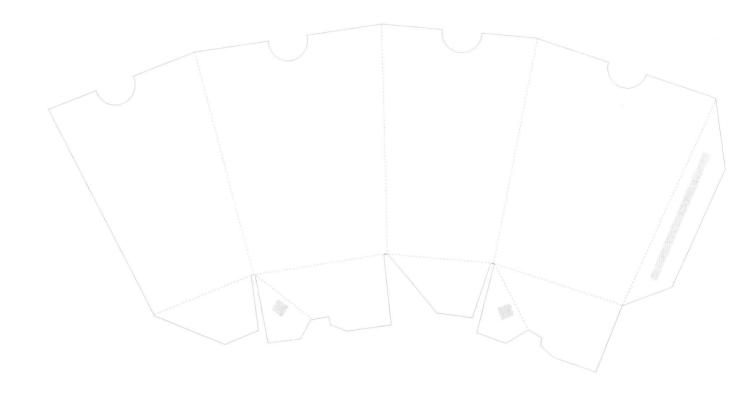

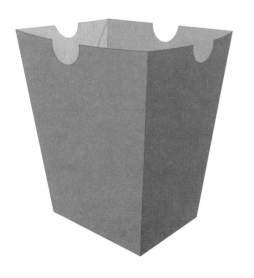

Office wastepaper bin with glued self-assembly base. Model 1 · Corbeille à papier avec base dépliable à coller. Modèle 1 · Papierkorb fürs Büro mit zusammensteckbarem, geklebtem Boden. Modell 1 · Papelera para oficina con base automontable encolada. Modelo 1 · Cestino gettacarte da ufficio con base automontante incollata. Modello 1 · Cesto de papéis para escritório com base automontável colada. Modelo 1 · Prullenbak voor kantoor met vaste vouwbodem. Model 1

·

Office wastepaper bin with glued self-assembly base.
Model 2 • Corbeille à papier avec base dépliable à coller.
Modèle 2 • Papierkorb fürs Büro mit zusammensteckbarem,
geklebtem Boden. Modell 2 • Papelera para oficina con base
automontable encolada. Modelo 2 • Cestino gettacarte da
ufficio con base automontante incollata. Modello 2 • Cesto de
papéis para escritório com base automontável colada. Modelo 2 •
Prullenbak voor kantoor met vaste vouwbodem. Model 2

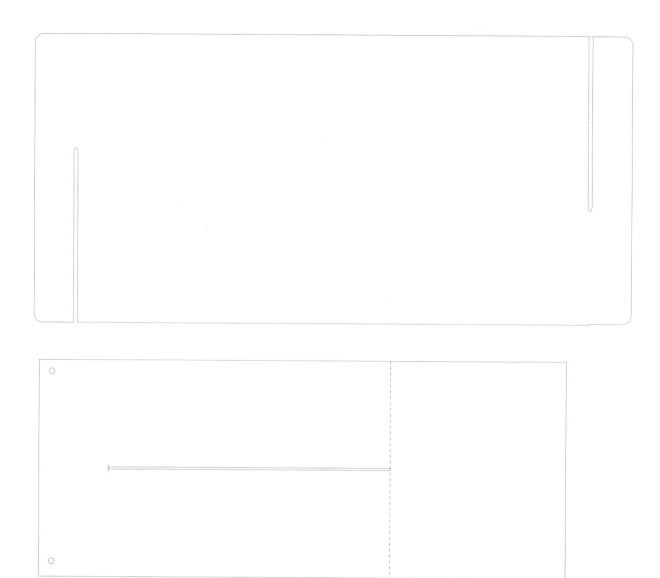

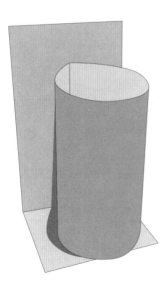

Cylinder-shaped wall container box • Boîte vide-poche cylindrique à fixer au mur • Zylindrischer Wandbehälter • Caja contenedora cilíndrica de pared • Scatola-contenitore cilindrico a parete • Caixa para conteúdo cilíndrica de parede • Ronde bewaardoos voor aan de wand

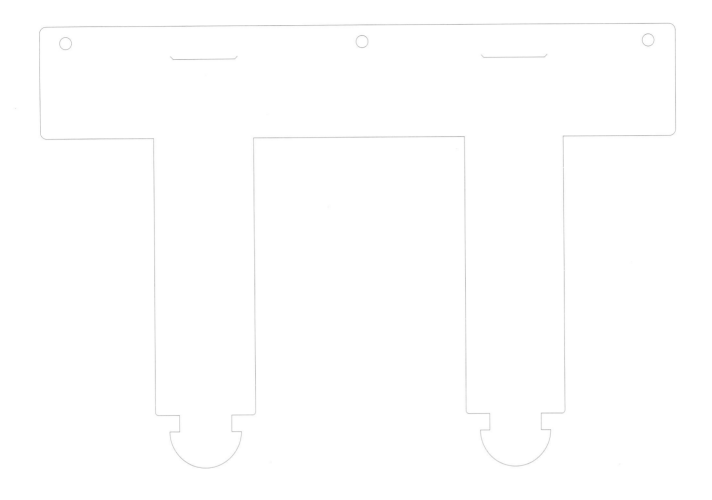

Wall-mounted plan-holder • Boîte de rangement pour
les plans avec support mural • Wandhalterung mit zwei
Vorrichtungen zum Aufbewahren von Plänen • Contenedor
soporte pared guardaplanos • Contenitore per planimetrie
con supporto a parete • Contentor suporte parede guarda
projectos • Kaartenhouder voor aan de wand

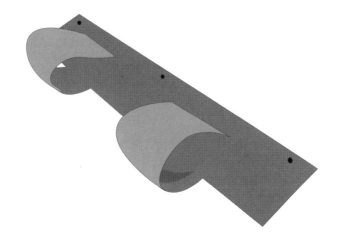

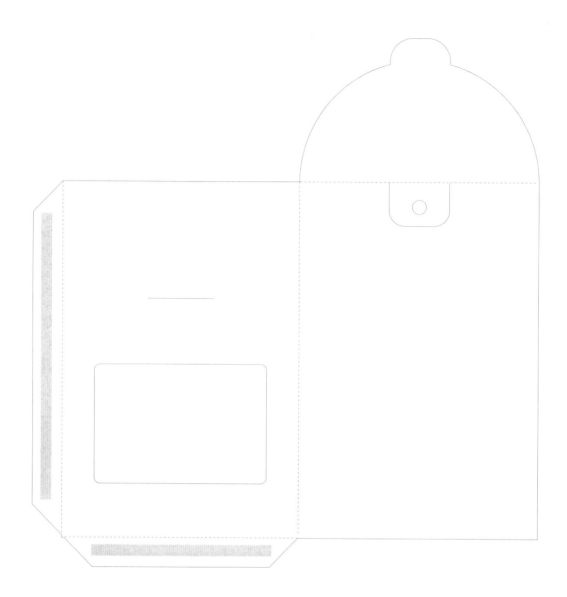

Basic wall-mounted folder · Dossier à suspendre
classique · Hängemappe für die Wandmontage · Carpeta
colgante básica · Cartella sospesa base · Pasta de pendurar
básica · Basismodel hangmap

Self-assembly CD box with tuck-in closure. Model 1 ·
Boîte dépliable pour un CD avec languette de fermeture.
Modèle 1 · CD-Box mit Laschenverschluss. Modell 1 · Caja
automontable para un CD, con cierre de pestaña.
Modelo 1 · Scatola automontante per un CD con lembo di
chiusura. Modello 1 · Caixa automontável para um CD com
fecho de língua. Modelo 1 · Zelfbouwdoos voor een cd, met
flapsluiting. Model 1

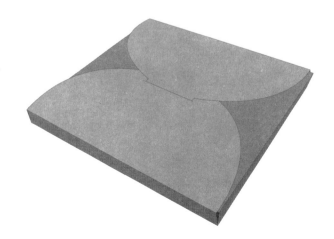

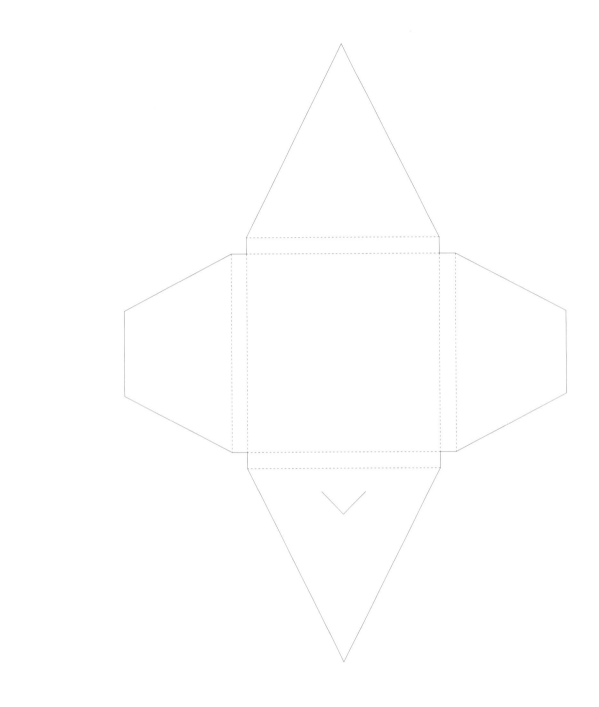

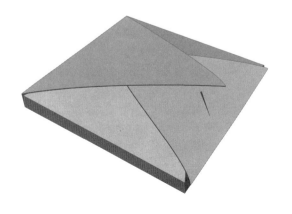

Self-assembly CD box with tuck-in closure. Model 2 • Boîte dépliable pour un CD avec languette de fermeture. Modèle 2 • CD-Box mit Laschenverschluss. Modell 2 • Caja automontable para un CD, con cierre de pestaña. Modelo 2 • Scatola automontante per un CD con lembo di chiusura. Modello 2 • Caixa automontável para um CD com fecho de língua. Modelo 2 • Zelfbouwdoos voor een cd, met flapsluiting. Model 2

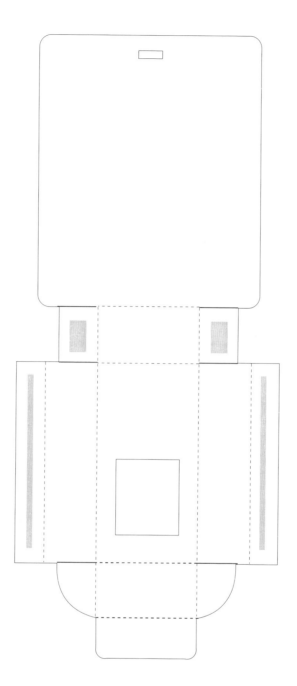

Wall-mounted box with back display. Model 1 • Boîte à suspendre au mur avec fenêtre arrière. Modèle 1 • Display für die Wandmontage. Modell 1 • Caja colgante para pared, con display posterior. Modelo 1 • Scatola sospesa da parete con display posteriore. Modello 1 • Caixa de pendurar para parede com display posterior. Modelo 1 • Wanddoos, met display. Model 1

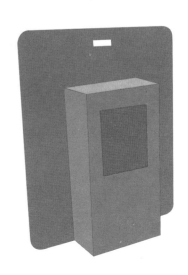

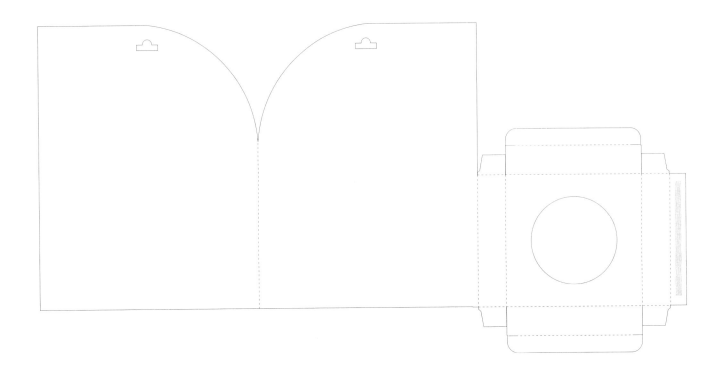

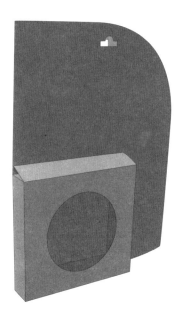

Wall-mounted box with back display. Model 2 • Boîte à suspendre au mur avec fenêtre arrière. Modèle 2 • Display für die Wandmontage. Modell 2 • Caja colgante para pared, con display posterior. Modelo 2 • Scatola sospesa da parete con display posteriore. Modello 2 • Caixa de pendurar para parede com display posterior. Modelo 2 • Wanddoos, met display. Model 2

CD and document folder • Chemise pour CD et documents •
Mappe für CDs und Dokumente • Carpeta para CD y
documentos • Cartella per CD e documenti • Pasta para
CD e documentos • Map voor cd en documenten

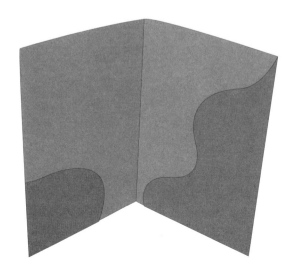

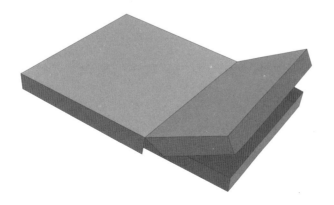

File box for documents with top access • Boîte archives pour documents avec ouverture supérieure • Archivbox für Dokumente mit Öffnung oben • Caja archivadora para documentos, con apertura superior • Scatola archivio per documenti con apertura superiore • Caixa arquivadora para documentos com abertura superior • Archiefdoos voor documenten, met grote opening

Wall-mounted folder with hook · Dossier à suspendre pour crochet · Hängemappe für die Wandmontage · Carpeta colgante para gancho · Cartella sospesa per gancio · Pasta de pendurar para gancho · Hangmap voor aan een haak

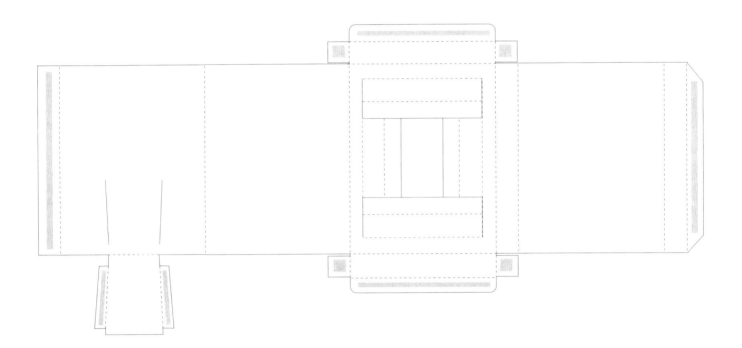

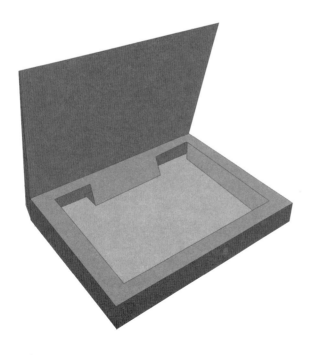

Double box for book • Boîte double pour livre • Doppelwandige
Bücherkassette • Caja de funda doble para libro • Scatola doppia
per libro • Caixa dupla para livro • Dubbele doos voor boek

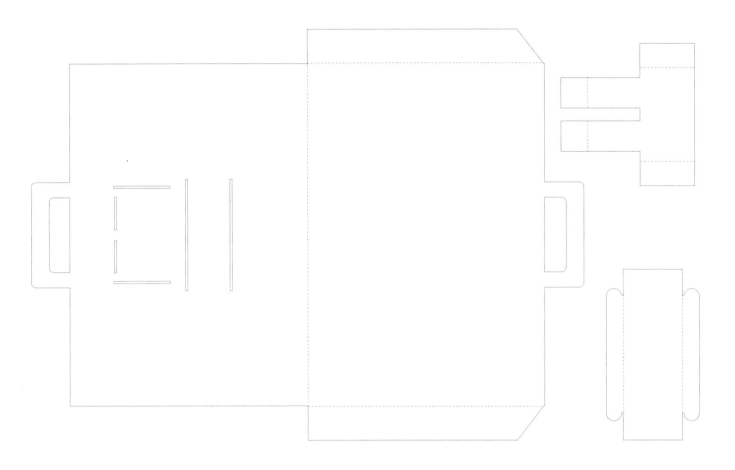

Sectioned document-holder box · Boîte porte-documents
avec compartiments · Dokumentenmappe mit zwei
Fächern · Caja portadocumentos compartimentada · Scatola
portadocumenti a scomparti · Caixa porta-documentos
compartimentada · Dossiermappen met sorteervakken

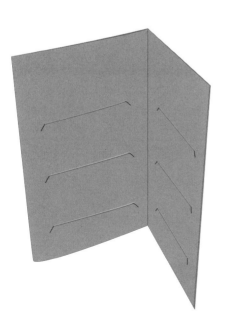

Card folder • Dossier porte-cartes • Mappe zum Einstecken von Karten • Carpeta tarjetera • Cartella portabiglietti da visita • Pasta para cartões • Portefeuillemap

Basic dossier folder with thumb index • Dossier basique avec intercalaires • Dossiermappe mit Greifausschnitt • Carpeta dossier simple con uñero • Cartella base per dossier con fessura • Pasta básica para dossier com puxador • Basisdossiermap, met duimgreep

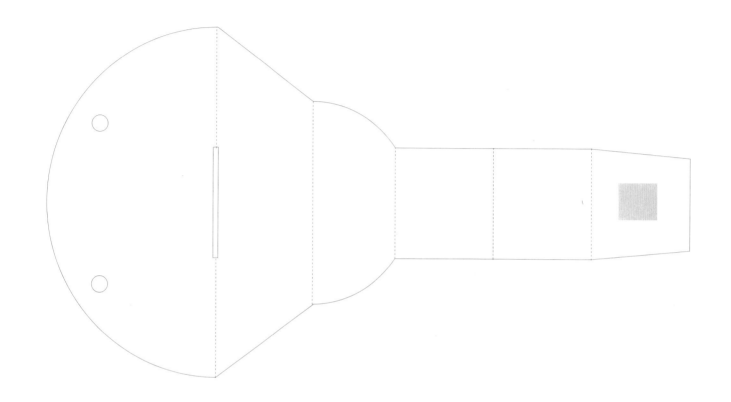

Wall-mounted box for newspapers and magazines • Boîte à suspendre pour journaux et revues • Hängebox für Zeitungen und Zeitschriften • Caja colgante para periódicos y revistas • Scatola sospesa per quotidiani e riviste • Caixa de pendurar para jornais e revistas • Hangdoos voor kranten en tijdschriften

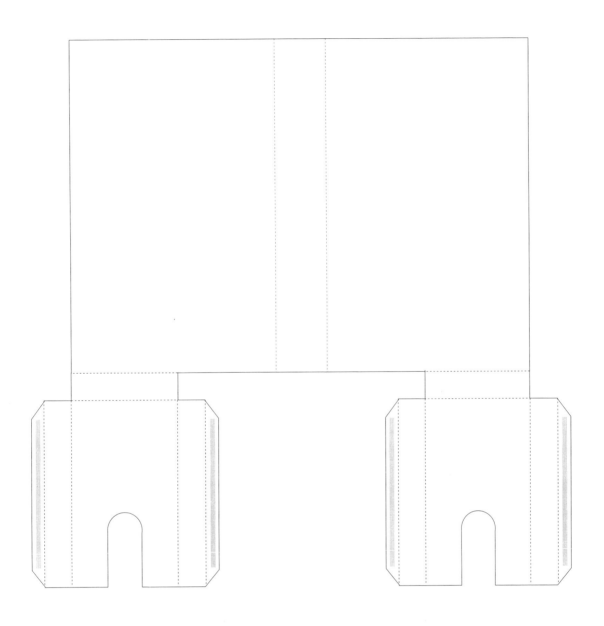

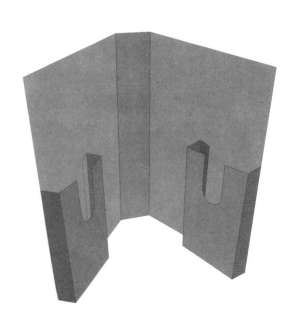

File box with dispenser display • Boîte archives avec fenêtre de distribution • Archivmappe mit zwei Einsteckfächern • Carpeta archivadora con display dispensador • Cartella per archiviazione con display • Pasta arquivadora com display dispensador • Archiefmap met display

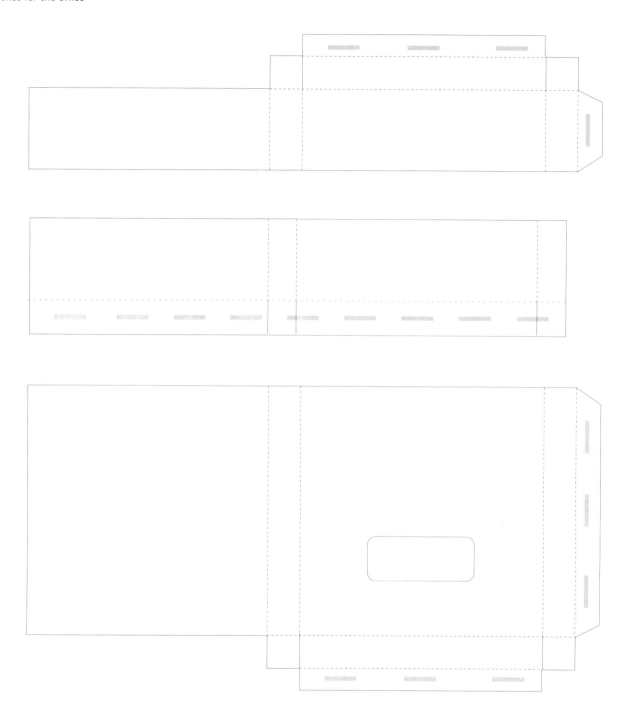

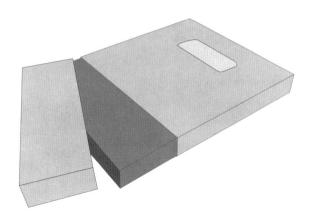

Document-holder telescopic box with window • Boîte porte-documents télescopiques avec fenêtre • Ausziehbare Dokumentenbox mit Fenster • Caja telescópica portadocumentos con ventana • Scatola portadocumenti telescopica con finestra • Caixa telescópica porta-documentos com janela • Telescopische doos voor dossiermappen met venster

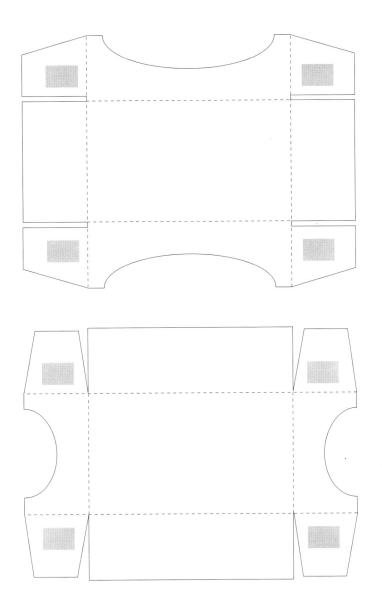

Box for visitors cards • Boîte pour cartes de visite • Schachtel für Visitenkarten • Caja para tarjetas de visita • Scatola portabiglietti da visita • Caixa para cartões de visita • Doos voor visitekaartjes

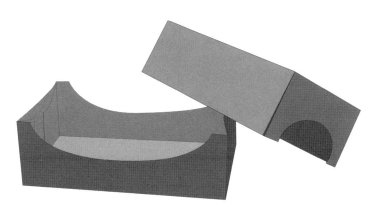

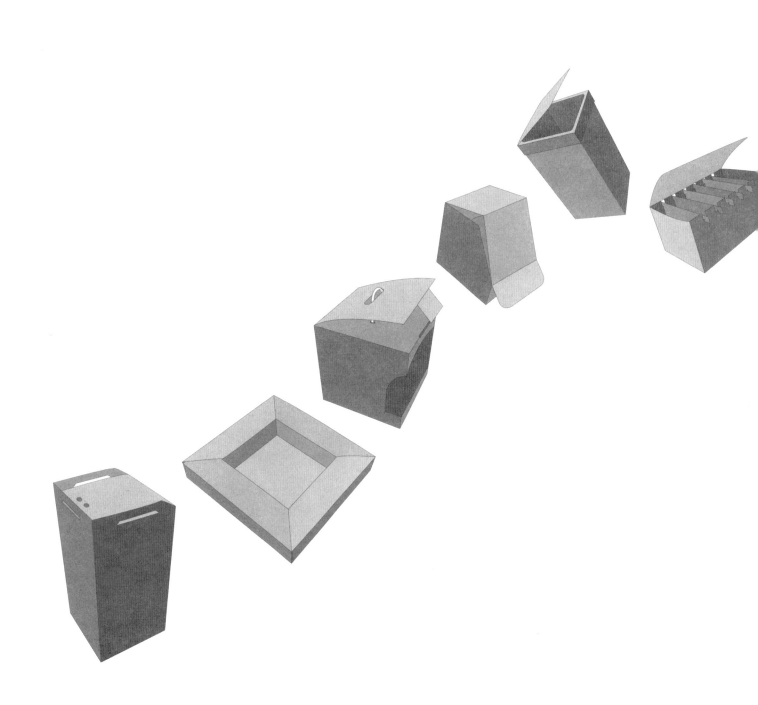

Boxes for storing clothes and accessories
Boîtes de rangement pour vêtements et accessoires
Boxen zum Aufbewahren von Textilien und Accessoires
Cajas para el almacenaje textil y de complementos
Scatole per l'imballaggio di tessuti e complementi
Caixas para a armazenagem têxtil e de complementos
Dozen voor het opbergen van textiel en toebehoren

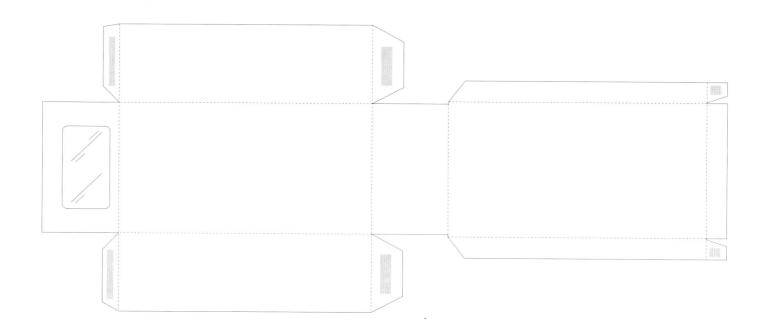

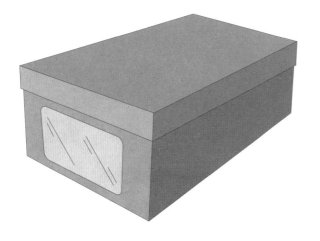

Shoe box with lift up lid and side window • Boîte à chaussures avec couvercle rabattable et fenêtre latérale • Schuhbox mit Klappdeckel und seitlichem Fenster • Caja para zapatos, con tapa basculante y ventana lateral • Scatola per scarpe con coperchio basculante e finestrella laterale • Caixa para sapatos com tampa móvel e janela lateral • Doos voor schoenen, met kanteldeksel en zijvenster

Box for storing gloves and hats • Boîte de rangement
pour gants et casquettes • Box zum Aufbewahren von
Handschuhen und Mützen • Caja para almacenaje de guantes
y gorras • Scatola per imballaggio di guanti e berretti • Caixa
para armazenagem de luvas e gorros • Doos voor het opbergen
van handschoenen en mutsen

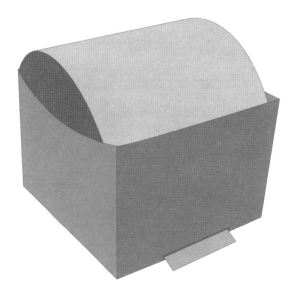

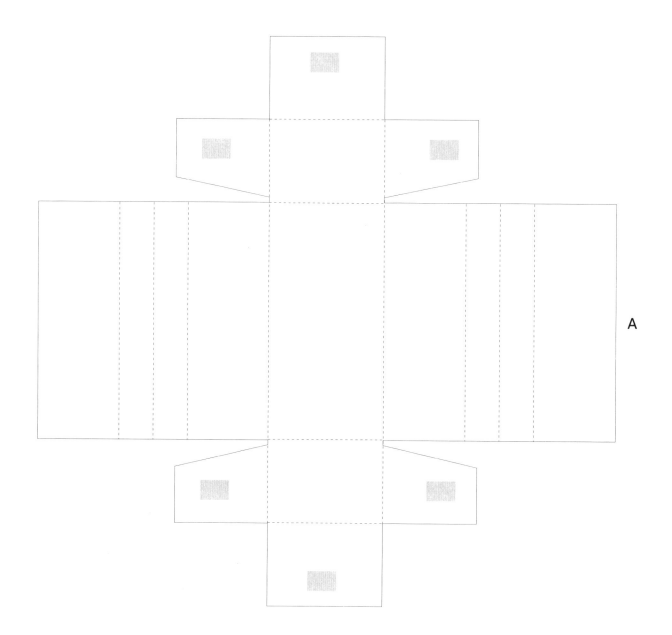

A

Shoe box with lid. Part 1 • Boîte à chaussures avec couvercle. Partie 1 • Schuhbox mit Deckel. Teil 1 • Caja con tapa para zapatos. Parte 1 • Scatola da scarpe con coperchio. Parte 1 • Caixa com tampa para sapatos. Parte 1 • Schoenendoos met deksel. Deel 1

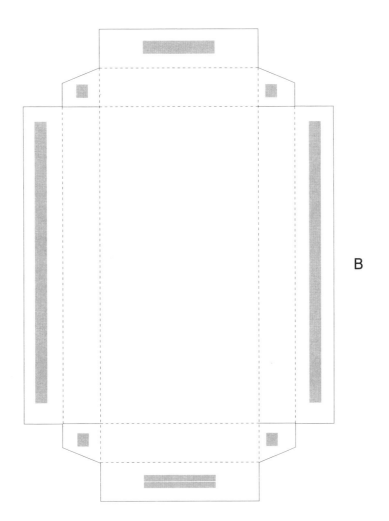

Shoe box with lid. Part 2 • Boîte à chaussures avec couvercle. Partie 2 • Schuhbox mit Deckel. Teil 2 • Caja con tapa para zapatos. Parte 2 • Scatola da scarpe con coperchio. Parte 2 • Caixa com tampa para sapatos. Parte 2 • Schoenendoos met deksel. Deel 2

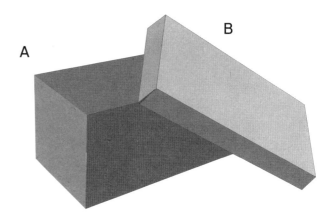

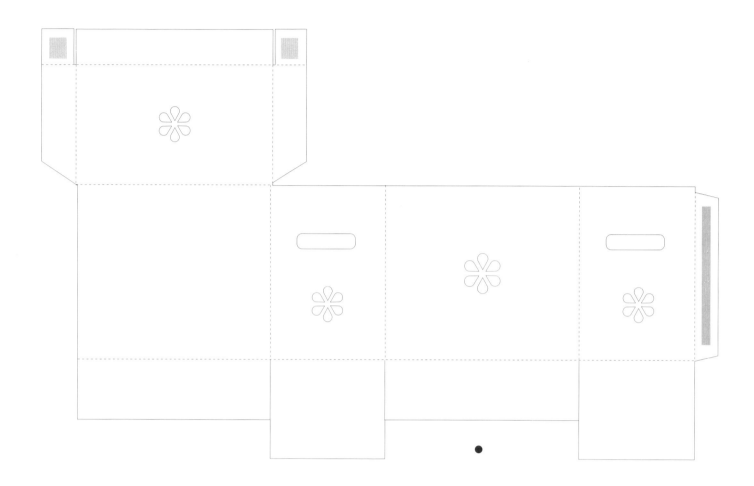

Box for storing clothes with lift up lid and springtime decoration · Boîte de rangement pour vêtements avec couvercle rabattable et image de la saison printemps · Box zum Aufbewahren von Kleidung mit Klappdeckel und Frühjahrsdeko · Caja para almacenaje de ropa, con tapa basculante y detalle de temporada primavera · Scatola per imballaggio abbigliamento, con coperchio basculante e decorazione primaverile · Caixa para armazenagem de roupa, com tampa móvel e motivo de temporada Primavera · Doos voor het opbergen van kleding, met kanteldeksel en voorjaarsdetail

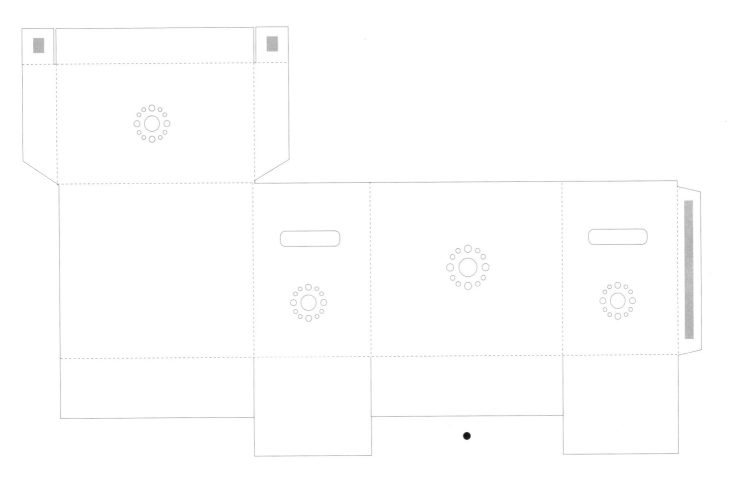

Box for storing clothes with lift up lid and summertime decoration · Boîte de rangement pour vêtements avec couvercle rabattable et image de la saison été · Box zum Aufbewahren von Kleidung mit Klappdeckel und Sommerdeko · Caja para almacenaje de ropa, con tapa basculante y detalle de temporada verano · Scatola per imballaggio abbigliamento, con coperchio basculante e decorazione estiva · Caixa para armazenagem de roupa, com tampa móvel e motivo de temporada Verão · Doos voor het opbergen van kleding, met kanteldeksel en zomerdetail

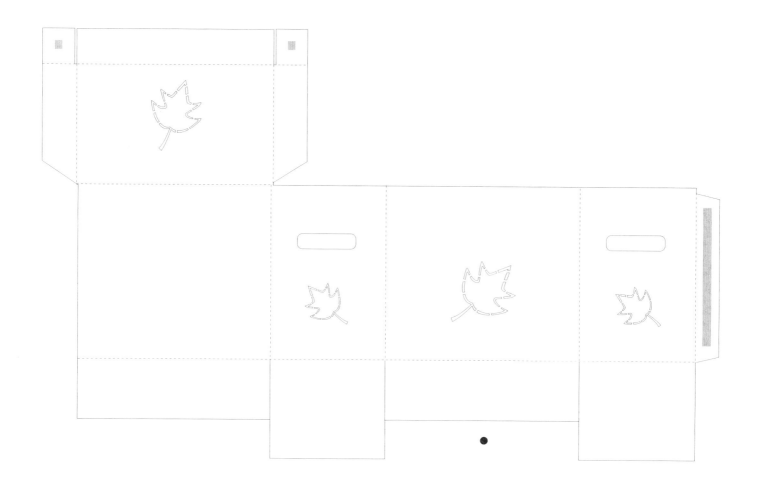

Box for storing clothes with lift up lid and autumn time decoration • Boîte de rangement pour vêtements avec couvercle rabattable et image de la saison automne • Box zum Aufbewahren von Kleidung mit Klappdeckel und Herbstdeko • Caja para almacenaje de ropa, con tapa basculante y detalle de temporada otoño • Scatola per imballaggio abbigliamento, con coperchio basculante e decorazione autunnale • Caixa para armazenagem de roupa, com tampa móvel e motivo de temporada Outono • Doos voor het opbergen van kleding, met kanteldeksel en najaarsdetail

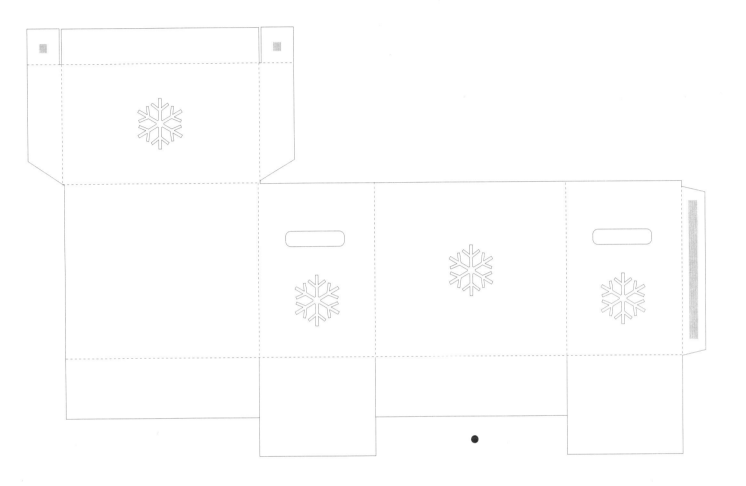

Box for storing clothes with lift up lid and wintertime decoration · Boîte de rangement pour vêtements avec couvercle rabattable et image de la saison hiver · Box zum Aufbewahren von Kleidung mit Klappdeckel und Winterdeko · Caja para almacenaje de ropa, con tapa basculante y detalle de temporada invierno · Scatola per imballaggio abbigliamento, con coperchio basculante e decorazione invernale · Caixa para armazenagem de roupa, com tampa móvel e motivo de temporada Inverno · Doos voor het opbergen van kleding, met kanteldeksel en winterdetail

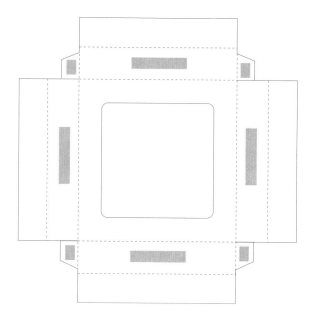

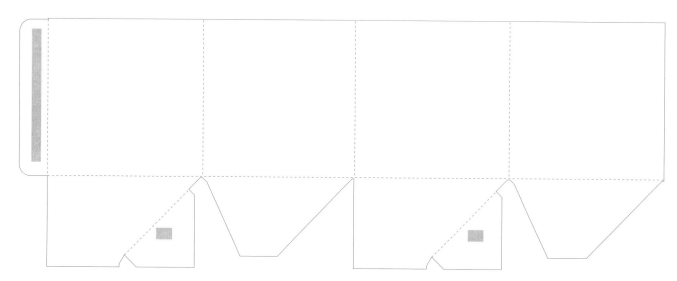

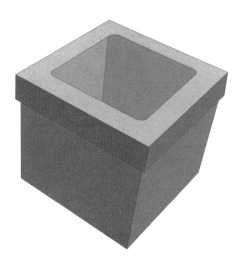

Box for storing underwear with upper window • Boîte de rangement pour sous-vêtements, avec fenêtre supérieure • Box mit Sichtfenster zum Aufbewahren von Unterwäsche • Caja para almacenaje de ropa interior, con ventana superior • Scatola per imballaggio biancheria intima, con finestrella superiore • Caixa para armazenagem de roupa interior, com janela superior • Doos voor het opbergen van ondergoed, met venster aan de bovenkant

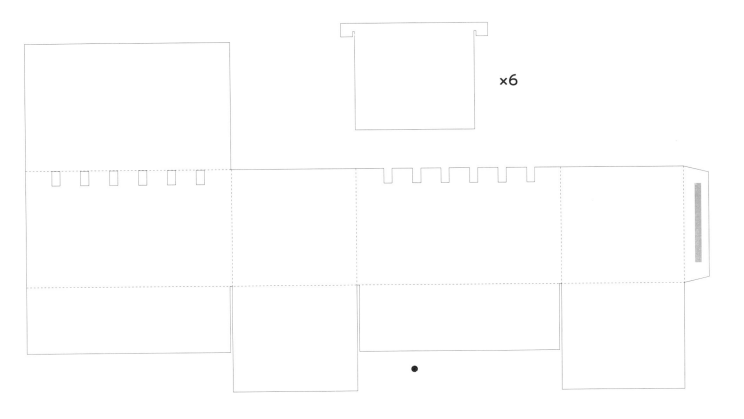

×6

Box for storing bags with interior dividers • Boîte pour le rangement des sacs à mains avec intercalaires intérieurs • Box mit Abtrennungen zum Aufbewahren von Taschen • Caja para almacenaje de bolsos, con separadores interiores • Scatola per imballaggio di borse con divisori interni • Caixa para armazenagem de sacos com separadores interiores • Doos voor het opbergen van tassen

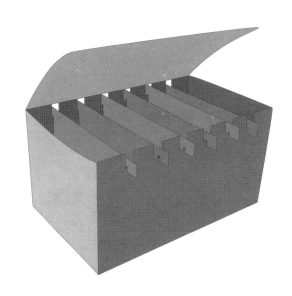

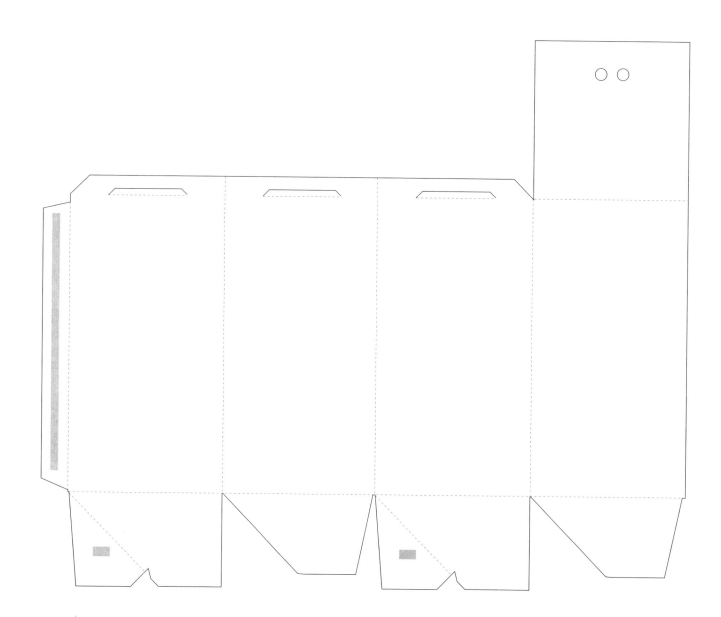

Clothes basket with lift lid • Panier à linge avec couvercle à bascule • Wäschekorb mit Klappdeckel • Cesto para la ropa, con tapa basculante • Cesto per biancheria con coperchio basculante • Cesto para a roupa com tampa móvel • Mand voor kleding, met kanteldeksel

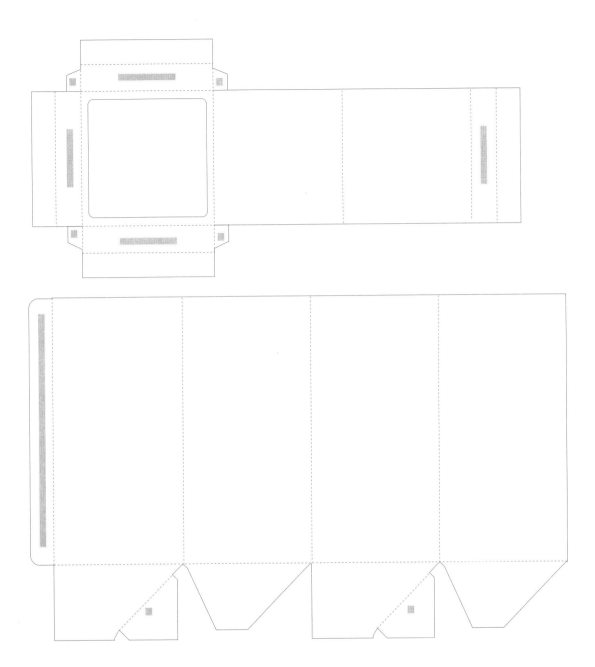

Clothes basket · Panier à linge · Wäschekorb · Cesto para la
ropa · Cesto per biancheria · Cesto para a roupa · Mand voor kleding

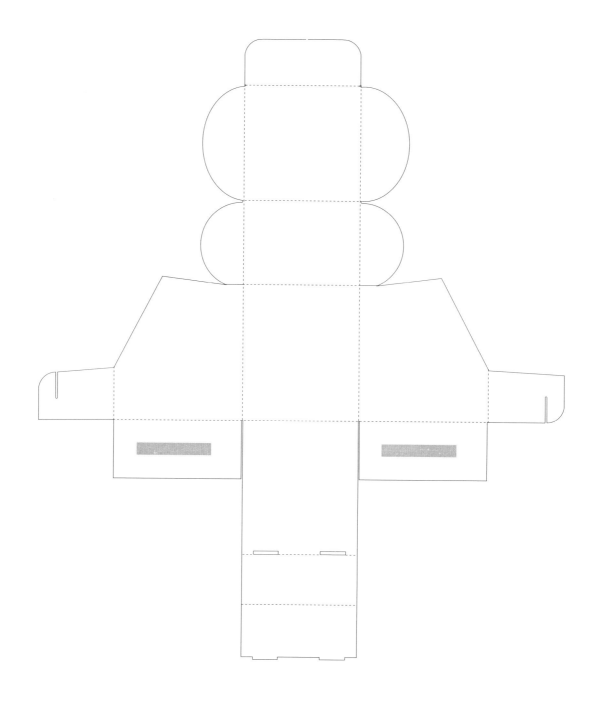

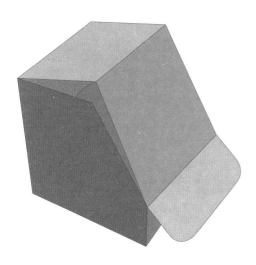

Box for ski boots • Boîte pour chaussures de ski • Box für Skischuhe • Caja para botas de esquiar • Scatola per scarponi da sci • Caixa para botas de esquiar • Doos voor skischoenen

Box for bed clothes with handle • Boîte pour la chambre avec poignée • Box mit Griff für Bettwäsche • Caja para dormitorio, con asa • Scatola per camera da letto con maniglia • Caixa para quarto com asa • Doos voor slaapkamer, met handgreep

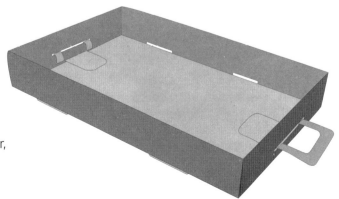

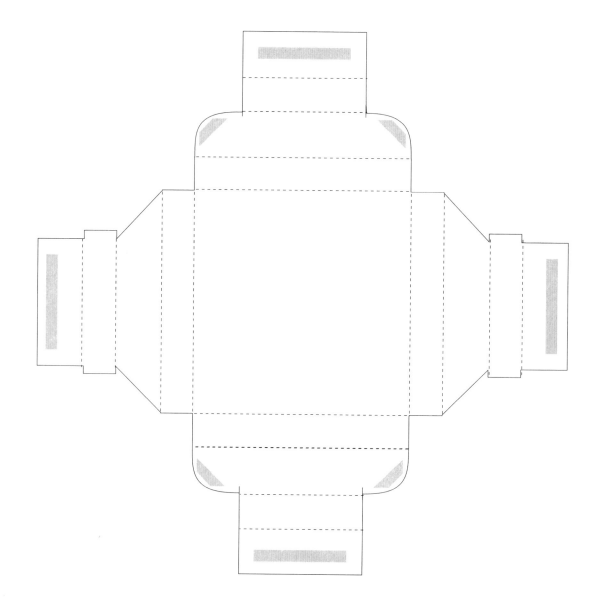

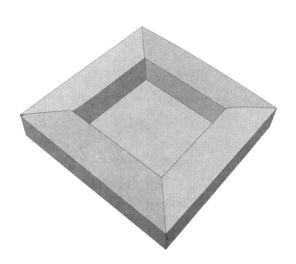

Double tray for jewellery · Plateau double porte-bijoux · Doppelwandige Ablage für Schmuck · Bandeja doble para la bisutería · Vaschetta portagioie doppia · Bandeja dupla para a bijutaria · Dubbelwandig snuisterijenbakje

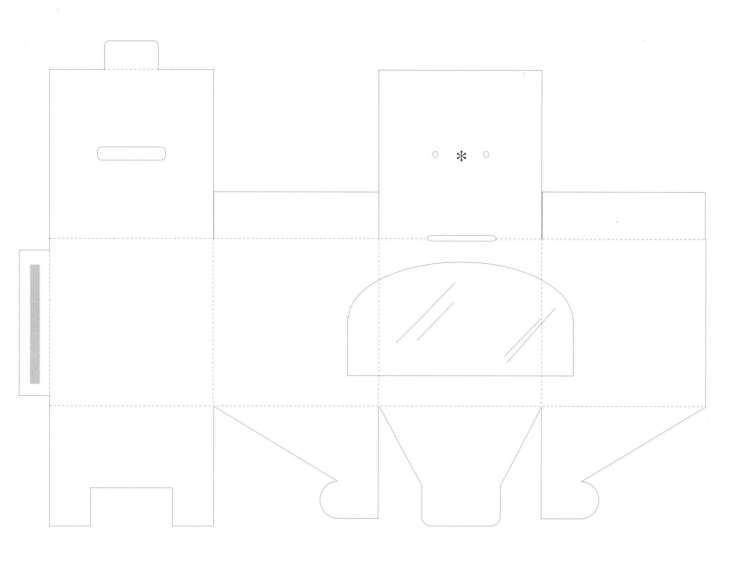

Box for helmets • Boîte pour ranger les casques • Box für
Helme • Caja para cascos • Scatola per caschi • Caixa para
capacetes • Doos voor helmen

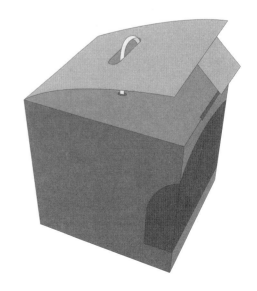

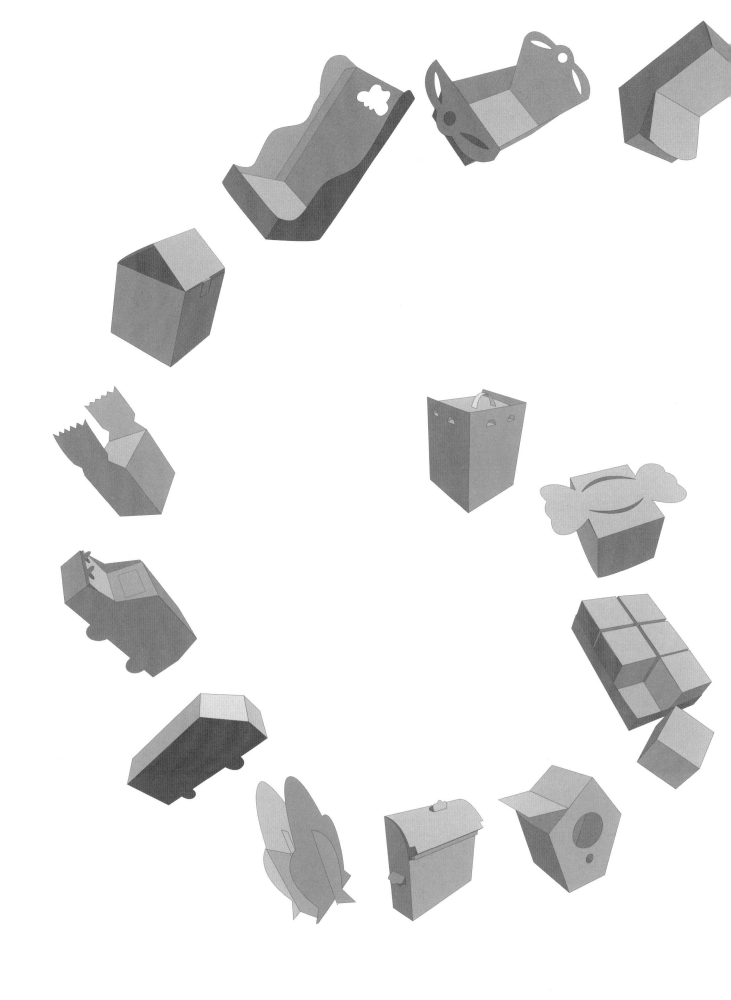

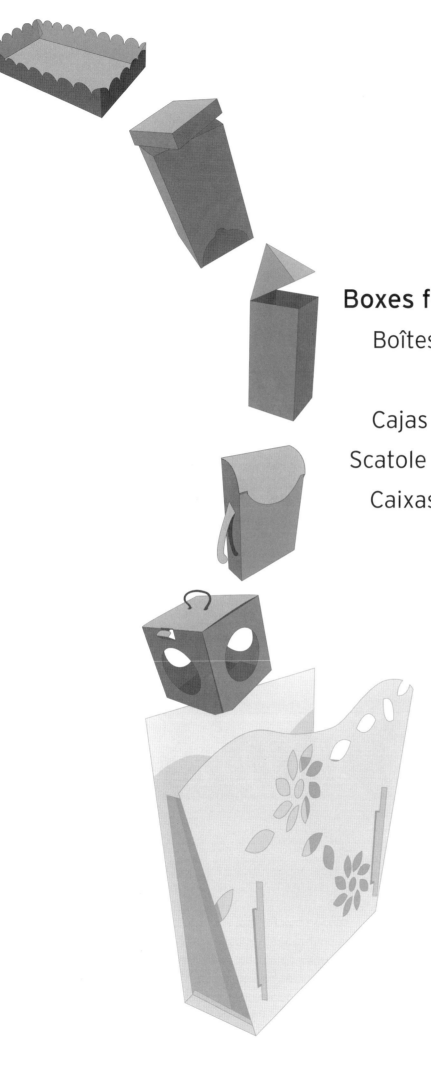

Boxes for children's bedrooms

Boîtes pour chambres d'enfants

Boxen fürs Kinderzimmer

Cajas para dormitorios de niños

Scatole per la camera dei bambini

Caixas para quartos de crianças

Dozen voor kinderkamers

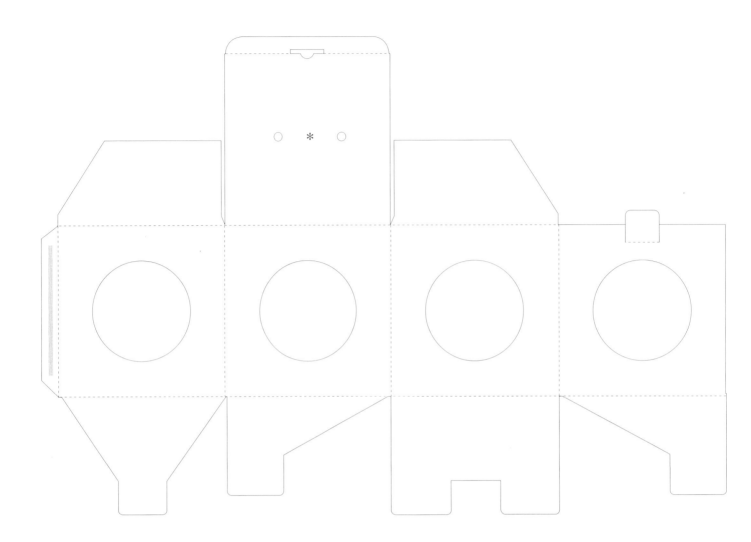

Cube-shaped box for ball with handle • Boîte cubique avec poignée pour ranger les balles • Quadratische Box mit Griff für einen Ball • Caja cúbica para pelota, con asa • Scatola cubica per pallone con maniglia • Caixa cúbica para bola com asa • Vierkante doos voor bal, met handgreep

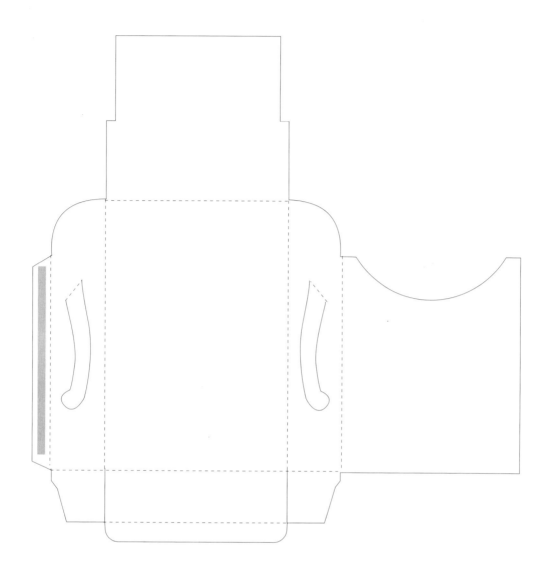

Box for sweets with flaps, ears and arms with button closure • Boîte à bonbons avec rabats, languettes et pattes à fermeture clic clac • Bonbonschachtel mit Laschen, Seitenarmen und Klickverschluss • Caja para caramelos, con solapas, orejas y brazos de cierre click • Scatola per caramelle, con alette, linguette e bracci con chiusura a bottone • Caixa para caramelos, com abas, orelhas e braços de fecho clic • Snoepjesdoos, met flappen, oren en beugels met kliksluiting

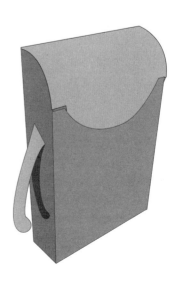

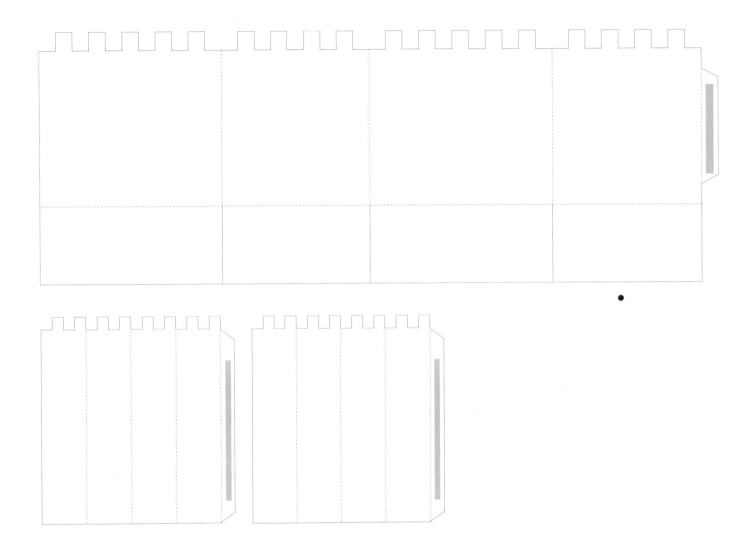

Castle-shaped basket for storing toys · Coffre à jouets en forme de château · Burgförmige Box zum Aufbewahren von Spielzeug · Cesta para almacenaje de juguetes, con forma de castillo · Cesto per riporre i giocattoli a forma di castello · Cesta para armazenagem de brinquedos com forma de castelo · Opbergdoos voor speelgoed, in de vorm van een kasteel

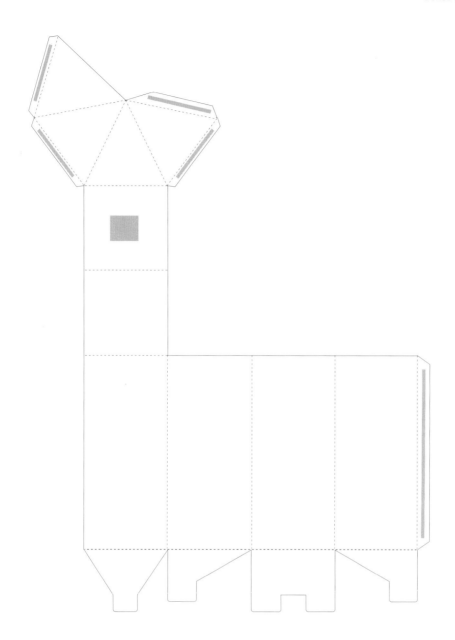

Tower-shaped box with lift up lid • Boîte à couvercle à bascule, en forme de tour • Turmförmige Box mit Klappdeckel • Caja con tapa basculante y con forma de torreón • Scatola con coperchio basculante a forma di torre • Caixa com tampa móvel e com forma de torreão • Doos in de vorm van een grote toren met kanteldeksel

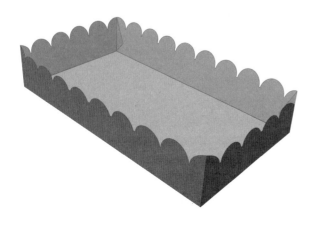

Cloud-shaped tray with rounded edges • Plateau à rebords, en forme de nuage • Ablage mit wolkenförmigem Abschluss • Bandeja con remate y con forma de nube • Vaschetta con rifinitura a forma di nuvola • Bandeja com remate e com forma de nuvem • Wolkvormig bakje met sierrand

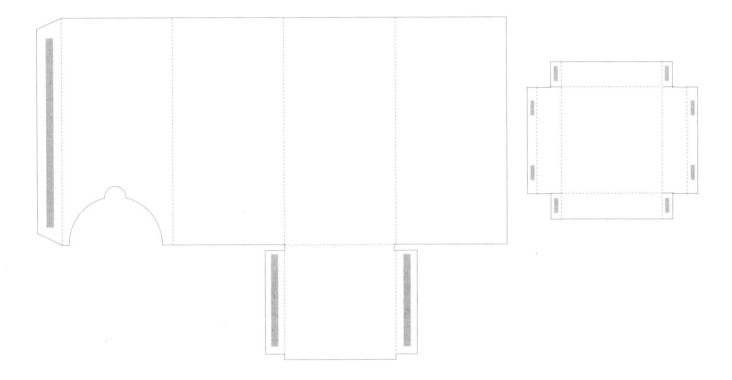

Nappy-dispenser box with lower access and interior telescopic lid • Boîte à mouchoirs avec ouverture inférieure et couvercle télescopique intérieur • Windelspenderbox mit Öffnung unten und Deckel • Caja dispensadora de pañales, con apertura inferior y tapa telescópica interior • Scatola dispenser di pannolini, con apertura inferiore e coperchio interno telescopico • Caixa dispensadora de fraldas, com abertura inferior e tampa telescópica interior • Dispenser voor luiers, met kleine opening en telescopisch deksel

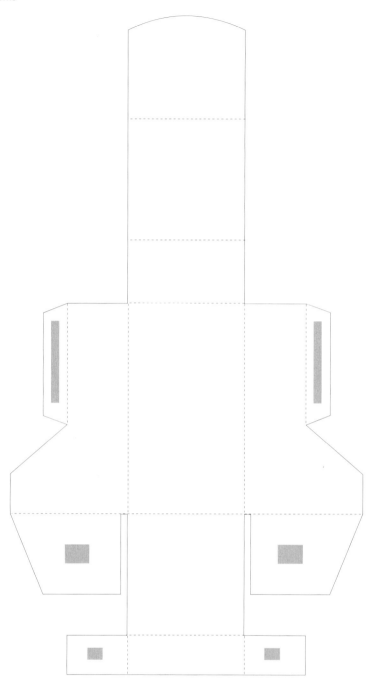

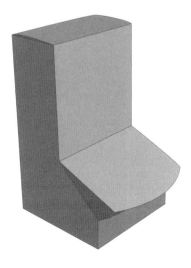

Sweet dispenser box with lower lift up lid • Boîte à bonbons avec couvercle inférieur à bascule • Bonbonspenderbox mit Klappdeckel unten • Caja dispensadora de caramelos, con tapa inferior basculante • Scatola dispenser di caramelle con coperchio inferiore basculante • Caixa dispensadora de caramelos com tampa inferior móvel • Dispenser voor snoepjes, met klein kanteldeksel

Crib-shaped box for dolls • Boîte de rangement pour les poupées, en forme de berceau. • Wiegenförmige Puppenbox • Caja para muñecos, con forma de cuna • Scatola per bambole a forma di culla • Caixa para bonecos com forma de berço • Poppendoos, in de vorm van een wieg

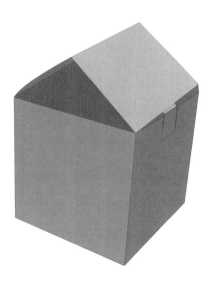

House-shaped box for sweets • Boîte à bonbons en forme de maison • Hausförmige Bonbonschachtel • Caja para caramelos, con forma de casa • Scatola per caramelle a forma di casa • Caixa para caramelos com forma de casa • Snoepjesdoos, in de vorm van een huis

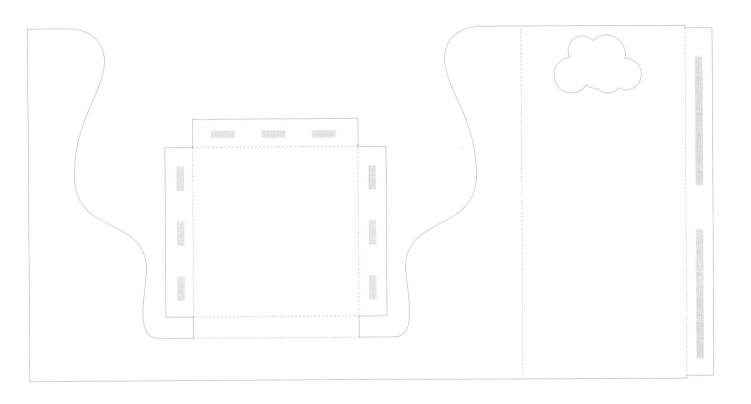

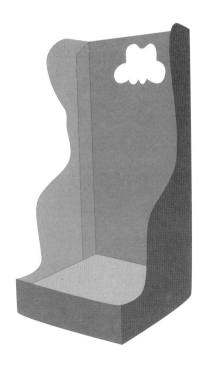

Dispenser box with cloud detail · Distributeur avec détail
en forme de nuage · Spenderbox mit Wolkendeko · Caja
dispensadora con detalle de nubes · Scatola dispenser con
decorazione di nuvole · Caixa dispensadora com motivo de
nuvens · Sorteerdoos met wolkmotief

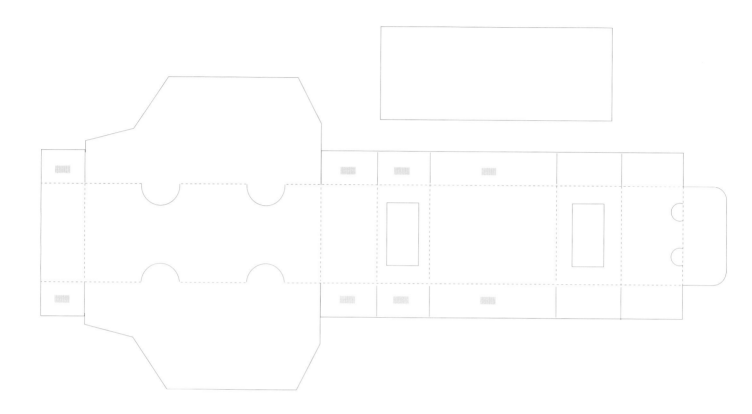

Car-shaped gift box • Boîte à cadeau en forme de voiture • Geschenkbox in Form eines Autos • Caja para regalo, con forma de coche • Scatola da regalo a forma di automobile • Caixa para presente com forma de carro • Geschenkdoos, in de vorm van een auto

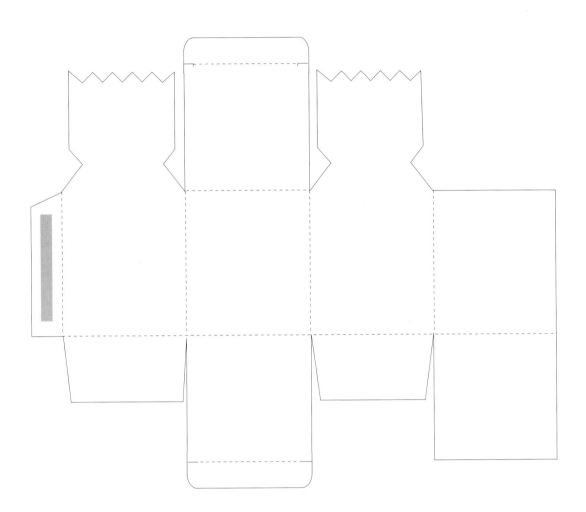

Box for sweets in the shape of a king's head and straight-forward base • Boîte à bonbons avec tête de roi et base simple • Bonbonschachtel mit Königskopf und einfachem Boden • Caja para caramelos, con cabeza de rey y base simple • Scatola per caramelle con testa di re e base semplice • Caixa para caramelos com cabeça de rei e base simples • Snoepjesdoos, met kroon en eenvoudige basis

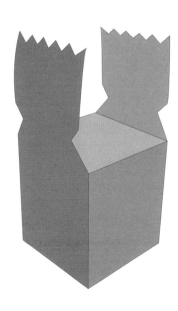

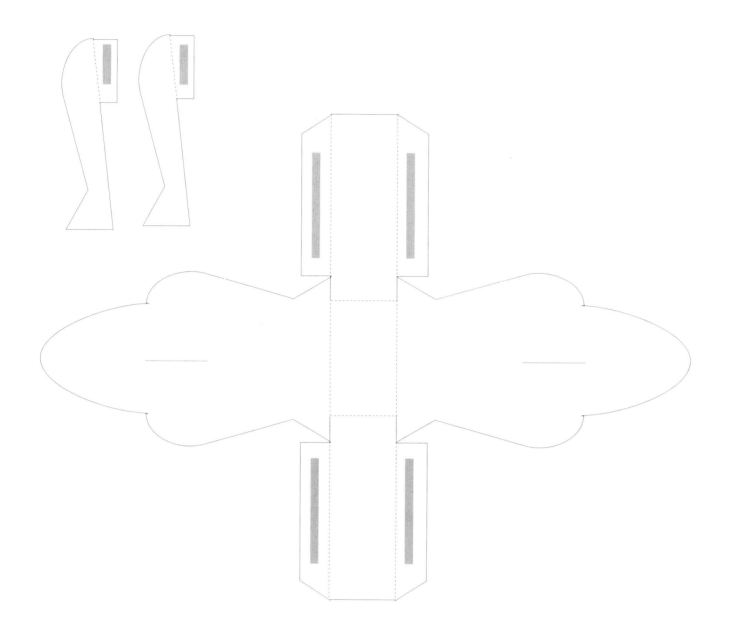

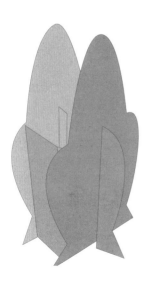

Rocket-shaped gift box • Boîte à cadeau en forme de fusée • Geschenkbox in Form einer Rakete • Caja para regalo, con forma de cohete • Scatola da regalo a forma di razzo • Caixa para presentes com forma de foguete • Geschenkdoos, in de vorm van een raket

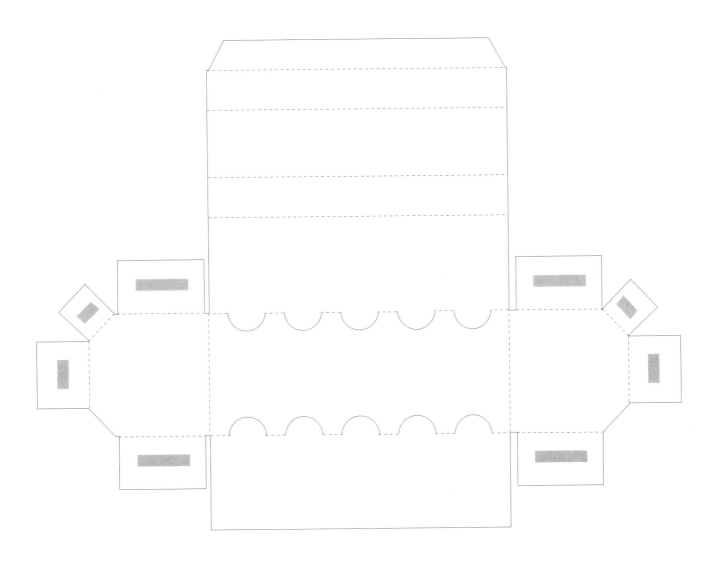

Train carriage-shaped gift box • Boîte à cadeau en forme de wagon de train • Geschenkbox in Form eines Waggons • Caja para regalo, con forma de vagón de tren • Scatola da regalo a forma di vagone ferroviario • Caixa para presentes com forma de vagão de comboio • Geschenkdoos, in de vorm van een treinwagon

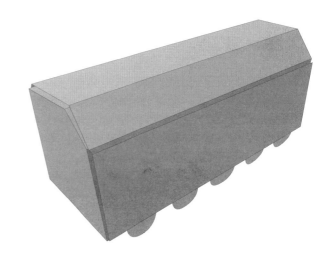

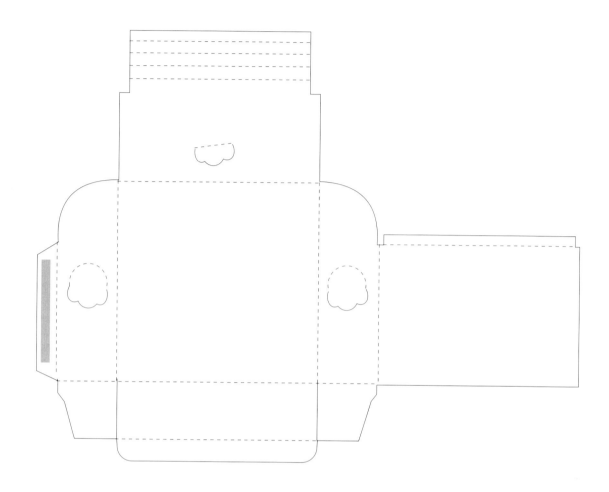

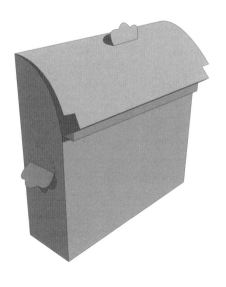

Mailbox-shaped gift box • Emballage cadeau en forme de boîte aux lettres • Geschenkbox in Form eines Briefkastens • Caja para regalo con forma de buzón de correo • Confezione regalo a forma di cassetta delle lettere • Caixa para presente com forma de caixa postal • Geschenkdoos in de vorm van een brievenbus

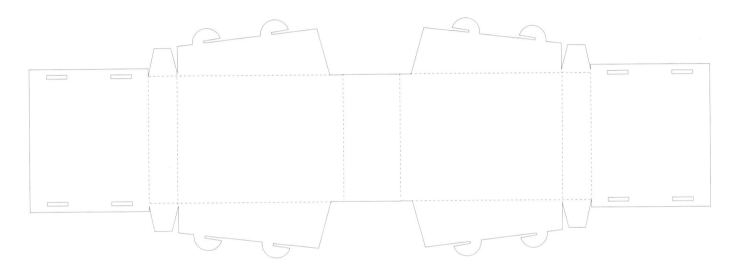

Double saddlebags for bicycle • Sacoches doubles pour bicyclette • Doppelte Satteltaschen fürs Fahrrad • Alforjas dobles para bicicleta • Borse portaoggetti doppie per bicicletta • Cestos duplos para bicicleta • Dubbele fietstassen

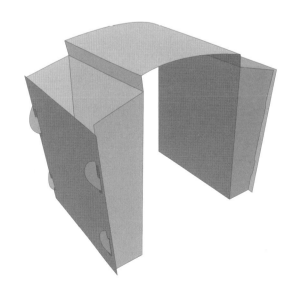

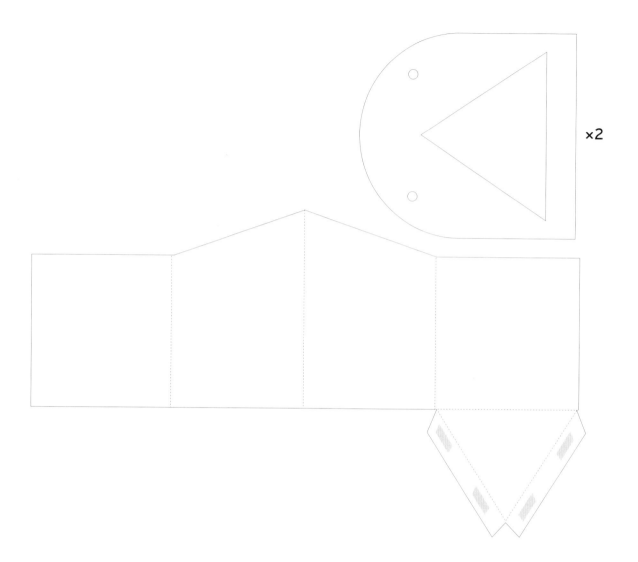

×2

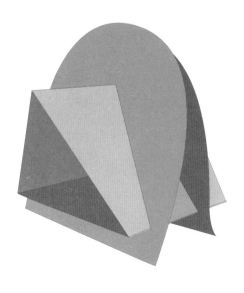

Hanging box for birds. Model 1 • Abri pour les oiseaux, à suspendre. Modèle 1 • Vogelhäuschen. Modell 1 • Caja colgante para pájaros. Modelo 1 • Scatola sospesa per uccelli. Modello 1 • Caixa de pendurar para pássaros. Modelo 1 • Vogelhuisje. Model 1

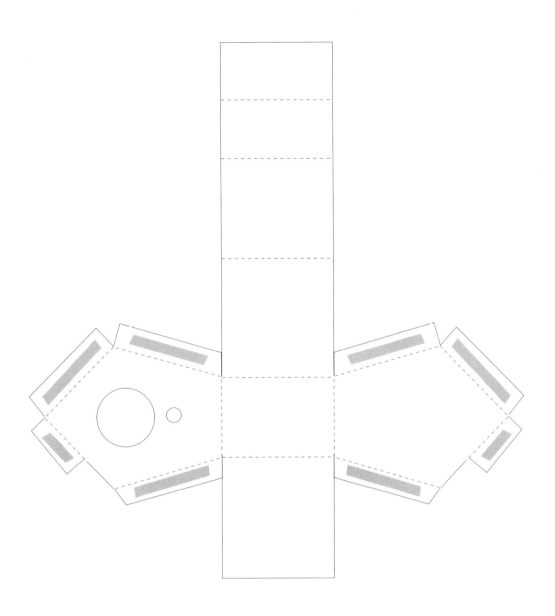

Hanging box for birds. Model 2 • Abri pour les oiseaux, à suspendre. Modèle 2 • Vogelhäuschen. Modell 2 • Caja colgante para pájaros. Modelo 2 • Scatola sospesa per uccelli. Modello 2 • Caixa de pendurar para pássaros. Modelo 2 • Vogelhuisje. Model 2

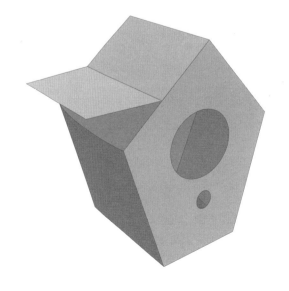

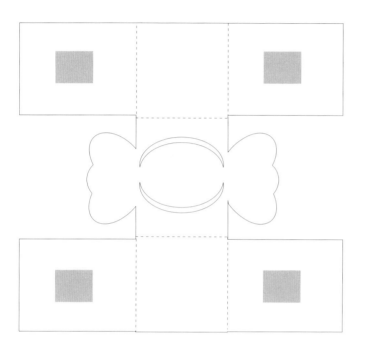

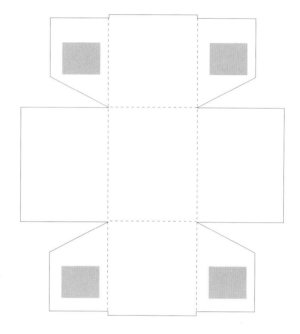

Sweet-shaped gift box • Boîte à cadeau en forme de bonbon • Geschenkbox in Form eines Bonbons • Caja para regalo, con forma de caramelo • Scatola da regalo a forma di caramella • Caixa para presente com forma de caramelo • Geschenkdoos, in de vorm van een snoepje

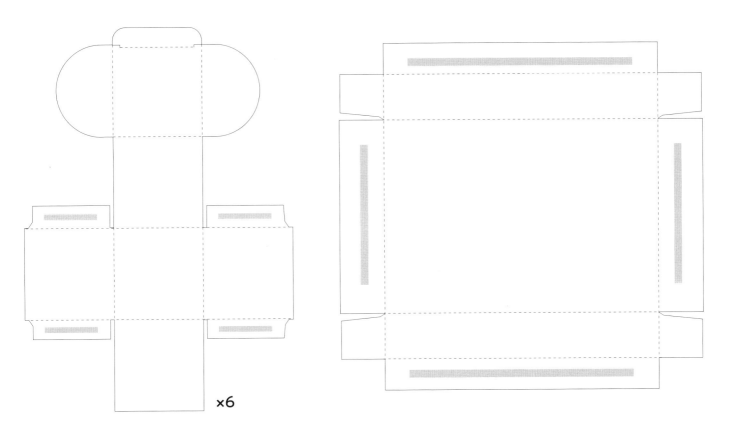

×6

Gift box in shape of six-cubed puzzle • Boîte à cadeau en forme de casse-tête à six cubes • Geschenkbox in Form eines Puzzles aus sechs Würfeln • Caja para regalo, con forma de rompecabezas de seis cubos • Scatola da regalo a forma di rompicapo a sei cubi • Caixa para presente com forma de quebra-cabeças de seis cubos • Geschenkdoos, in de vorm van een puzzel met zes kubussen

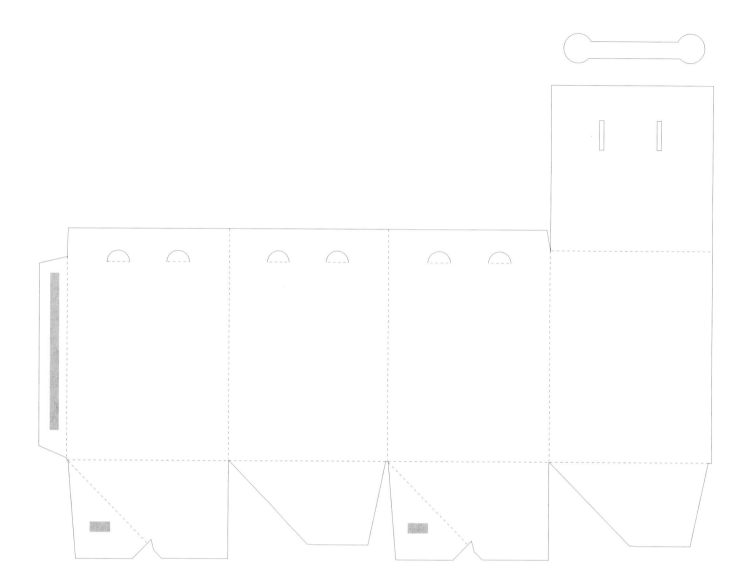

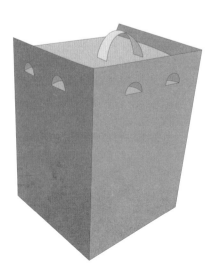

Nappy bin · Poubelle pour les couches · Windelbehälter · Papelera para pañales · Cestino per pannolini · Cesto do lixo para fraldas · Prullenbak voor luiers

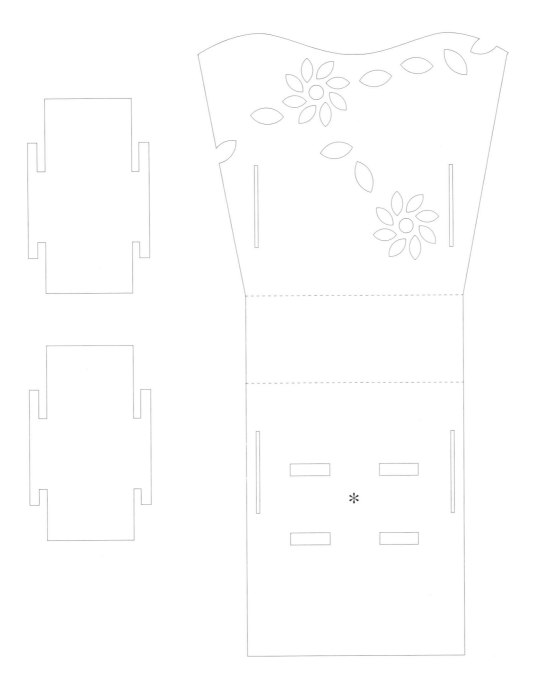

Bicycle basket · Panier à bicyclette · Fahrradkorb · Cesto para bicicleta · Cesto per bicicletta · Cesto para bicicleta · Fietsmand

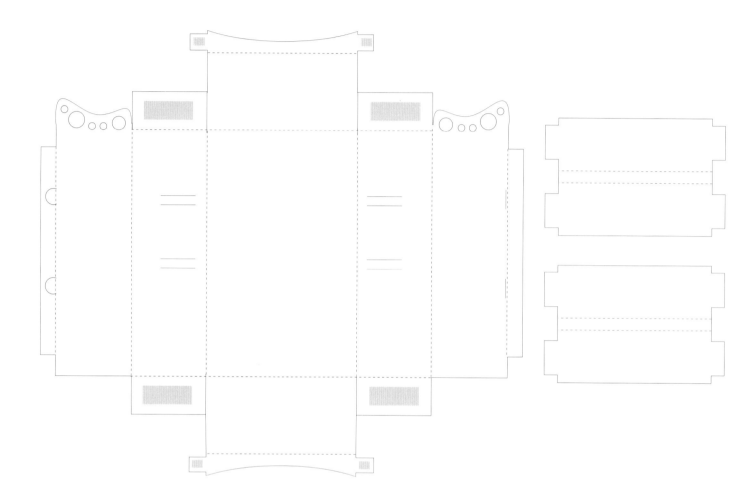

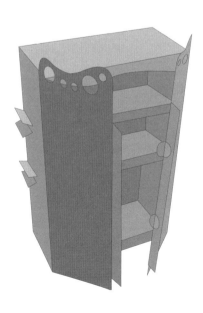

Wardrobe-shaped box for dolls clothing • Boîte en forme d'armoire pour vêtements de poupées • Box in Form eines Puppenschrankes • Caja con forma de armario para ropa de muñecas • Scatola a forma di armadio delle bambole • Caixa em forma de roupeiro para roupa de bonecas • Klerenkast voor poppenkleding

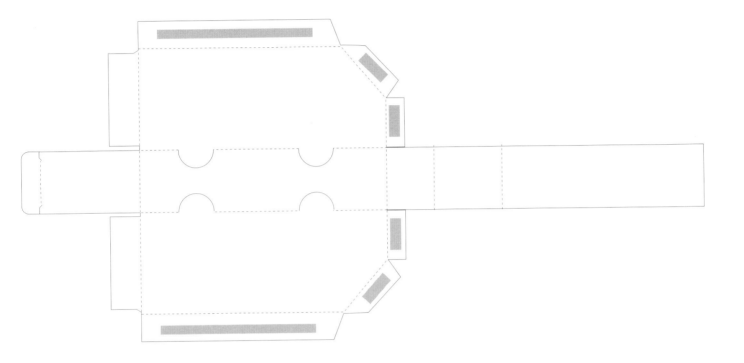

Lorry-shaped gift box • Boîte à cadeau en forme de camion • Geschenkbox in Form eines Lastwagens • Caja para regalo, con forma de camión • Scatola da regalo a forma di camion • Caixa para presente com forma de camião • Geschenkdoos, in de vorm van een vrachtauto

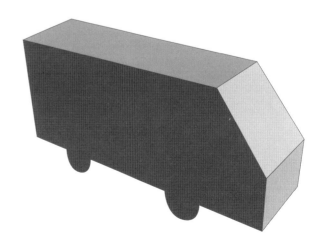

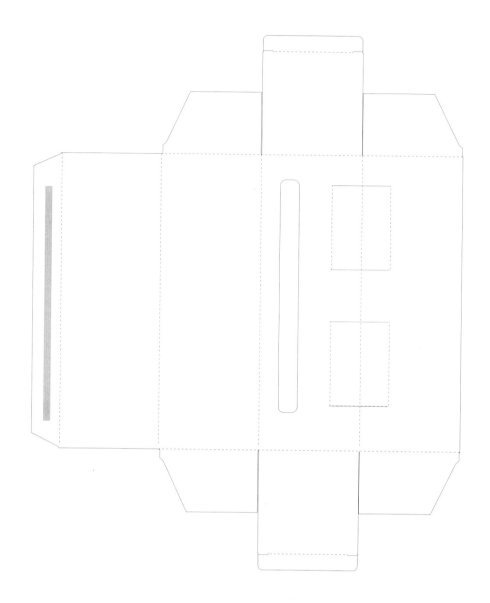

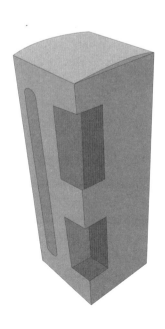

Sectioned box for paints and paintbrushes with lid ·
Coffret à compartiments avec couvercle, pour peintures
et pinceaux · Box mit Fächern für Farben und Pinsel · Caja
compartimentada para pinturas y pinceles, con tapa · Scatola
a scomparti con coperchio per colori e pennelli · Caixa
compartimentada para pinturas e pincéis com tampa · Doos
met vakken voor verf en pencelen, met deksel

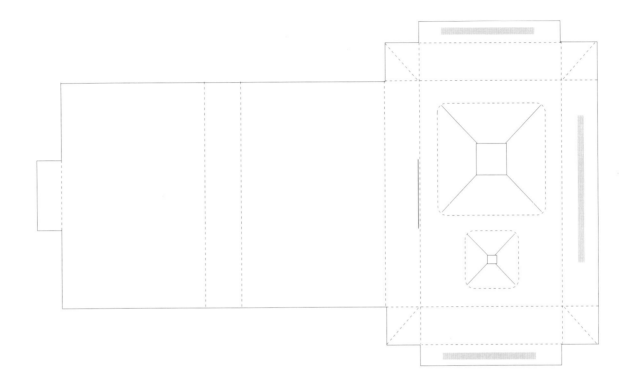

MP3 box • Coffret pour MP3 • Box für MP3-Player • Caja para MP3 • Scatola per lettore MP3 • Caixa para MP3 • Doos voor MP3-player

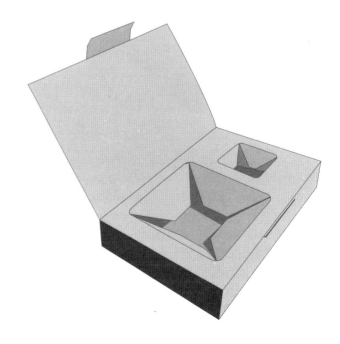

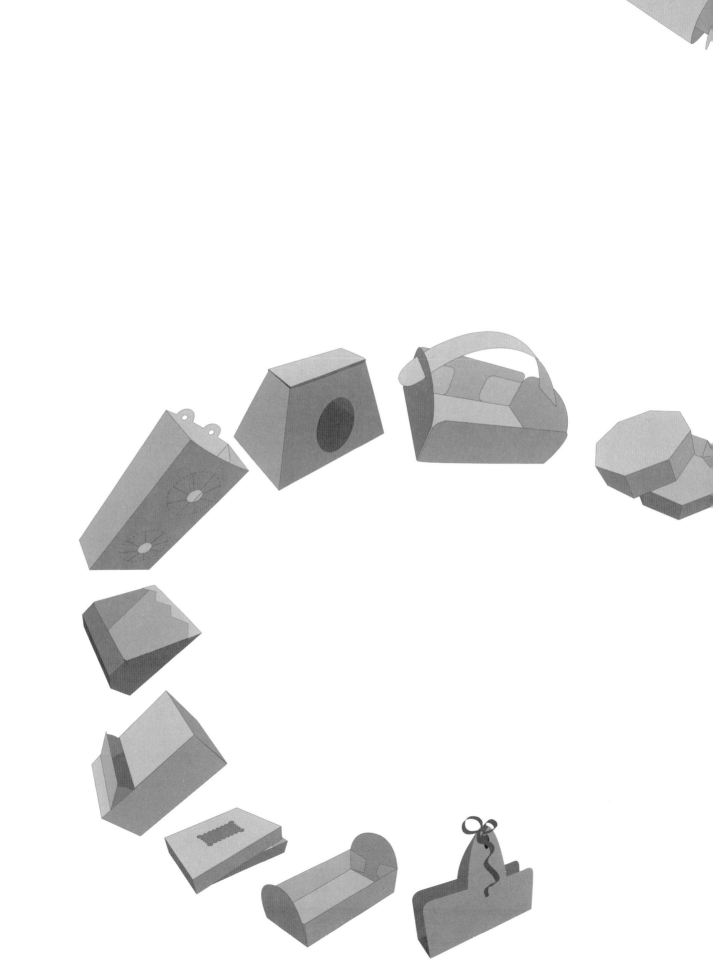

Boxes for food and drinks

Boîtes pour nourriture et boissons

Verpackungen für Speisen und Getränke

Cajas para alimentos y bebidas

Scatole per alimenti e bevande

Caixas para alimentos e bebidas

Dozen voor spijs en drank

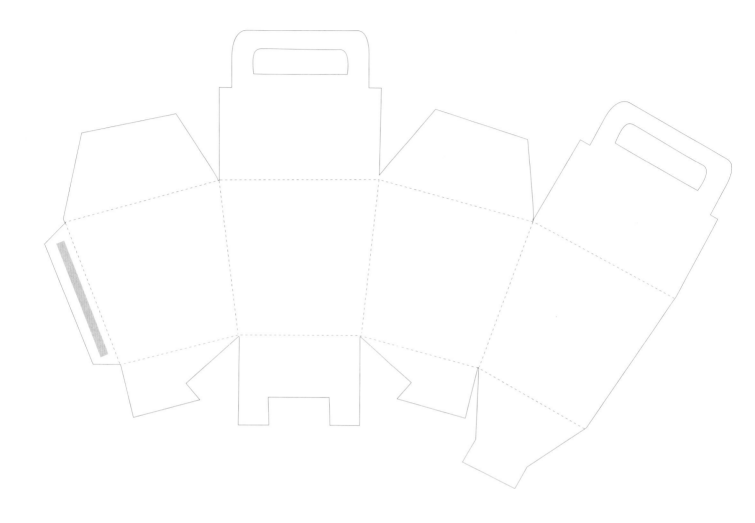

Trapezium-shaped box for picnic with handle • Boîte trapézoïdale à pique-nique, avec poignée • Trapezförmige Picknickbox mit Griff • Caja trapezoidal para picnic, con asa • Scatola trapezoidale da picnic con maniglia • Caixa trapezoidal para piquenique com asa • Trapeziumvormige picknickdoos, met handgreep

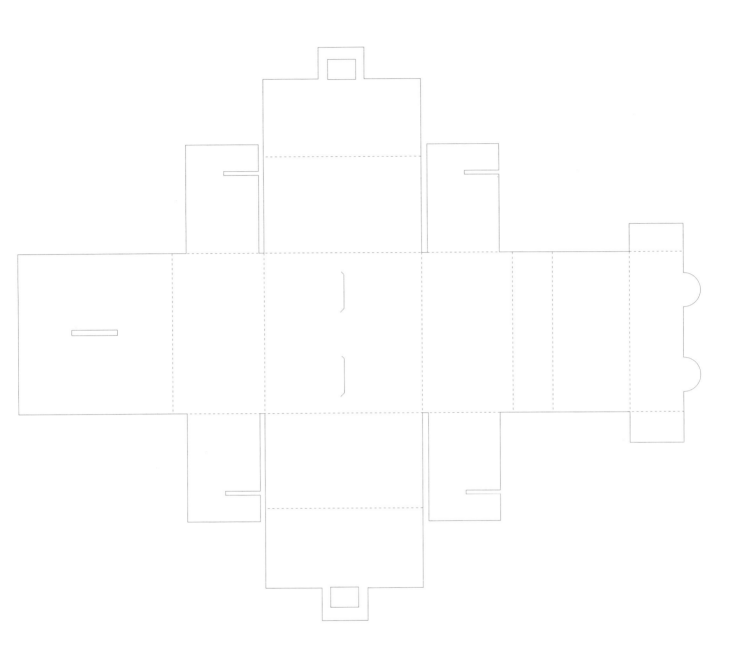

Double box for picnic • Boîte à pique-nique double • Doppelbox fürs Picknick • Caja doble para picnic • Scatola doppia da picnic • Caixa dupla para piquenique • Dubbele picknickdoos

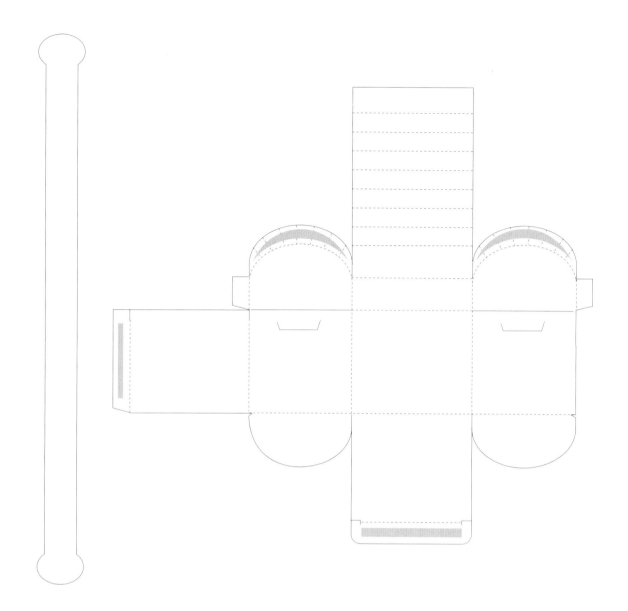

Letter box-shaped box with handle • Boîte à pique-nique avec poignée, en forme de boîte aux lettres • Picknickbox mit Griff in Briefkastenform • Caja para picnic, con forma de buzón y con asa • Scatola da picnic a forma di cassetta per le lettere con maniglia • Caixa para piquenique com forma de caixa de correio e com asa • Picknickdoos, in de vorm van een brievenbus en met hengsel

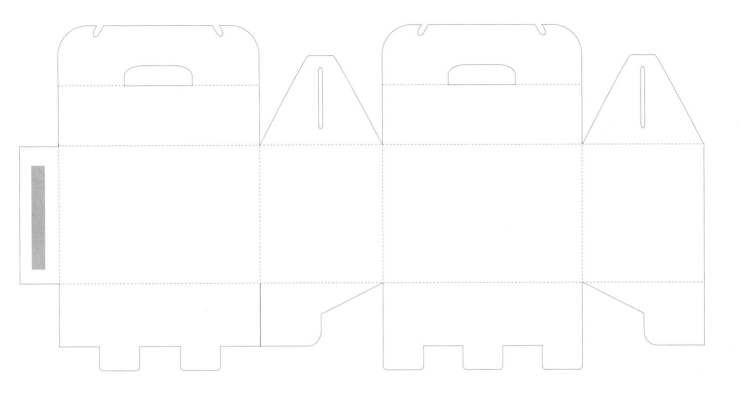

Picnic box with handle and ear-shaped closure • Boîte
à pique-nique avec poignée et fermeture à languettes •
Picknickbox mit Griff und Ohrenverschluss • Caja para picnic,
con asa y cierre de orejas • Scatola da picnic con maniglia e
chiusura «a orecchie» • Caixa para piquenique com asa e fecho
de orelhas • Picknickdoos, met hengsel en met beugelsluiting

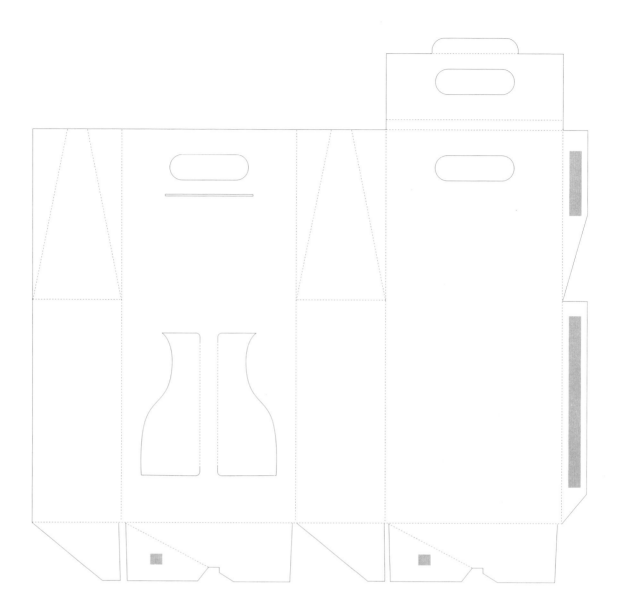

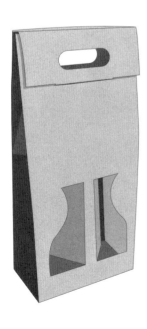

Two-bottle die cut box with handle • Casier ajouré pour deux bouteilles, avec poignée • Box für zwei Flaschen mit Ausstanzung und Griff • Caja troquelada para dos botellas, con asa • Scatola fustellata per due bottiglie con maniglia • Caixa cunhada para duas garrafas com asa • Gestanste doos voor twee flessen, met handgreep

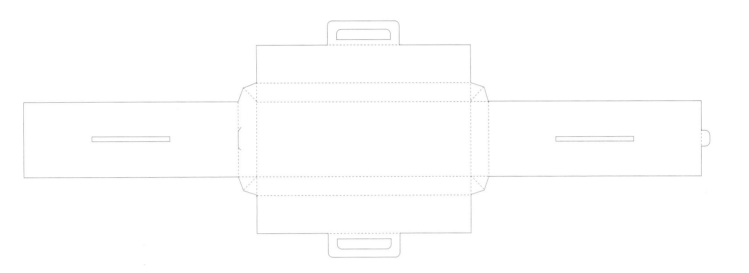

Rectangular self-assembly cake box with handle • Boîte
rectangulaire dépliable pour tarte, avec poignée • Rechteckige
Tortenschachtel mit Griff zum Zusammenstecken • Caja
automontable rectangular para tarta, con asa • Scatola
rettangolare automontante per torta con maniglia • Caixa
automontável rectangular para tarte com asa • Rechthoekige
zelfbouwdoos voor taart, met handgreep

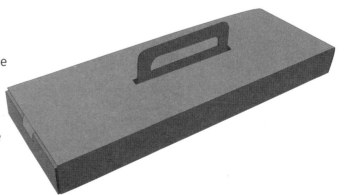

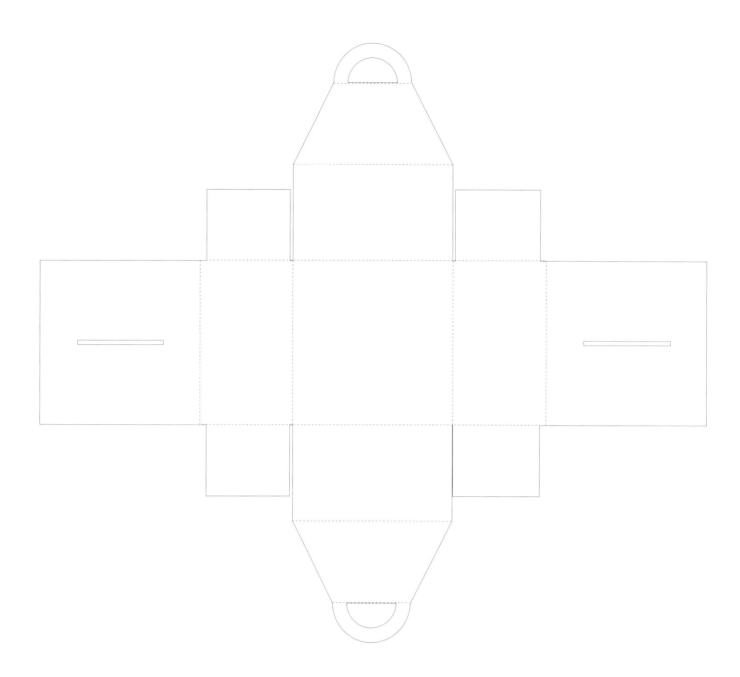

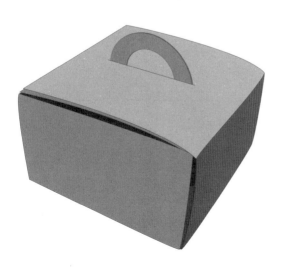

Cake box with handle • Boîte à gâteau avec poignée • Kuchenschachtel mit Griff • Caja para pastel, con asa • Scatola per dolce con maniglia • Caixa para bolo com asa • Doos voor koekjes, met handgreep

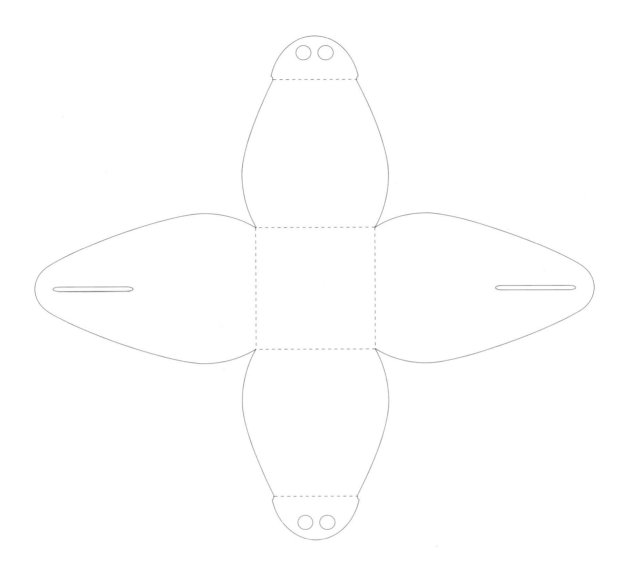

Circular self-assembly cake box with handle • Boîte dépliable pour tarte ronde, avec poignée • Runde Tortenschachtel zum Zusammenstecken • Caja automontable para tarta redonda, con asa • Scatola automontante per torta rotonda con maniglia • Caixa automontável para tarte redonda com asa • Zelfbouwdoos voor ronde taart, met handgreep

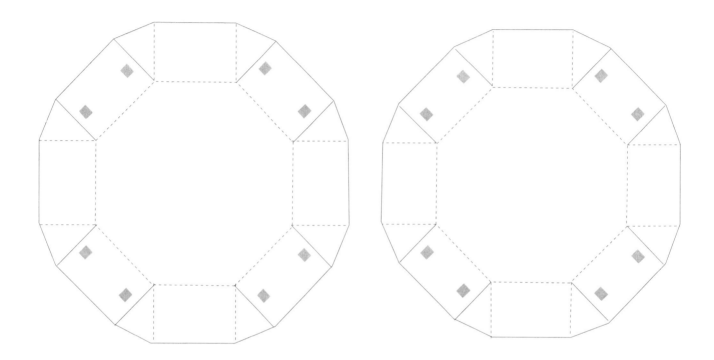

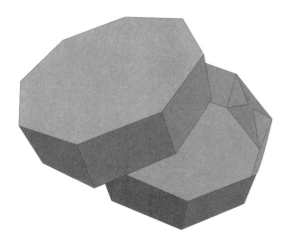

Octagonal cake box • Boîte octogonale à gâteau dépliable • Achteckige Kuchenschachtel • Caja octogonal para pastel • Scatola ottagonale per dolce • Caixa octogonal para bolo • Achthoekige taartdoos

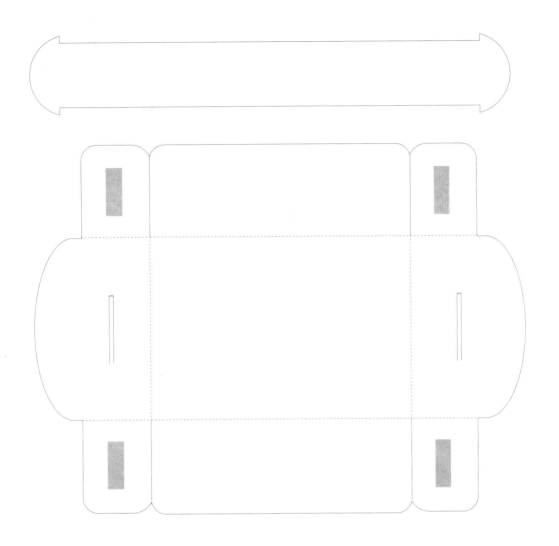

Fruit basket with handle • Panier à fruit avec anse • Obstkorb
mit Griff • Cesta para fruta, con asa • Cesto portafrutta con
maniglia • Cesta para fruta com asa • Fruitmand, met hengsel

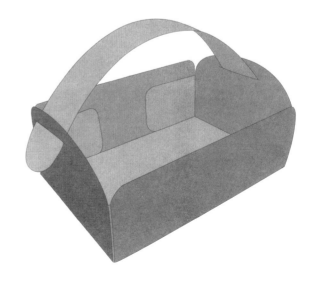

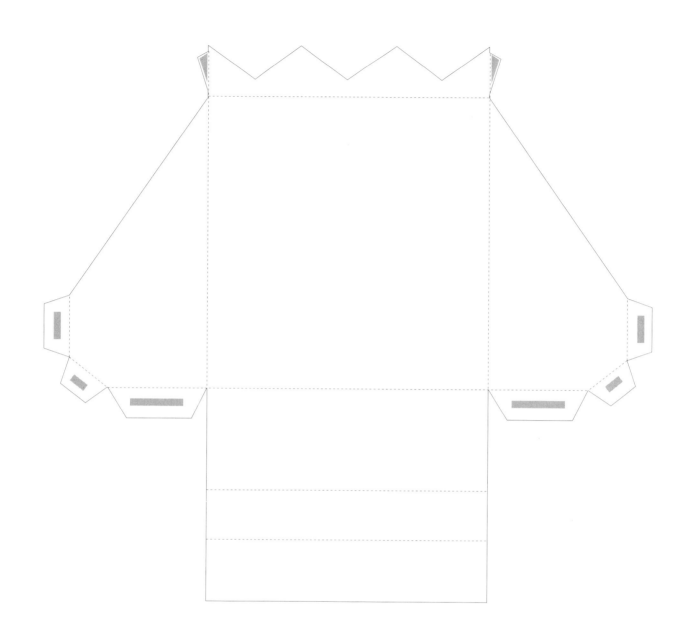

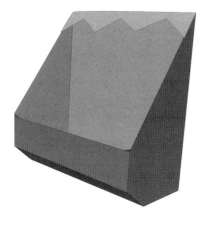

Wall-mounted spice rack • Range-épices à fixer au mur • Gewürzregal für die Wandmontage • Especiero colgante para pared • Portaspezie sospeso da parete • Porta-especiarias de pendurar para parede • Hangend kruidenrekje

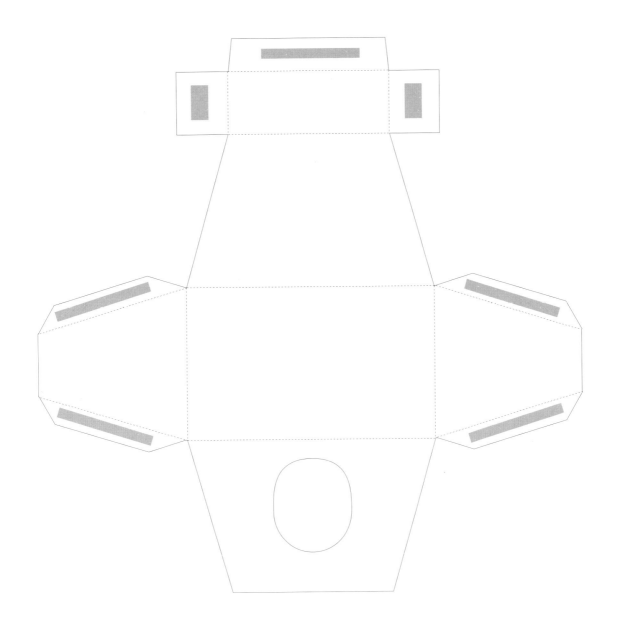

Plastic bag dispenser · Distributeur de sacs plastique ·
Plastiktütenspender · Dispensadora de bolsas de
plástico · Dispenser per sacchetti di plastica · Dispensadora
de sacos de plástico · Plastic-zakkendispenser

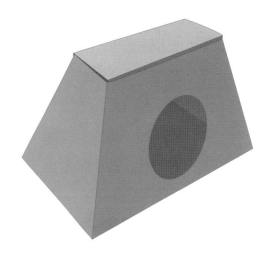

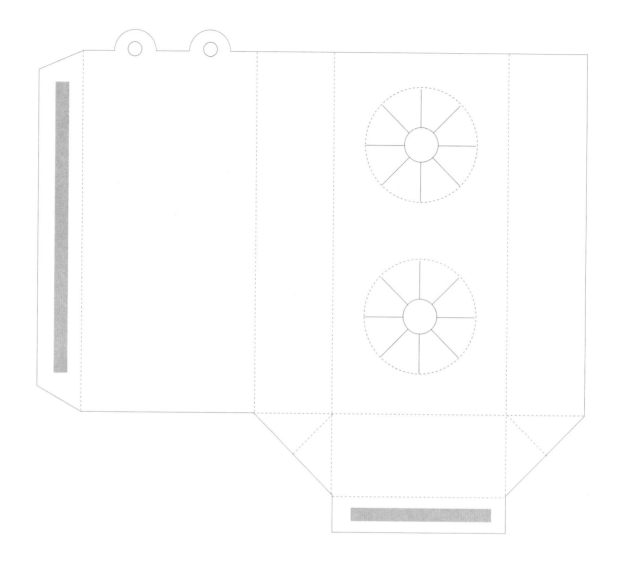

Hanging plastic bag dispenser • Distributeur de sacs plastique à suspendre • Hängender Plastiktütenspender • Dispensadora colgante de bolsas de plástico • Dispenser sospeso per sacchetti di plastica • Dispensadora de pendurar de sacos de plástico • Hangende dispenser voor plastic zakjes

Semi-cylinder plastic bag dispenser • Distributeur
semi-cylindrique de sacs plastique • Halbzylindrischer
Plastiktütenspender • Dispensadora semicilíndrica de
bolsas de plástico • Dispenser semicilindrico per sacchetti
di plastica • Dispensadora semicilíndrica de sacos de
plástico • Halfronde dispenser voor plastic zakjes

Bottle rack • Casier à bouteilles • Geschenkbox für Flaschen • Botellero • Portabottiglie • Garrafeira • Flessenhouder

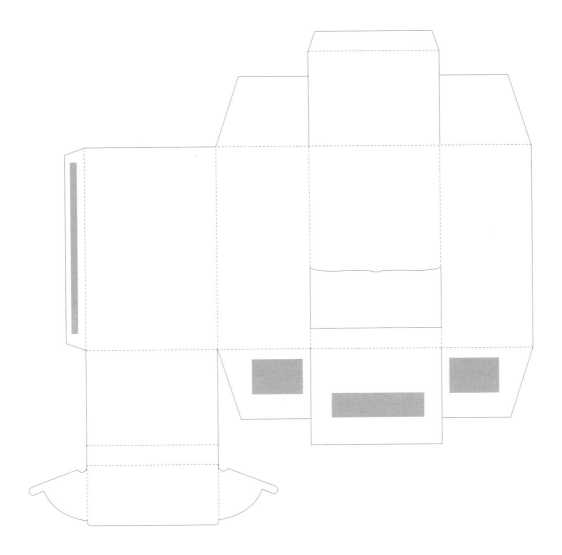

Sugar sachet dispenser with lower opening • Distributeur de sachets de sucre avec ouverture inférieure • Zuckertütenspender mit Klappe unten • Dispensadora de sobres de azúcar, con trampilla inferior • Dispenser per bustine di zucchero con sportellino inferiore • Dispensadora de pacotinhos de açúcar com escotilha inferior • Dispenser voor suikerzakjes, met opening aan de onderkant

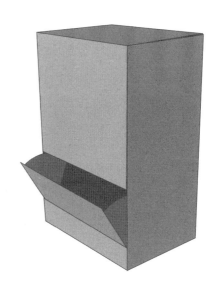

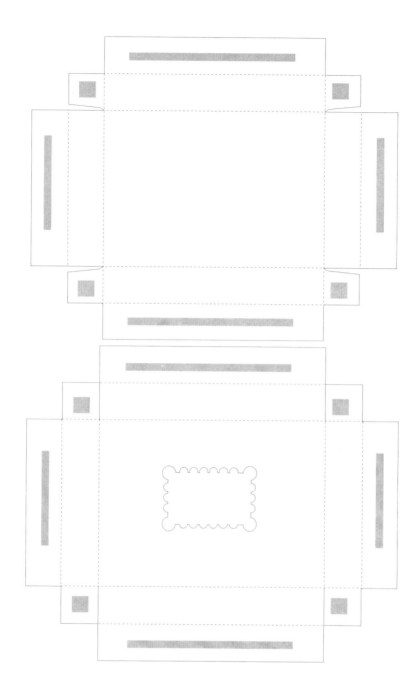

Biscuit box • Boîte à biscuits • Keksschachtel • Caja para galletas • Scatola per biscotti • Caixa para bolachas • Doos voor koekjes

Self-assembly pizza box · Boîte à pizza dépliable ·
Pizzaschachtel zum Zusammenstecken · Caja automontable
para pizza · Scatola automontante per pizza · Caixa automontável para pizza · Pizzadoos

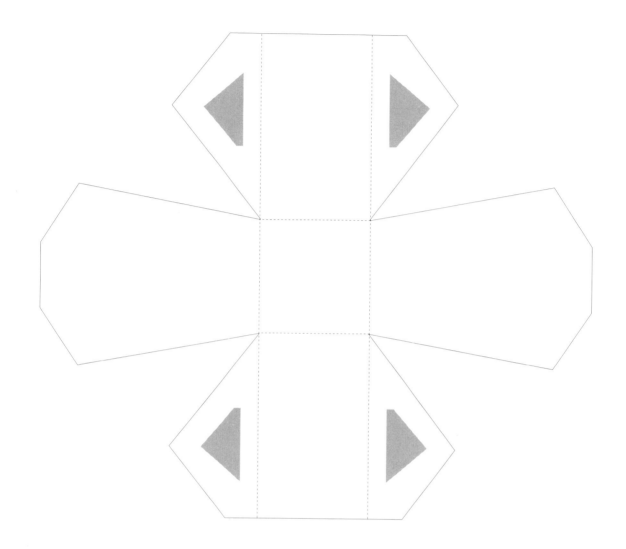

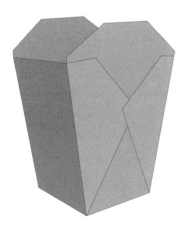

Traditional open box for Chinese food • Boîte classique ouverte pour nourriture chinoise • Offene Box für chinesisches Essen • Caja clásica abierta para comida china • Scatola classica aperta per cibo cinese • Caixa clássica aberta para comida chinesa • Klassieke open doos voor Chinese gerechten

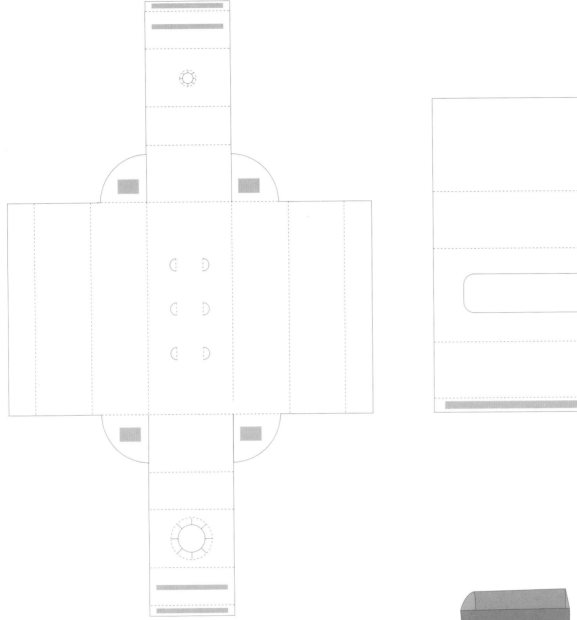

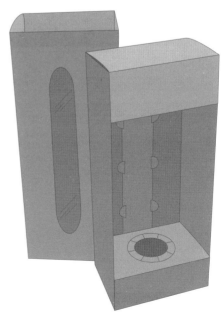

Flat box for bottle with exterior sleeve • Boîte plate pour bouteille avec étui extérieur • Flaschenverpackung mit Schuber • Caja plana para botella, con faja exterior • Scatola piana per bottiglia con aletta esterna • Caixa lisa para garrafa com faixa exterior • Platte doos voor fles, met hoes

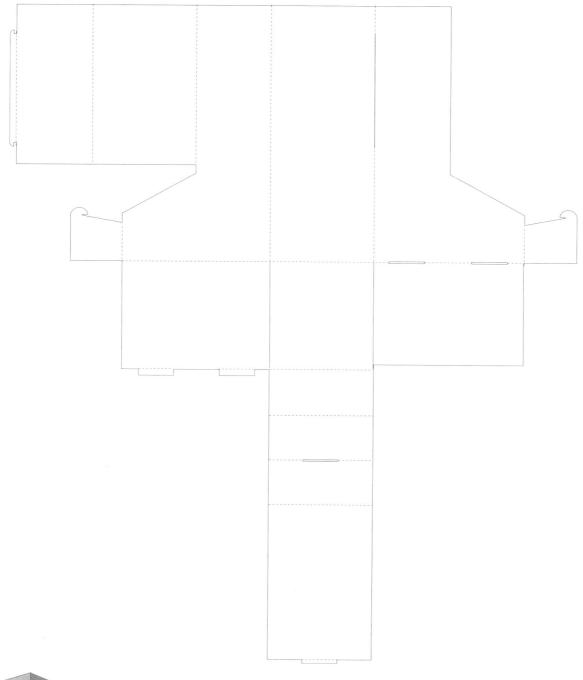

Can dispenser • Distributeur de boîtes de conserve •
Büchsenspender • Dispensadora de latas • Dispenser per
lattine • Dispensadora de latas • Dispenser voor blikjes

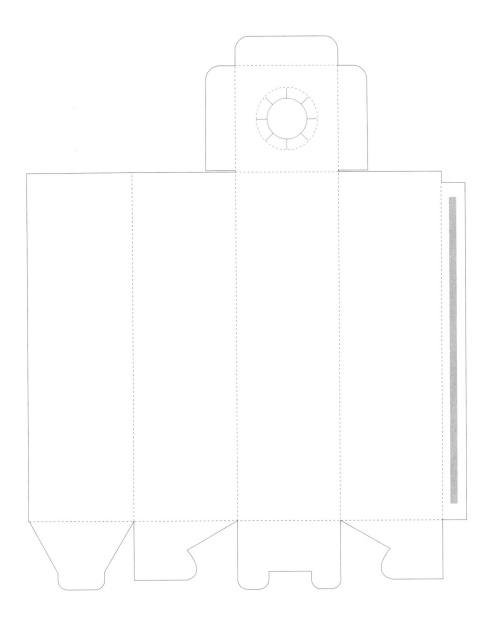

Open top wine box · Boîte pour bouteille laissant apparaître le col de la bouteille · Box für eine Weinflasche mit Öffnung für den Flaschenhals · Caja para botella de vino, con cuello al aire · Scatola per bottiglia di vino con collo a vista · Caixa para garrafa de vinho com gargalo à mostra · Doos voor wijnfles, met opening aan de bovenkant

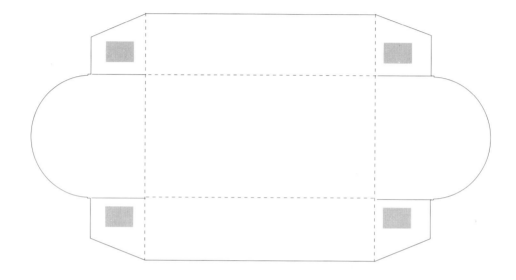

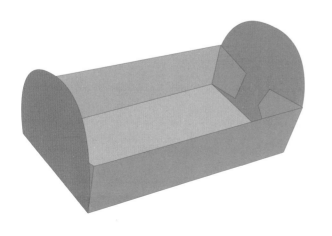

Salt and pepper shaker. Model 1 • Salière et poivrier. Modèle 1 • Tablett für Salz- und Pfefferstreuer. Modell 1 • Salero y pimentero. Modelo 1 • Portasale e pepe. Modello 1 • Saleiro e pimenteiro. Modelo 1 • Peper-en-zoutstel. Model 1

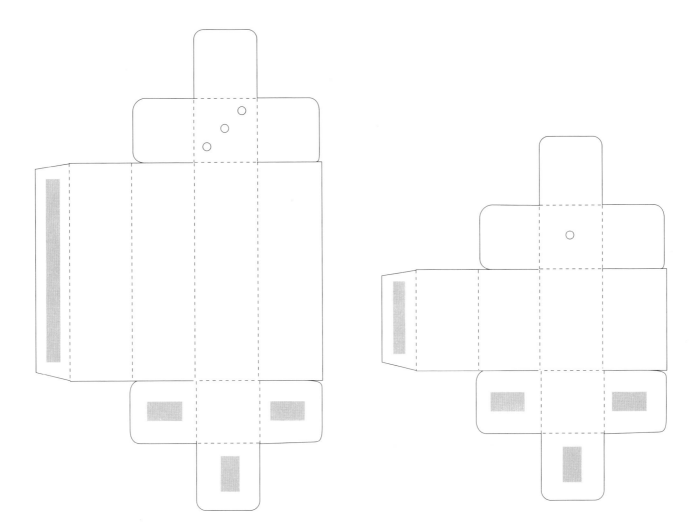

Salt and pepper shaker. Model 2 • Salière et poivrier. Modèle 2 • Salz- und Pfefferstreuer. Modell 2 • Salero y pimentero. Modelo 2 • Portasale e pepe. Modello 2 • Saleiro e pimenteiro. Modelo 2 • Peper-en-zoutstel. Model 2

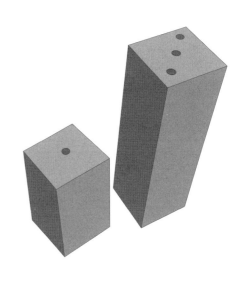

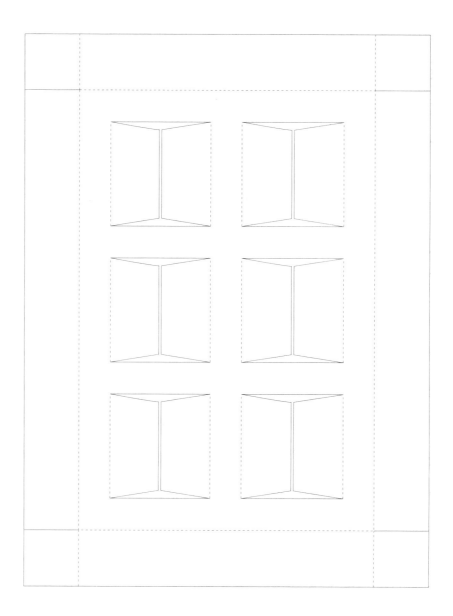

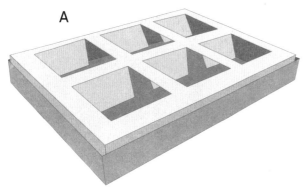

A

Sectioned box for teabags. Part 1 • Coffret compartimenté pour sachets de thé. Partie 1 • Box mit sechs Fächern für Teebeutel. Teil 1 • Caja compartimentada para bolsitas de té. Parte 1 • Scatola a scomparti per bustine di tè. Parte 1 • Caixa compartimentada para saquetas de chá. Parte 1 • Vakkendoos voor theezakjes. Deel 1

Sectioned box for teabags. Part 2 · Coffret compartimenté pour sachets de thé. Partie 2 · Box mit sechs Fächern für Teebeutel. Teil 2 · Caja compartimentada para bolsitas de té. Parte 2 · Scatola a scomparti per bustine di tè. Parte 2 · Caixa compartimentada para saquetas de chá. Parte 2 · Vakkendoos voor theezakjes. Deel 2

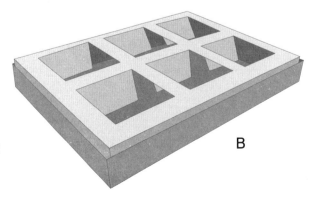

B

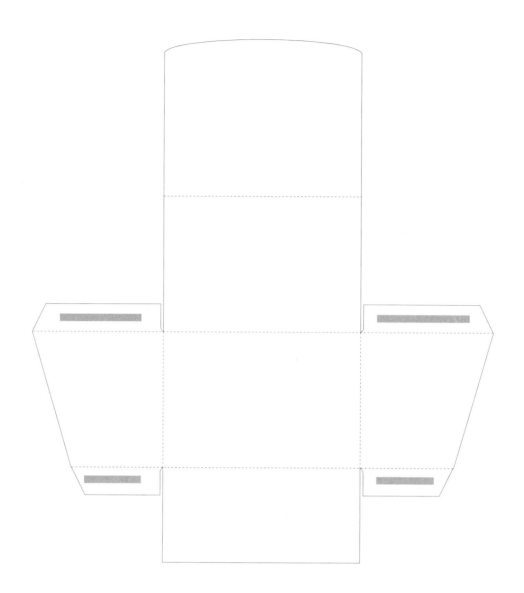

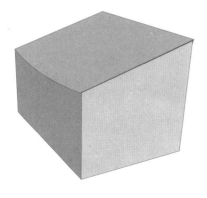

Salt shaker for kitchen with lift up lid • Salière de cuisine avec couvercle à bascule • Salzbehälter mit Klappdeckel für die Küche • Salero para cocina, con tapa basculante • Portasale da cucina, con coperchio basculante • Saleiro para cozinha, com tampa móvel • Zoutvaatje voor keuken, met kanteldeksel

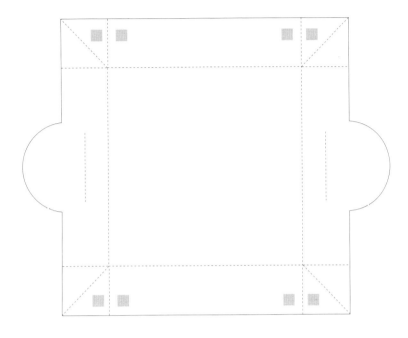

Napkin holder. Model 1 • Porte-serviettes de table. Modèle 1 •
Serviettenkorb. Modell 1 • Cesta servilletero. Modelo 1 • Cesto
portatovaglioli. Modello 1 • Cesta porta-guardanapos. Modelo 1 •
Servetringenmand. Model 1

*

Napkin holder. Model 2 • Porte-serviettes de table. Modèle 2 • Serviettenkorb. Modell 2 • Cesta servilletero. Modelo 2 • Cesto portatovaglioli. Modello 2 • Cesta porta-guardanapos. Modelo 2 • Servettenhouder. Model 2

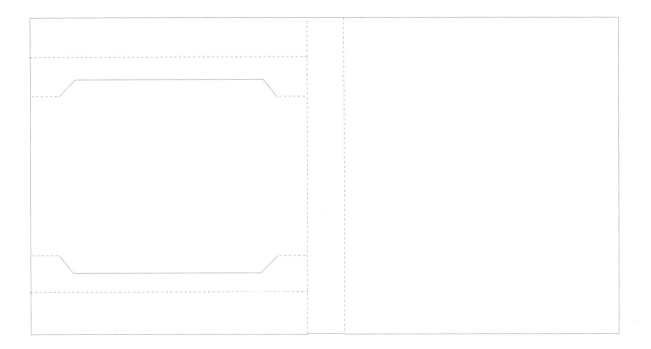

Box for plates with dividers · Casier pour assiettes ·
Tellerbox mit Unterteilungen · Caja para platos, con
separadores · Scatola per piatti con divisori · Caixa para
pratos com separadores · Doos voor borden

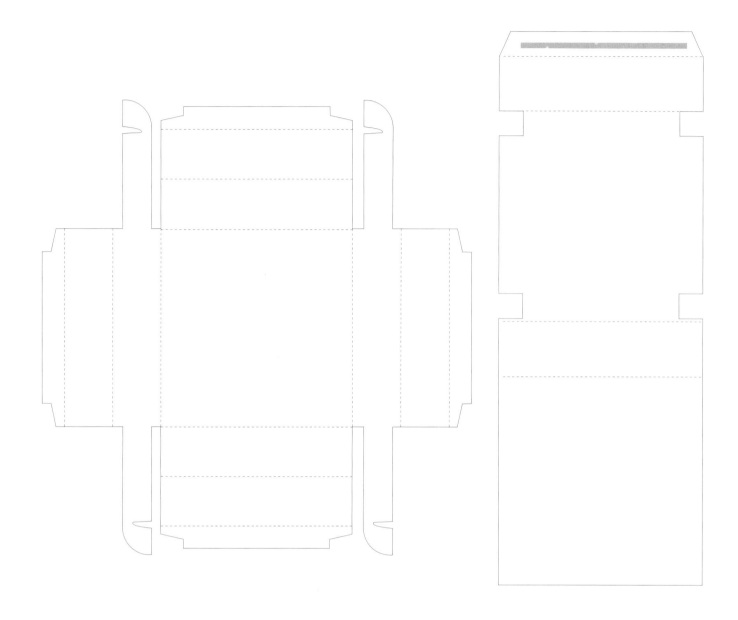

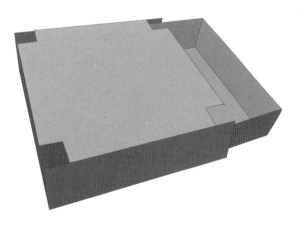

Sandwich tray with cover • Étui à sandwich • Sandwichtablett mit Schuber • Bandeja para sandwich, con faja • Vassoio per panini con fascetta • Bandeja para sanduíche com faixa • Bakje voor sandwich, met hoes

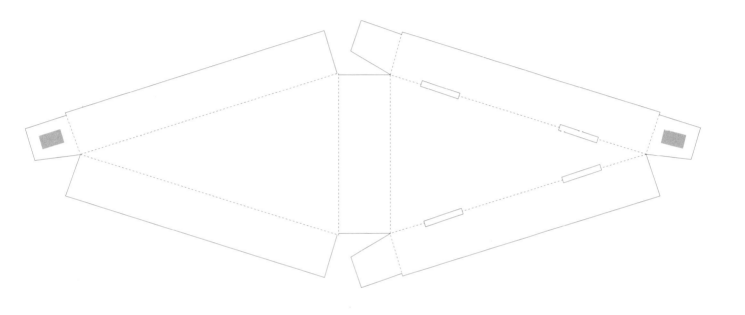

Triangular pizza portion box • Boîte à bascule triangulaire pour parts de pizza • Dreieckige Klappschachtel für Pizzaportionen • Caja basculante triangular para porciones de pizza • Scatola basculante triangolare per tranci di pizza • Caixa basculante triangular para fatias de pizza • Driehoekig kanteldeksel voor pizzaporties

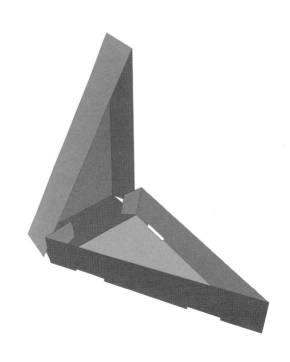

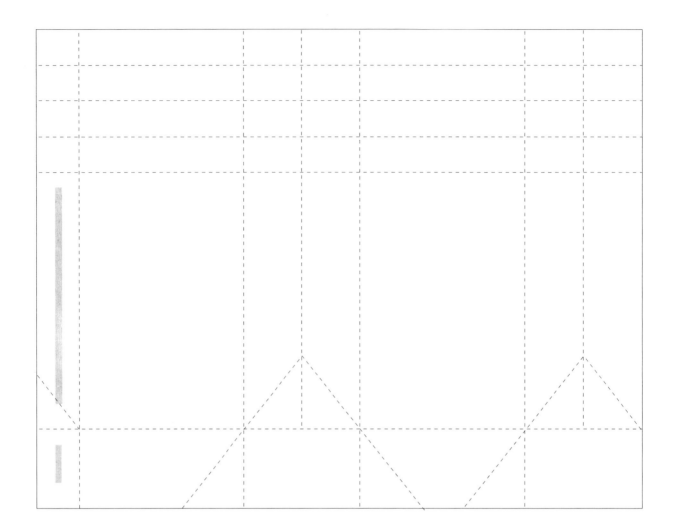

Closable takeaway food bag with closure • Sac avec fermeture pour nourriture à emporter • Tüte mit Verschluss für Speisen • Bolsa de comida para llevar, con cierre • Borsa per pranzo al sacco con chiusura • Saco de comida para levar com fecho • Draagtas voor eten, met sluiting

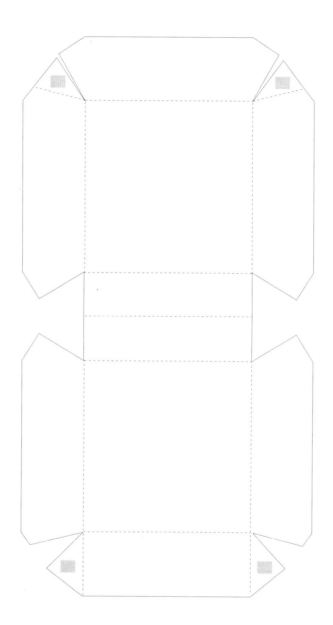

Self-assembly hamburger box • Boîte à hamburgers
dépliable • Hamburger-Box zum Zusammenstecken •
Caja automontable para hamburguesas • Scatola
automontante per hamburger • Caixa automontável para
hambúrgueres • Zelfbouwdoos voor hamburgers

Self-assembly hot dog box · Boîte à hotdogs dépliable ·
Hotdog-Box zum Zusammenstecken · Caja automontable
para hot dogs · Scatola automontante per hot dog · Caixa
automontável para cachorros · Zelfbouwdoos voor hotdogs

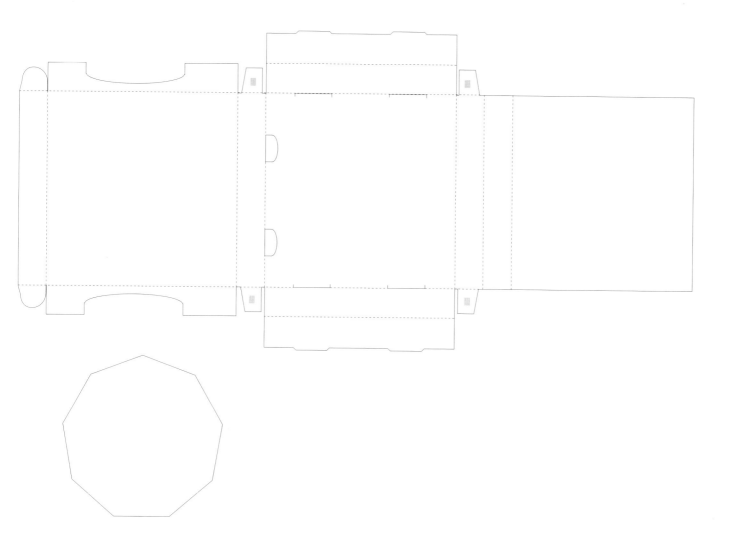

Box with tray for round cake • Boîte avec plateau pour tarte circulaire • Schachtel mit Tablett für eine runde Torte • Caja con bandeja para tarta circular • Scatola con vassoio per torta rotonda • Caixa com bandeja para tarte circular • Doos met bakje voor ronde taart

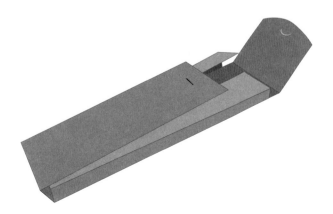

Box with tray for rectangular cake • Boîte avec plateau pour tarte rectangulaire • Rechteckige Kuchenschachtel mit Tablett • Caja con bandeja para tarta rectangular • Scatola con vassoio per torta rettangolare • Caixa com bandeja para tarte rectangular • Doos met bakje voor rechthoekige taart

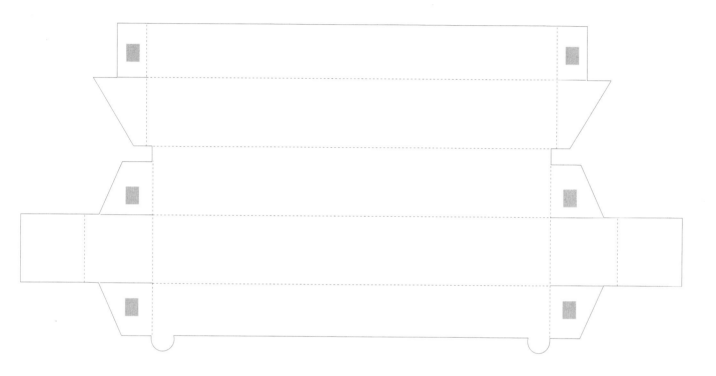

Kitchen paper dispenser • Dérouleur de papier absorbant • Küchenpapierspender • Dispensador de rollos de papel de cocina • Dispenser per rotoli di carta da cucina • Dispensador de rolos de papel de cozinha • Doos voor rollen keukenpapier

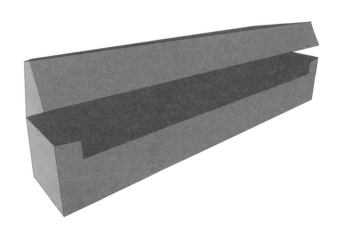

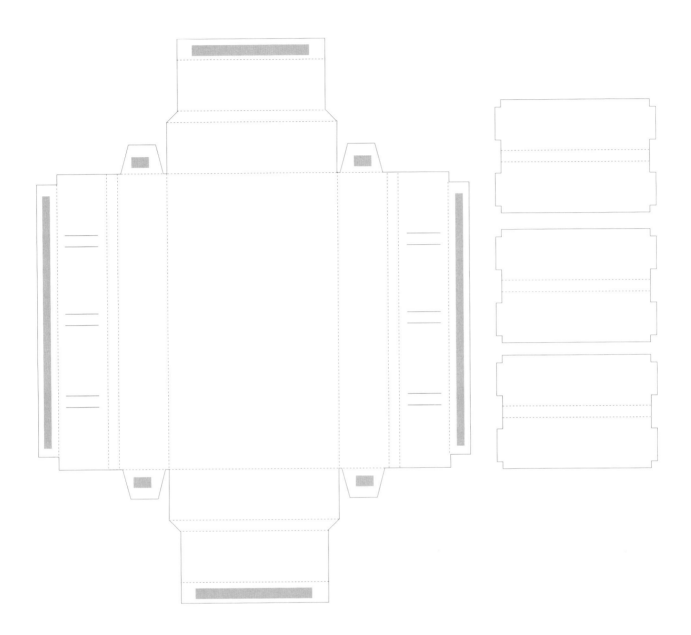

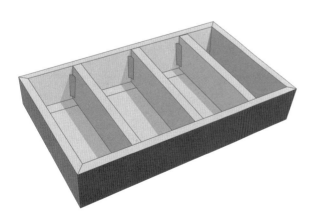

Sectioned cutlery box • Range-couverts • Besteckbox • Caja clasificadora de cubiertos • Scatola portaposate con divisori • Caixa classificadora de talheres • Verdeeldoos voor bestek

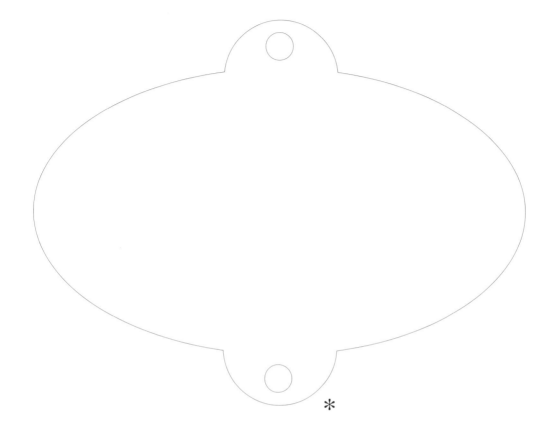

*

Bread basket • Huche à pain • Brotkorb • Cesta para el pan • Cesto per il pane • Cesta para o pão • Broodmandje

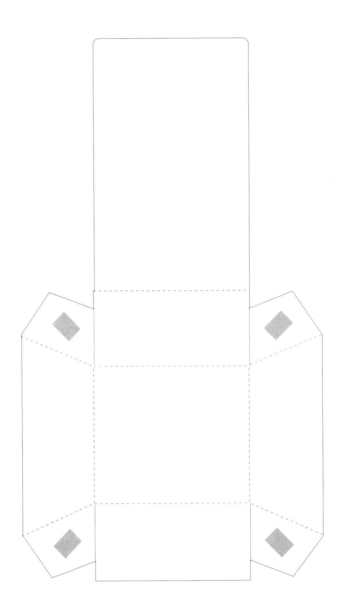

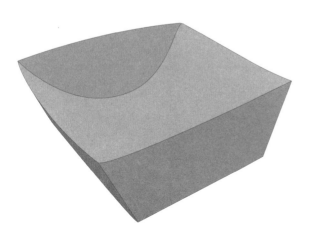

Jar. Model 1 • Bocal de rangement. Modèle 1 • Behälter. Modell 1 • Tarro contenedor. Modelo 1 • Barattolo contenitore. Modello 1 • Tarro para conteúdos. Modelo 1 • Trommelhouder. Model 1

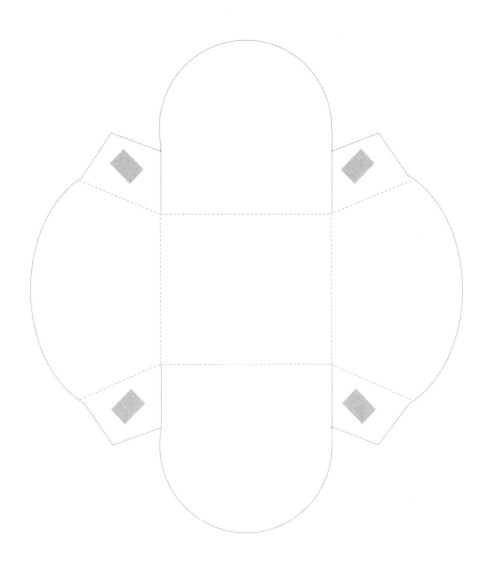

Jar. Model 2 • Bocal de rangement. Modèle 2 • Behälter.
Modell 2 • Tarro contenedor. Modelo 2 • Barattolo contenitore.
Modello 2 • Tarro para conteúdos. Modelo 2 • Trommelhouder.
Model 2

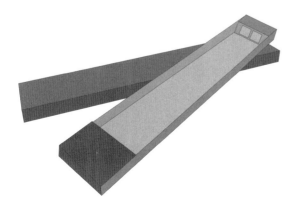

Box for Chinese chopsticks with interior support • Boîte pour baguettes chinoises avec support intérieur • Schachtel mit Innenhalterung für Essstäbchen • Caja para palillos chinos, con soporte interior • Scatola per bacchette cinesi con supporto interno • Caixa para palitos chineses com suporte interior • Doos voor Chinese stokjes, met binnensteun

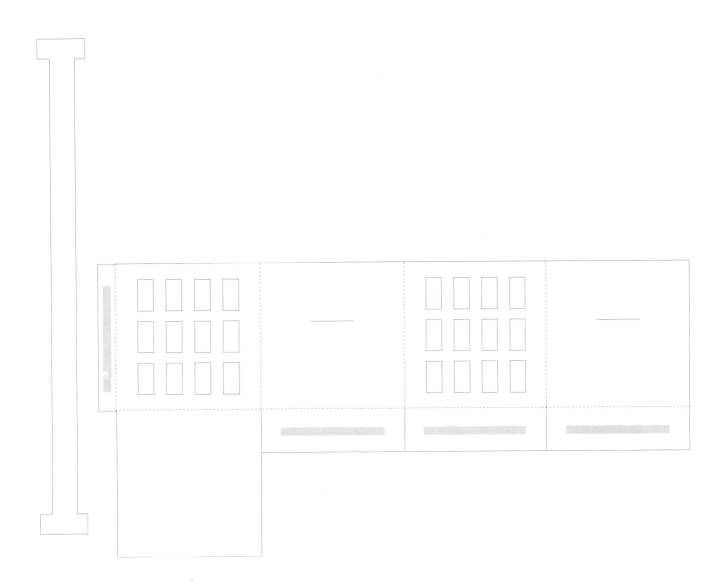

Garlic basket • Boîte pour conserver l'ail • Korb für
Knoblauch • Caja para ajos • Cesto porta-aglio • Caixa para
alhos • Knoflookmandje

×3

×4

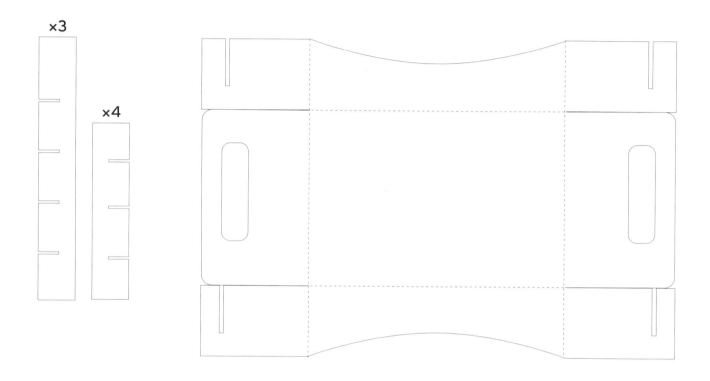

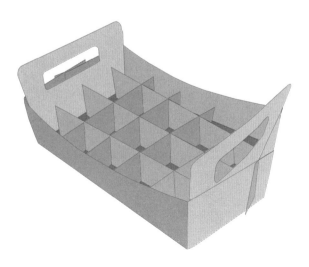

Fruit box • Coupe à fruits • Obstkiste • Caja para fruta • Scatola
per frutta • Caixa para fruta • Doos voor fruit

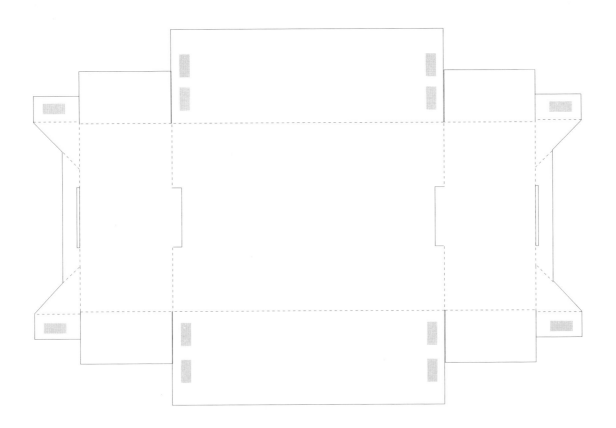

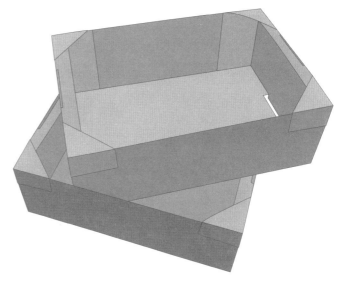

Stackable fruit box · Coupe à fruits empilable · Stapelbare Obstkiste · Caja apilable para fruta · Scatola impilabile per frutta · Caixa empilhável para fruta · Stapeldoos voor fruit

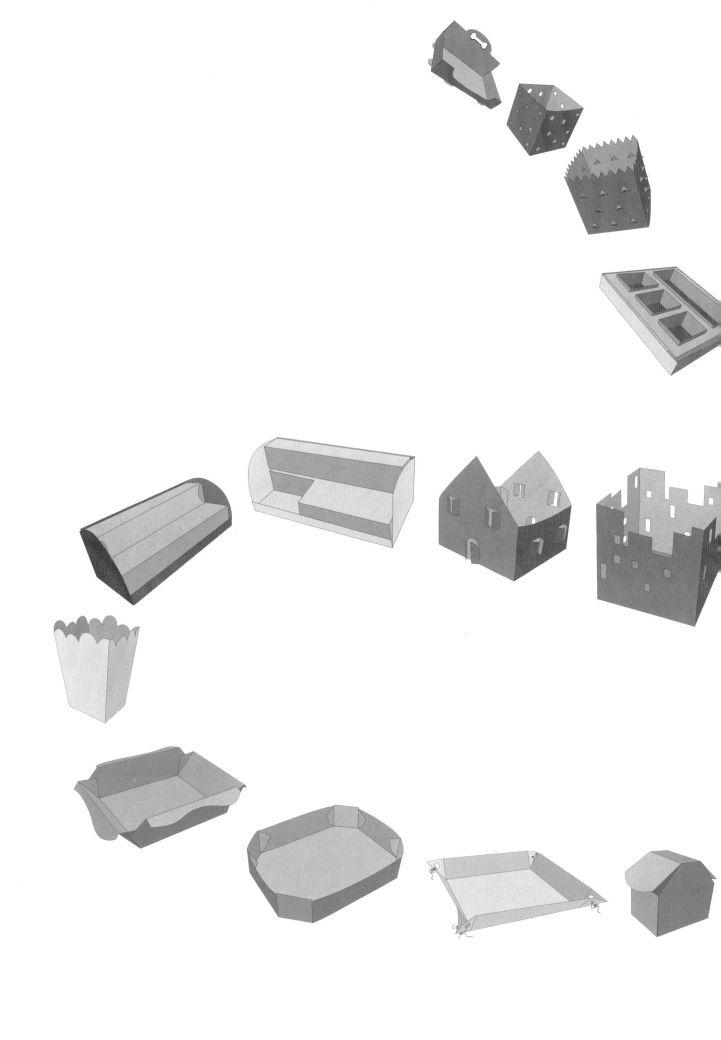

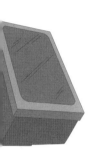

Decorative boxes. Accessories for the home
Boîtes décoratives. Accessoires pour la maison
Dekorative Boxen. Accessoires für die Wohnung
Cajas decorativas. Complementos para el hogar
Scatole decorative. Complementi d'arredo per la casa
Caixas decorativas. Complementos para o lar
Decoratieve dozen. Accessoires voor het huishouden

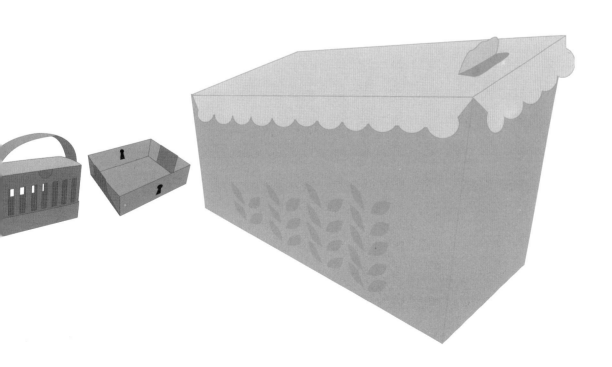

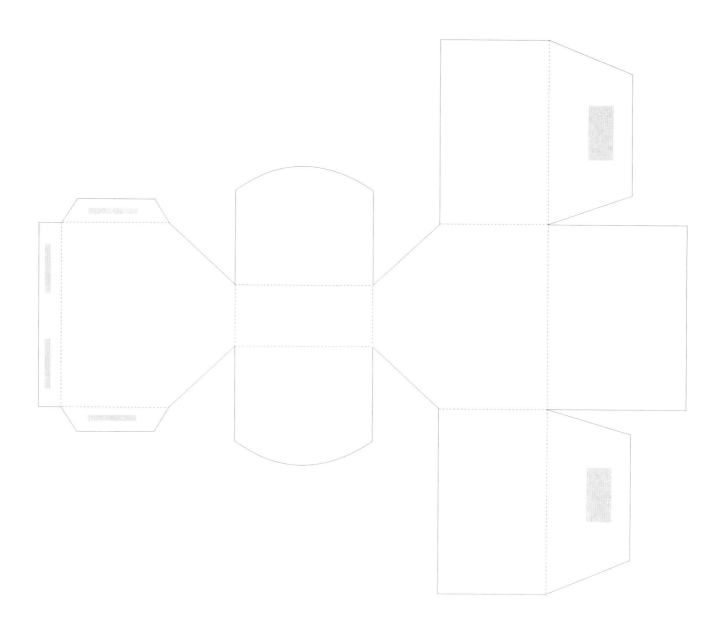

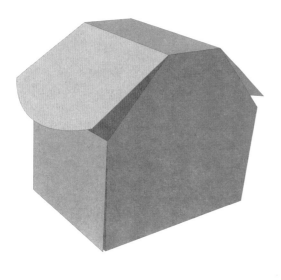

Sewing box with two lift up lids • Boîte à couture à deux rabats • Nähkasten mit zwei Klappdeckeln • Costurero con dos tapas basculantes • Cestino da cucito con coperchi basculanti • Caixa de costura com duas tampas móveis • Naaidoos met twee kanteldeksels

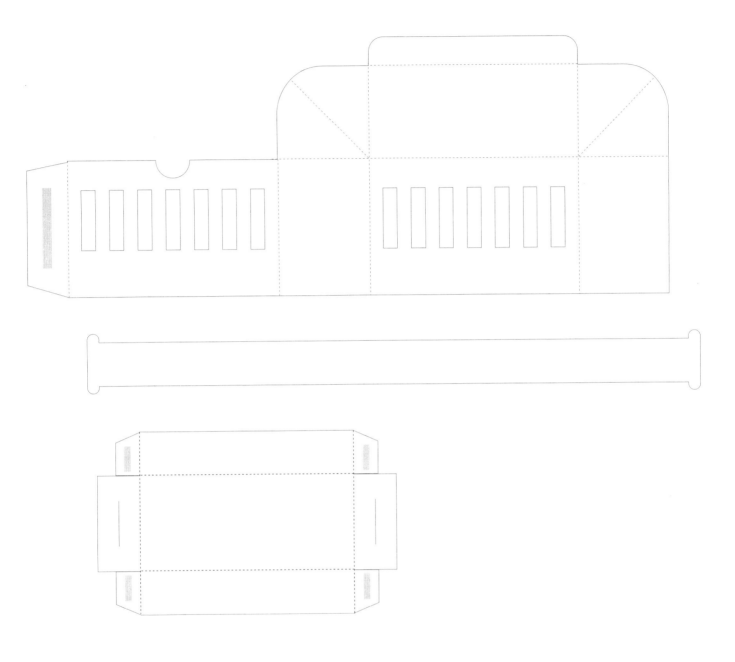

Cube-shaped box with vent and handle • Boîte cubique avec ouverture et poignée • Box mit Luftlöchern und Griff • Caja cúbica con respiradero y asa • Scatola cubica con fessura e maniglia • Caixa cúbica com respiradouro e asa • Rechthoekige doos met luchtgaten en hengsel

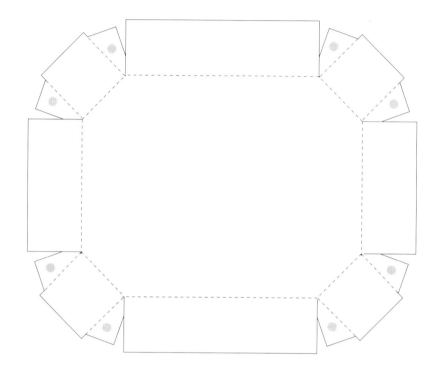

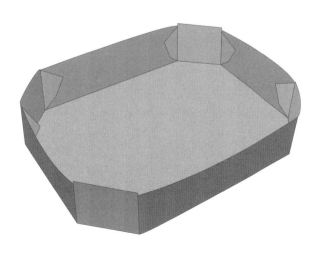

Coin tray with plain side and bevelled corners • Vide-poches à paroi unique et angles biseautés • Ablage mit einfacher Wand und abgeschrägten Ecken für Hosentascheninhalt • Bandeja vaciabolsillos con pared simple y esquinas biseladas • Vassoio vuotatasche con bordi semplici e angoli smussati • Bandeja esvazia bolsos com parede simples e cantos biselados • Dienblad met eenvoudige zijkanten en schuine hoeken

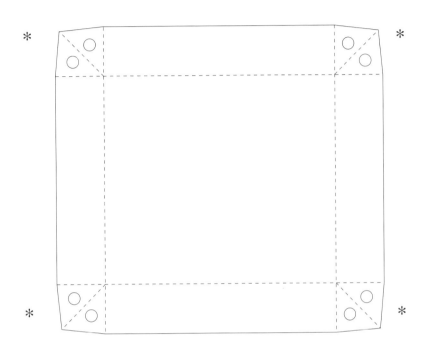

Coin tray with inclined corners • Vide-poches à bords inclinés • Ablage mit schrägen Ecken für Hosentascheninhalt • Bandeja vaciabolsillos con esquinas inclinadas • Vassoio vuotatasche con angoli inclinati • Bandeja esvazia bolsos com cantos inclinados • Dienblad met schuin aflopende hoeken

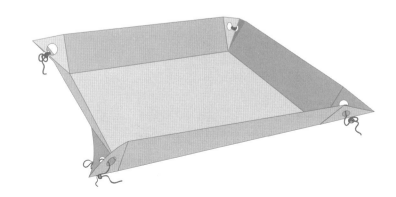

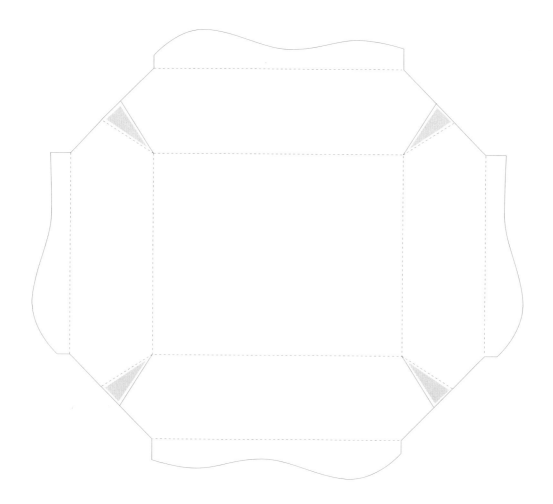

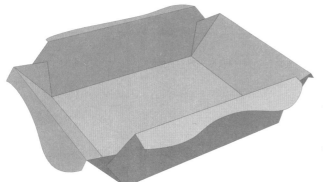

Tray with flap • Plateau à rebords fantaisie • Ablage mit Lasche • Bandeja con solapa • Vassoio con bordatura • Bandeja com aba • Dienblad met omgevouwen randen

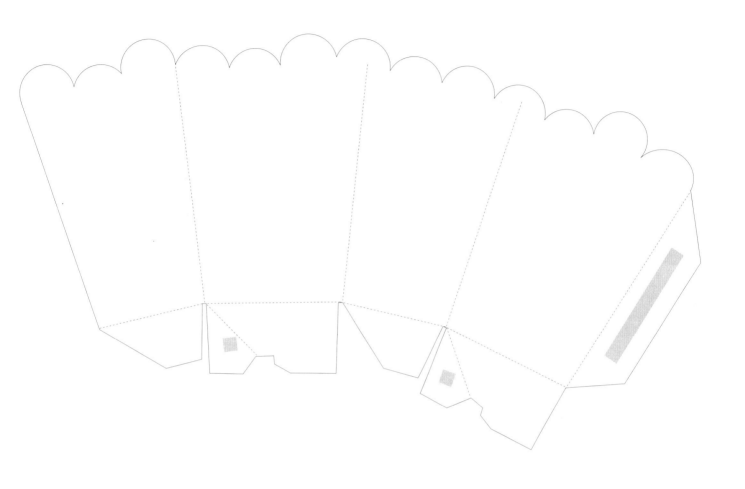

Wastepaper bin with glued self-assembly base • Corbeille à papier avec base automontable à coller • Papierkorb mit zusammensteckbarem, geklebtem Boden • Papelera con base automontable encolada • Cestino gettacarte con base automontante incollata • Cesto de papéis com base automontável colada • Prullenbak met vouwbodem

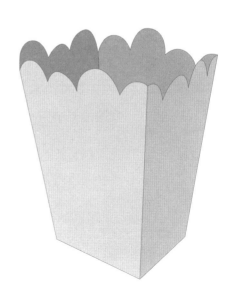

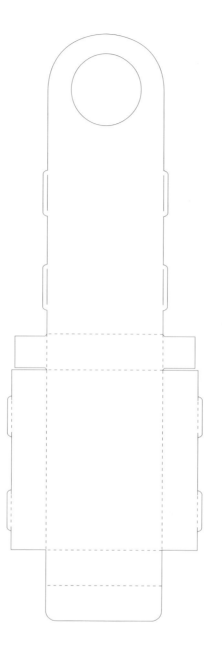

Wall-mounted note dispenser • Bloc-notes à suspendre •
Hängender Notizzettelspender • Dispensadora colgante de
notas • Dispenser sospeso per foglietti notes • Dispensadora
de notas de pendurar • Hangende dispenser voor briefjes

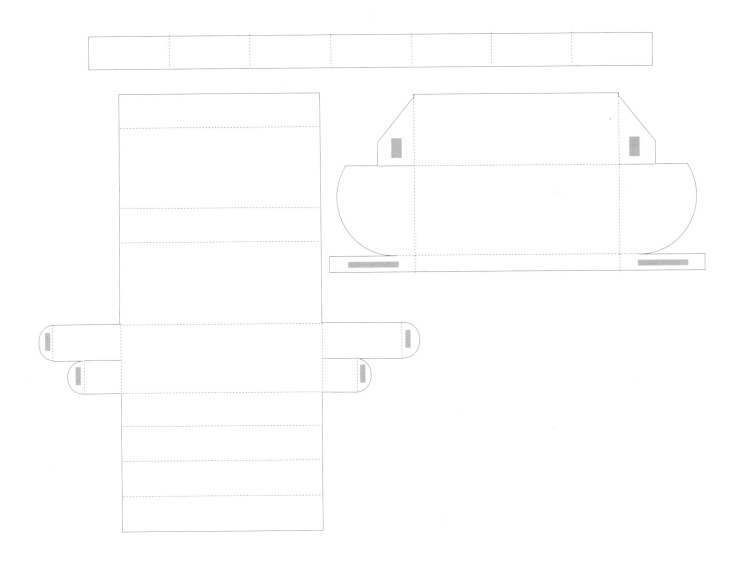

Small two shelf display box · Petite vitrine d'exposition à deux niveaux · Display mit zwei Ebenen · Caja expositora pequeña de dos niveles · Scatola espositore piccolo a due livelli · Caixa expositora pequena de dois níveis · Tentoonstellingsdoosje met twee schappen

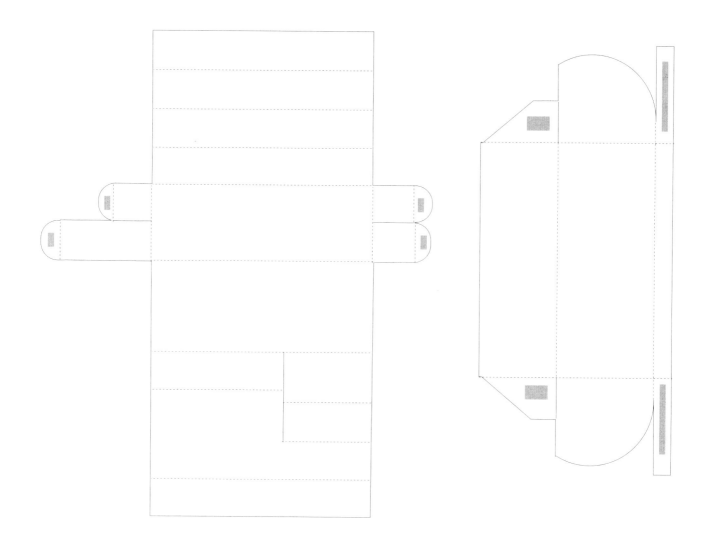

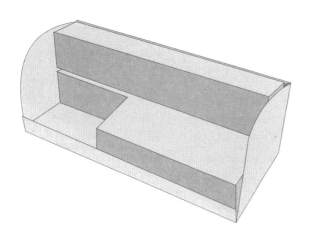

Small three shelf display box • Petite vitrine d'exposition à trois niveaux • Kleines Display mit drei Ebenen • Caja expositora pequeña de tres niveles • Scatola espositore piccolo a tre livelli • Caixa expositora pequena de três níveis • Tentoonstellingsdoosje met drie schappen

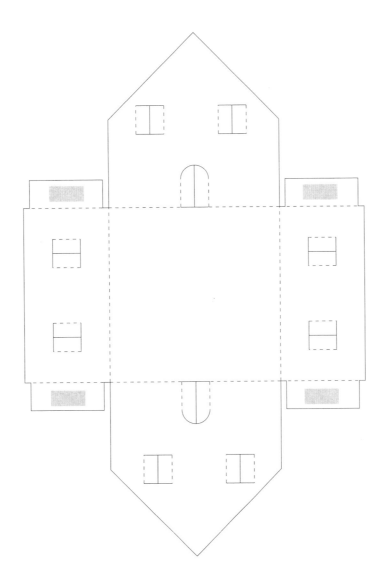

House-shaped open die cut box for candle • Photophore ajouré, en forme de maison • Hausförmige Box für eine Kerze • Caja troquelada abierta para vela, con forma de casa • Scatola fustellata aperta per candela a forma di casa • Caixa cunhada aberta para vela com forma de casa • Gestanste open doos voor kaars, in de vorm van een huis

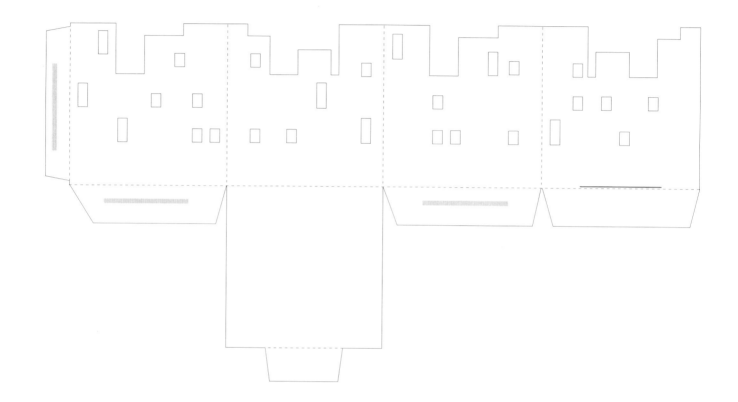

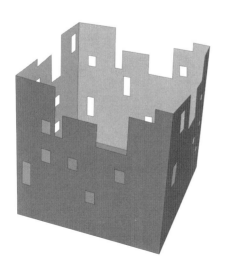

Urban-shaped open die cut box for candle • Photophore ajouré, aux formes urbaines • Hausförmige Box für eine Kerze • Caja troquelada abierta para vela, con forma urbana • Scatola fustellata aperta per candela a forma urbana • Caixa cunhada aberta para vela com forma urbana • Gestanste open doos voor kaars, in de vorm van een stad

×3

Sectioned jewellery box • Boîte à bijoux compartimentée •
Schmuckschachtel mit Fächern • Joyero compartimentado • Portagioie
a scomparti • Porta-jóias compartimentado • Bijouteriedoos met vakjes

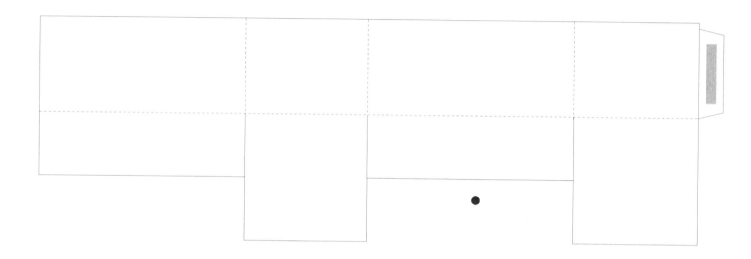

Photo box with lid Frame for one photo. Part 1 • Boîte à photos avec couvercle Cadre à photo. Partie 1 • Fotobox mit Deckel als Fotorahmen. Teil 1 • Caja con tapa para fotos. Marco para una foto. Parte 1 • Scatola per foto con coperchio. Cornice per una foto. Parte 1 • Caixa com tampa para fotos. Moldura para uma foto. Parte 1 • Doos met deksel voor foto's. Lijst voor een foto. Deel 1

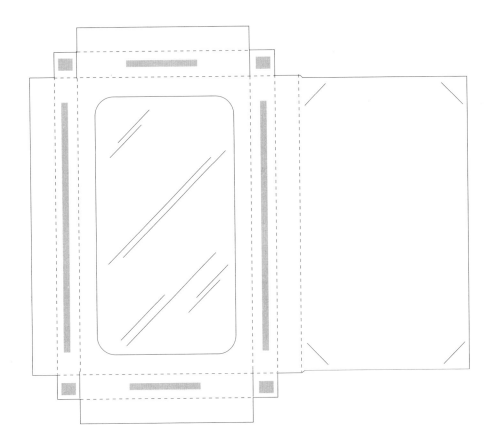

Photo box with lid Frame for one photo. Part 2 · Boîte à photos avec couvercle Cadre à photo. Partie 2 · Fotobox mit Deckel als Fotorahmen. Teil 2 · Caja con tapa para fotos. Marco para una foto. Parte 2 · Scatola per foto con coperchio. Cornice per una foto. Parte 2 · Caixa com tampa para fotos. Moldura para uma foto. Parte 2 · Doos met deksel voor foto's. Lijst voor een foto. Deel 2

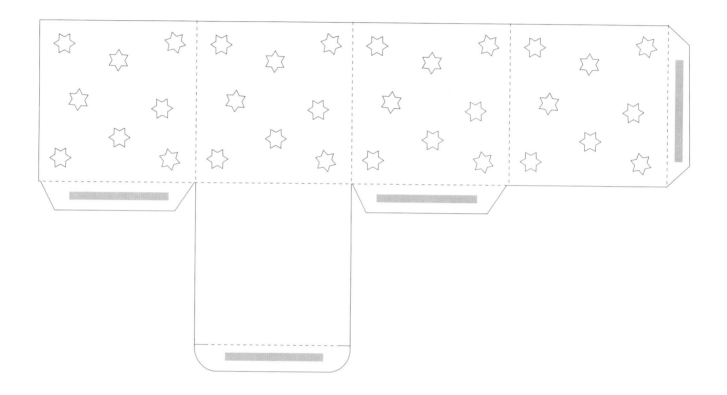

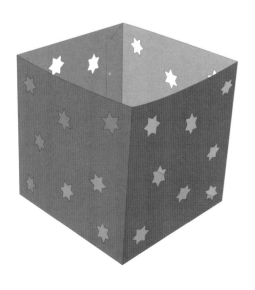

Decorated box for candle. Model 1 • Photophore décoré. Modèle 1 • Box mit Verzierungen für eine Kerze. Modell 1 • Caja decorada para vela. Modelo 1 • Scatola decorata per candela. Modello 1 • Caixa decorada para vela. Modelo 1 • Versierde doos voor kaars. Model 1

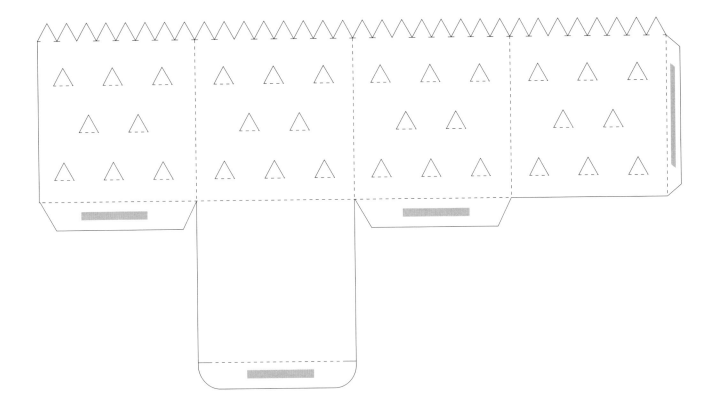

Decorated box for candle. Model 2 • Photophore décoré.
Modèle 2 • Box mit Verzierungen für eine Kerze. Modell 2 • Caja
decorada para vela. Modelo 2 • Scatola decorata per candela.
Modello 2 • Caixa decorada para vela. Modelo 2 • Versierde
doos voor kaars. Model 2

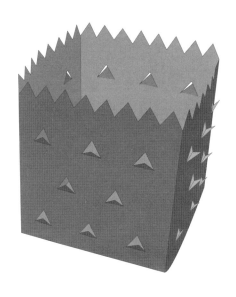

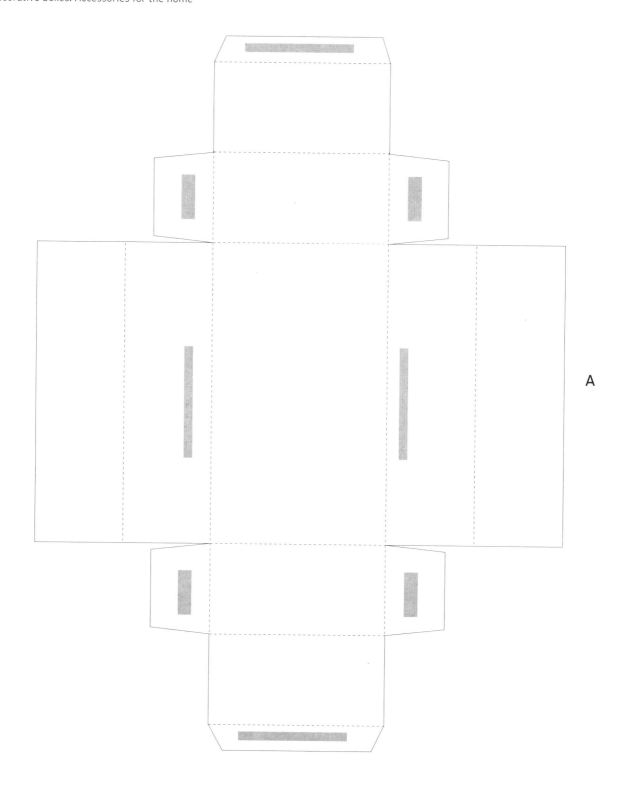

A

Sectioned box for rings. Part 1 • Boîte compartimentée pour les bagues. Partie 1 • Schachtel für Ringe. Teil 1 • Caja compartimentada para anillos. Parte 1 • Scatola a scomparti per anelli. Parte 1 • Caixa compartimentada para anéis. Parte 1 • Vakkendoos voor ringen. Deel 1

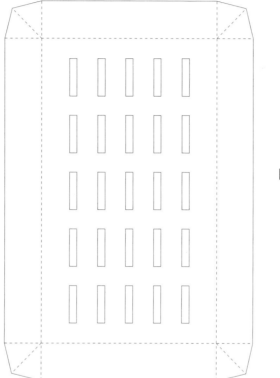

B

Sectioned box for rings. Part 2 • Boîte compartimentée pour les bagues. Partie 2 • Schachtel für Ringe. Teil 2 • Caja compartimentada para anillos. Parte 2 • Scatola a scomparti per anelli. Parte 2 • Caixa compartimentada para anéis. Parte 2 • Vakkendoos voor ringen. Deel 2

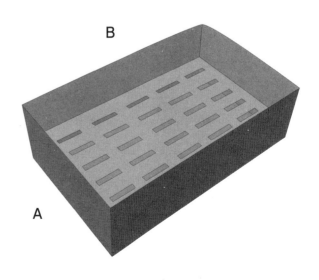

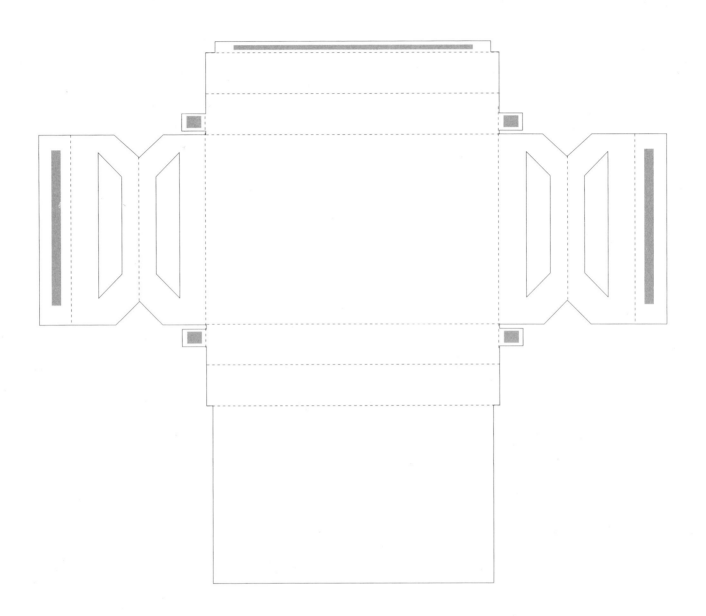

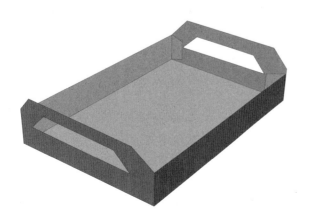

Tray. Model 1 • Plateau. Modèle 1 • Tablett. Modell 1 • Bandeja. Modelo 1 • Vassoio. Modello 1 • Bandeja. Modelo 1 • Dienblad. Model 1

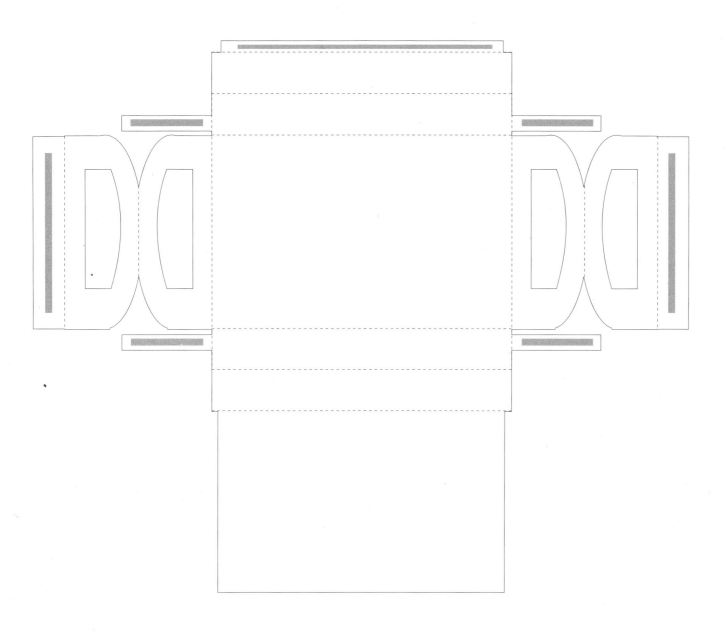

Tray. Model 2 • Plateau. Modèle 2 • Tablett. Modell 2 • Bandeja. Modelo 2 • Vassoio. Modello 2 • Bandeja. Modelo 2 • Dienblad. Model 2

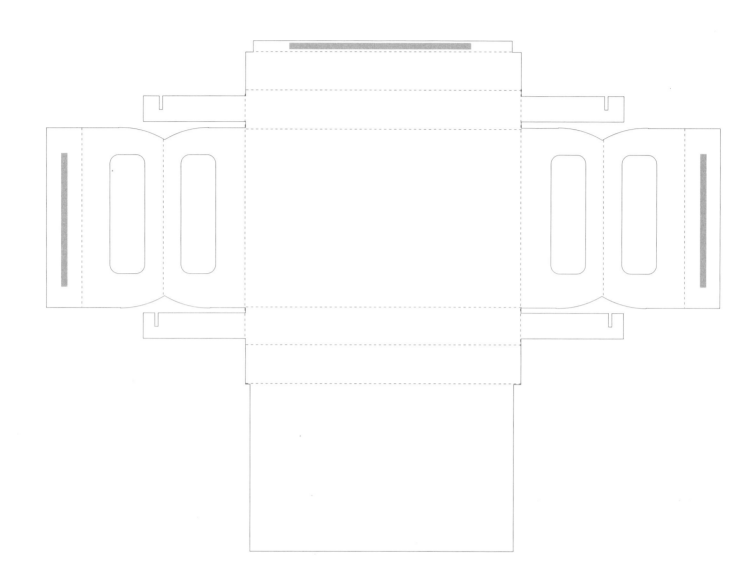

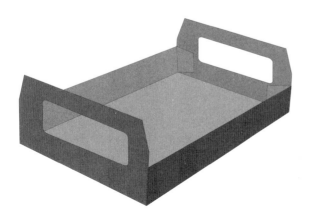

Tray. Model 3 • Plateau. Modèle 3 • Tablett. Modell 3 • Bandeja. Modelo 3 • Vassoio. Modello 3 • Bandeja. Modelo 3 • Dienblad. Model 3

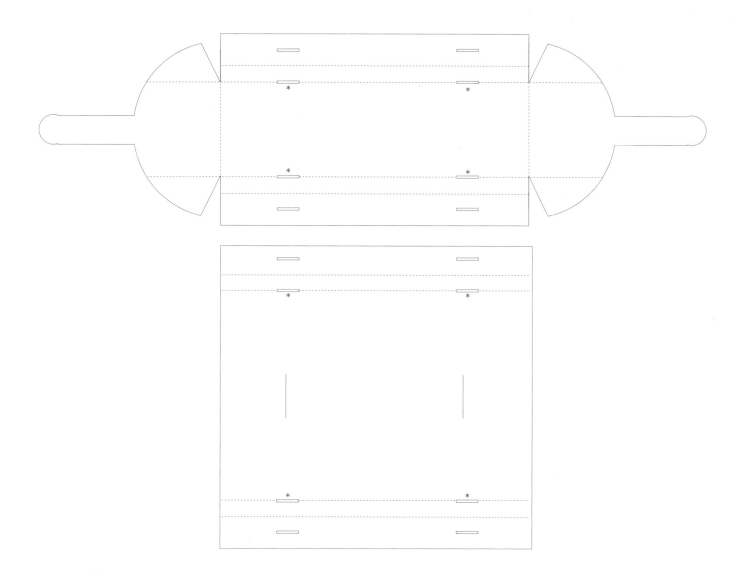

Classic semi-circle letterbox with side opening • Boîte aux lettres classique avec ouverture latérale • Klassischer, halbkreisförmiger Briefkasten mit seitlicher Öffnung • Buzón clásico semicircular con abertura lateral • Cassetta delle lettere classica semicircolare con apertura laterale • Caixa de correio clássica semicircular com abertura lateral • Halfronde klassieke brievenbus met zijopening

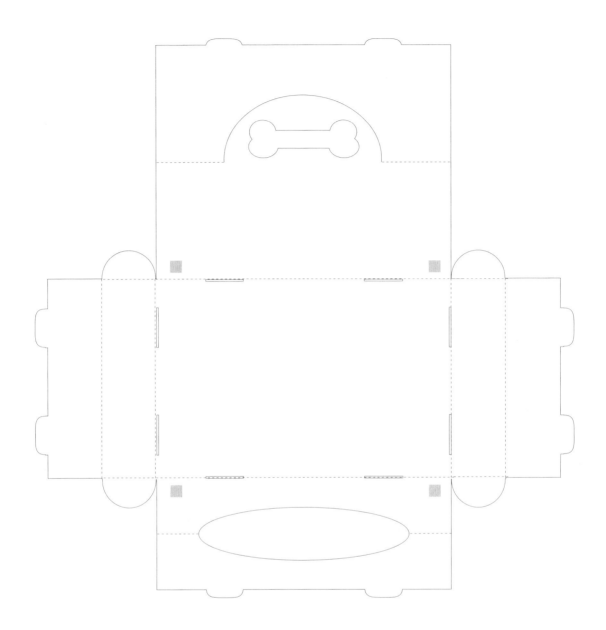

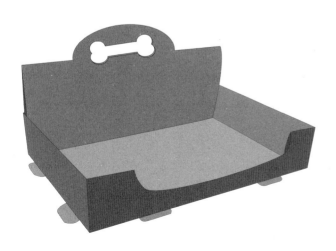

Pet tray. Model 1 (dog) • Plateau pour animal de compagnie. Modèle 1 (chien) • Haustierkorb. Modell 1 (Hund) • Bandeja para mascotas. Modelo 1 (perro) • Vaschetta per animali domestici. Modello 1 (cane) • Bandeja para animais de estimação. Modelo 1 (cão) • Dierenmand. Model 1 (hond)

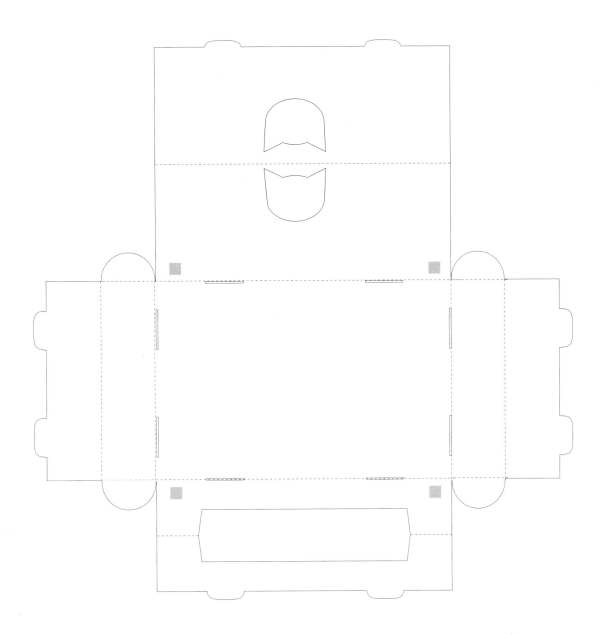

Pet tray. Model 2 (cat) • Plateau pour animal de compagnie. Modèle 2 (chat) • Haustierkorb. Modell 2 (Katze) • Bandeja para mascotas. Modelo 2 (gato) • Vaschetta per animali domestici. Modello 2 (gatto) • Bandeja para animais de estimação. Modelo 2 (gato) • Dierenmand. Model 2 (poes)

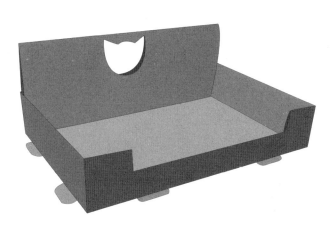

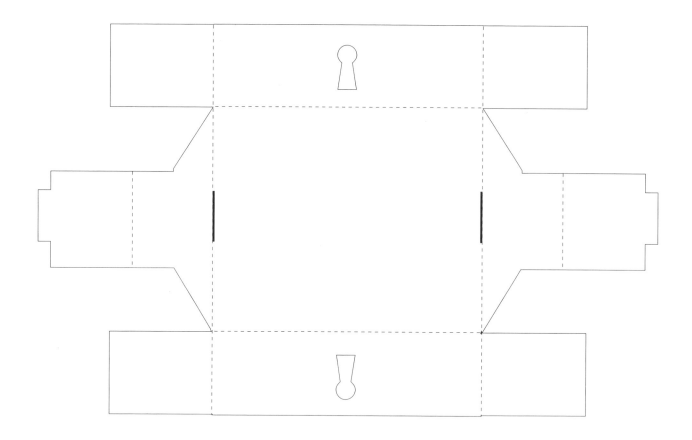

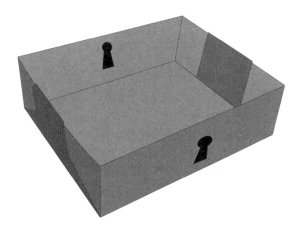

Key box • Boîte à clés • Schlüsselbox • Caja para llaves • Scatola per chiavi • Caixa para chaves • Doos voor sleutels

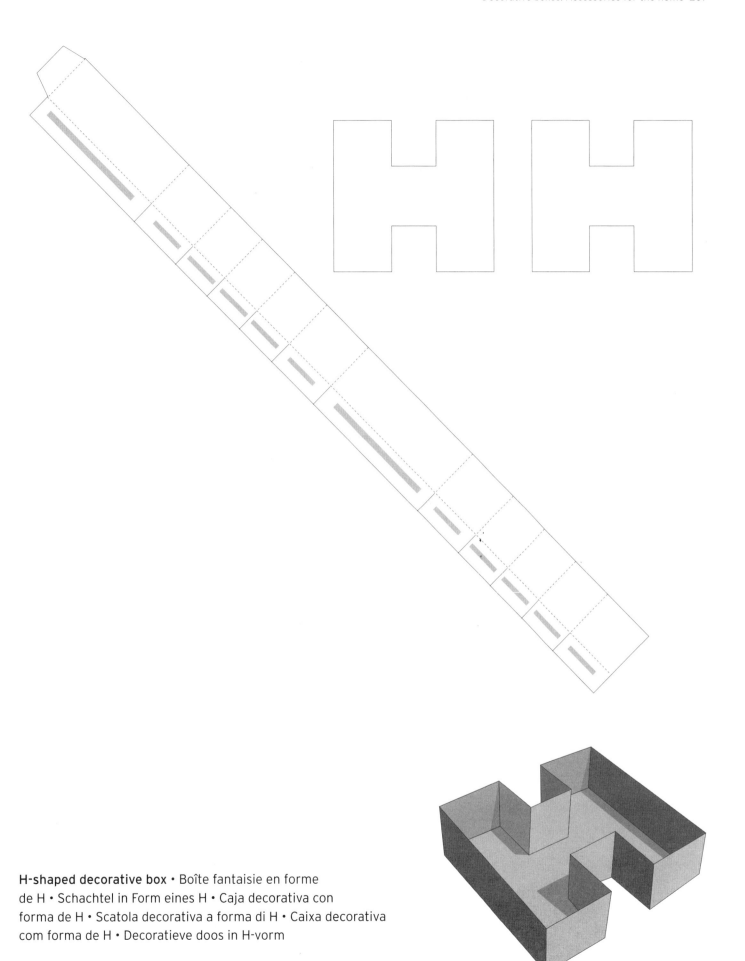

H-shaped decorative box • Boîte fantaisie en forme
de H • Schachtel in Form eines H • Caja decorativa con
forma de H • Scatola decorativa a forma di H • Caixa decorativa
com forma de H • Decoratieve doos in H-vorm

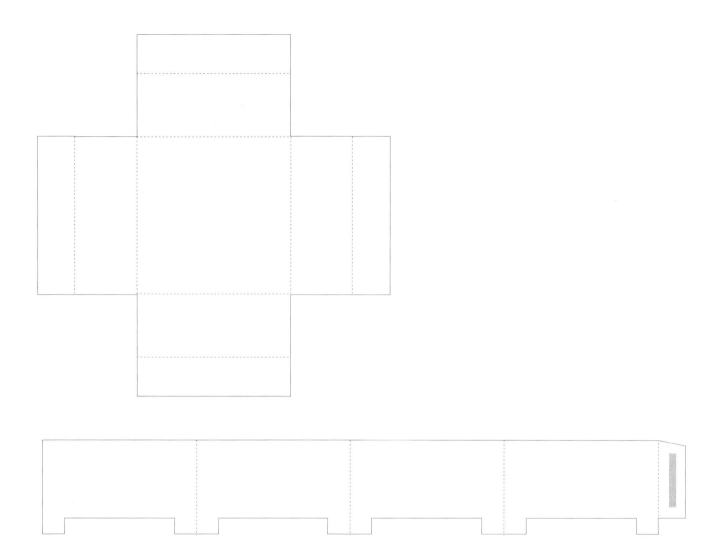

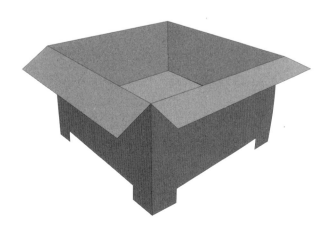

Decorative box with legs • Boîte fantaisie sur pattes • Dekorative Box mit Füßen • Caja decorativa con patas • Scatola decorativa con piedini • Caixa decorativa com pé • Decoratieve doos met pootjes

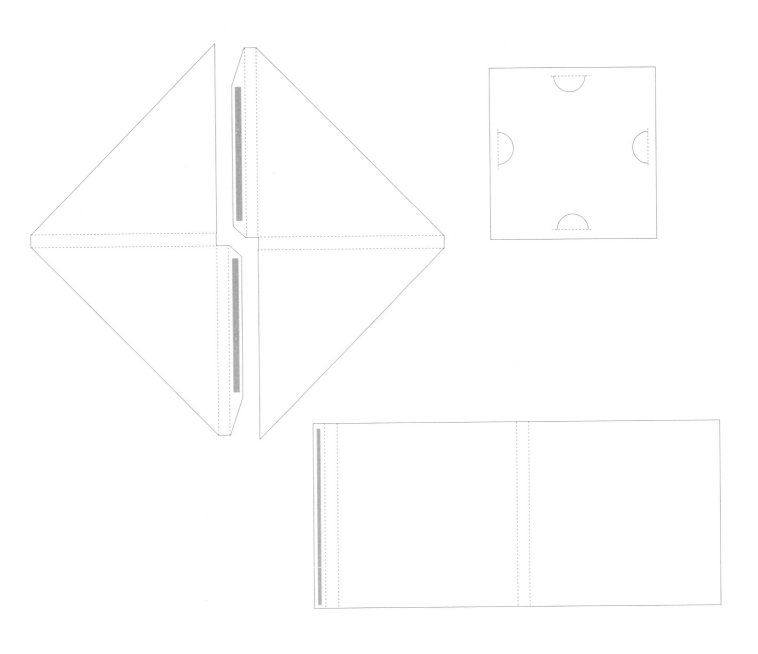

DVD box • Boîte à DVD • DVD-Hülle • Caja para DVD • Scatola per DVD • Caixa para DVD • Doos voor dvd

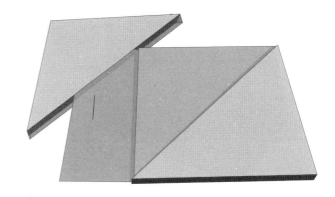

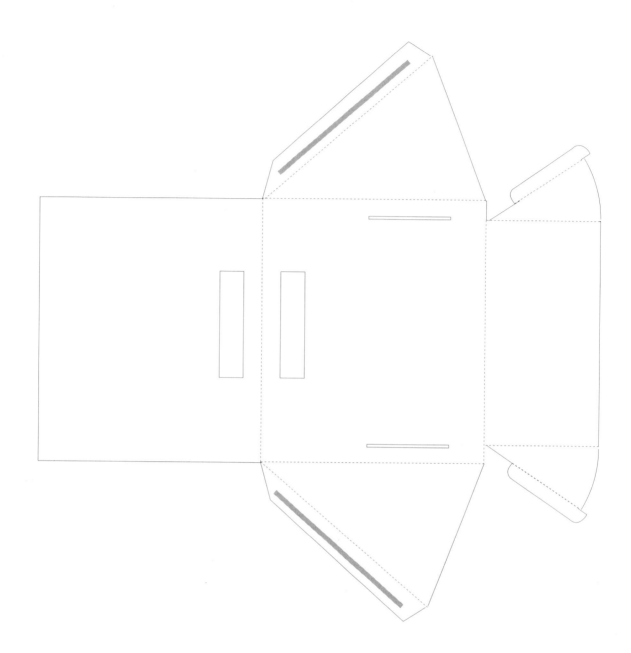

Floor magazine rack. Model 1 • Porte-revues à poser au sol.
Modèle 1 • Zeitschriftenständer. Modell 1 • Revistero de suelo.
Modelo 1 • Portariviste da pavimento. Modello 1 • Porta-revistas
de chão. Modelo 1 • Tijdschriftenstandaard. Model 1

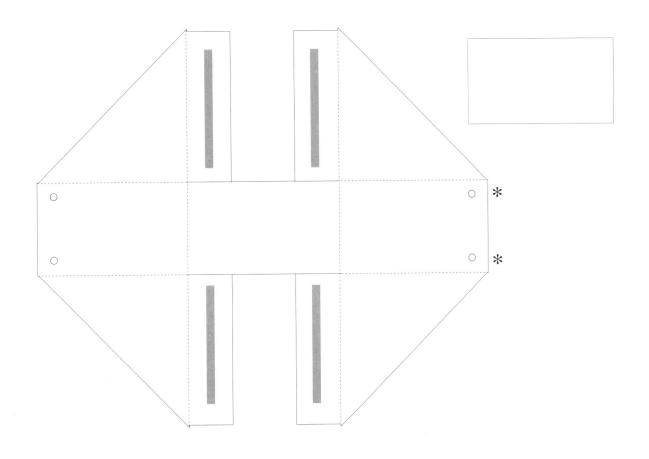

*

*

Floor magazine rack. Model 2 · Porte-revues à poser au sol.
Modèle 2 · Zeitschriftenständer. Modell 2 · Revistero de suelo.
Modelo 2 · Portariviste da pavimento. Modello 2 · Porta-revistas
de chão. Modelo 2 · Tijdschriftenstandaard. Model 2

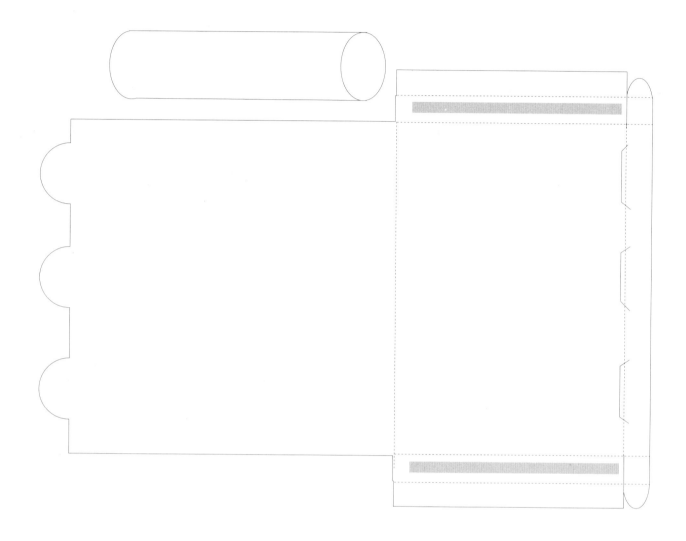

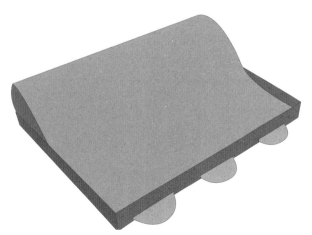

Magazine rack • Porte-revues • Zeitschriftenablage • Revistero • Portariviste • Porta-revistas • Tijdschriftenstandaard

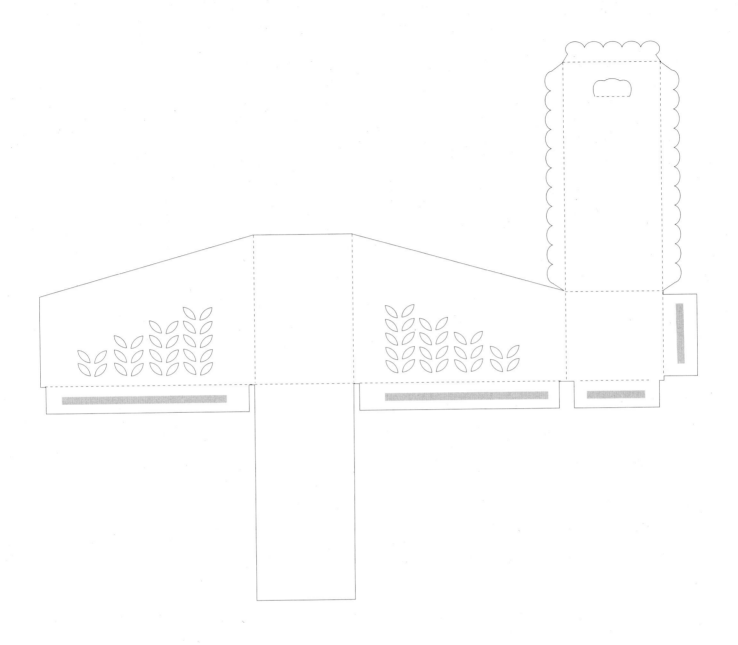

Decorative box for aromatic herbs with die cut and lid. Model 1 •
Boîte fantaisie pour herbes de Provence avec orifice et couvercle.
Modèle 1 • Dekorative Kräuterbox mit Ausstanzung und Deckel.
Modell 1 • Caja decorativa para hierbas aromáticas, con troquel
y tapa. Modelo 1 • Scatola decorativa per erbe aromatiche con
fustella e coperchio. Modello 1 • Caixa decorativa para ervas
aromáticas com cunha e tampa. Modelo 1 • Decoratieve doos voor
geurige kruiden, met gestanste decoratie en deksel. Model 1

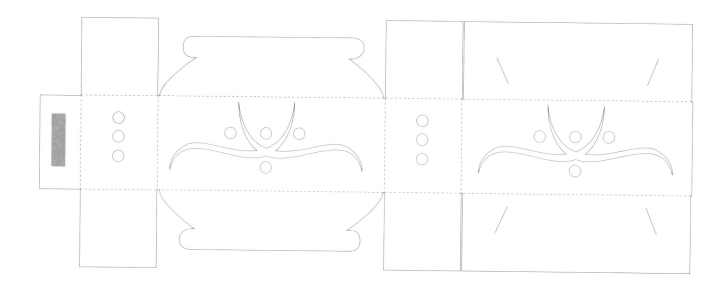

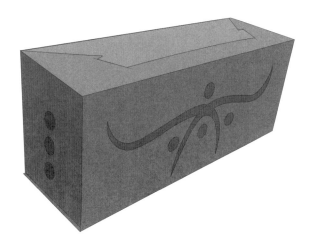

Decorative box for aromatic herbs with die cut. Model 2 • Boîte fantaisie pour herbes de Provence avec orifice. Modèle 2 • Dekorative Kräuterbox mit Ausstanzung. Modell 2 • Caja decorativa para hierbas aromáticas, con troquel. Modelo 2 • Scatola decorativa per erbe aromatiche con fustella. Modello 2 • Caixa decorativa para ervas aromáticas com cunha. Modelo 2 • Decoratieve doos voor geurige kruiden, met gestanste decoratie. Model 2

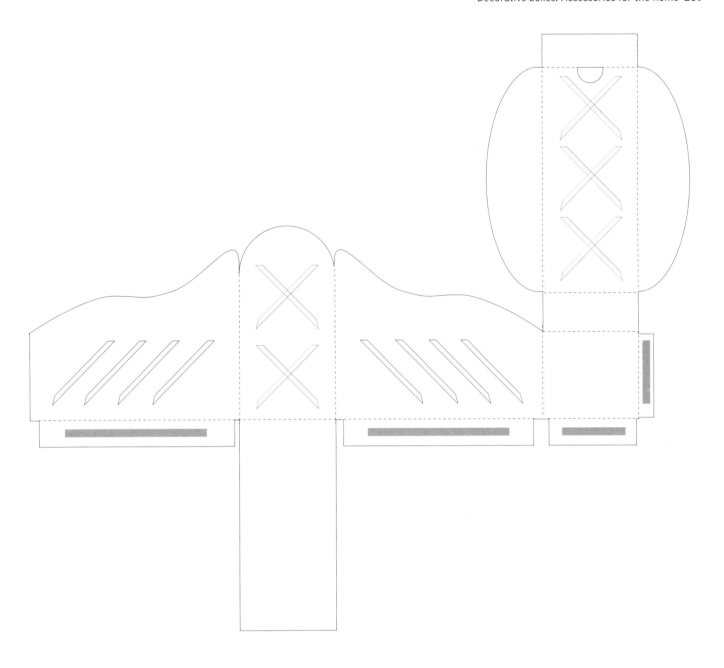

Decorative box for aromatic herbs with die cut and lid. Model 3 •
Boîte fantaisie pour herbes de Provence avec orifice et couvercle.
Modèle 3 • Dekorative Kräuterbox mit Ausstanzung und Deckel.
Modell 3 • Caja decorativa para hierbas aromáticas, con troquel
y tapa. Modelo 3 • Scatola decorativa per erbe aromatiche con
fustella e coperchio. Modello 3 • Caixa decorativa para ervas
aromáticas com cunha e tampa. Modelo 3 • Decoratieve doos voor
geurige kruiden, met gestanste decoratie en deksel. Model 3

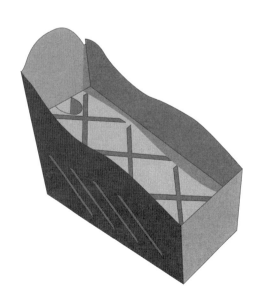

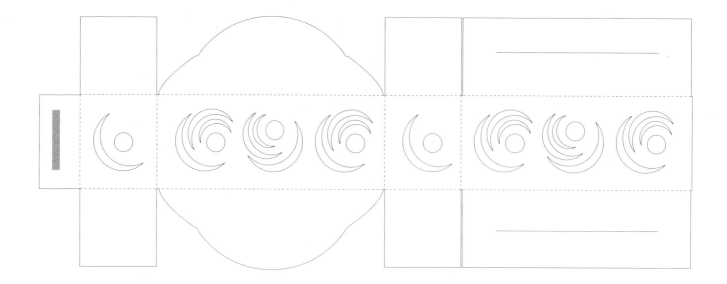

Decorative box for aromatic herbs with die cut. Model 4 •
Boîte fantaisie pour herbes de Provence avec orifice. Modèle 4 •
Dekorative Kräuterbox mit Ausstanzung. Modell 4 • Caja
decorativa para hierbas aromáticas, con troquel. Modelo 4 •
Scatola decorativa per erbe aromatiche con fustella.
Modello 4 • Caixa decorativa para ervas aromáticas com
cunha. Modelo 4 • Decoratieve doos voor geurige kruiden,
met gestanste decoratie. Model 4

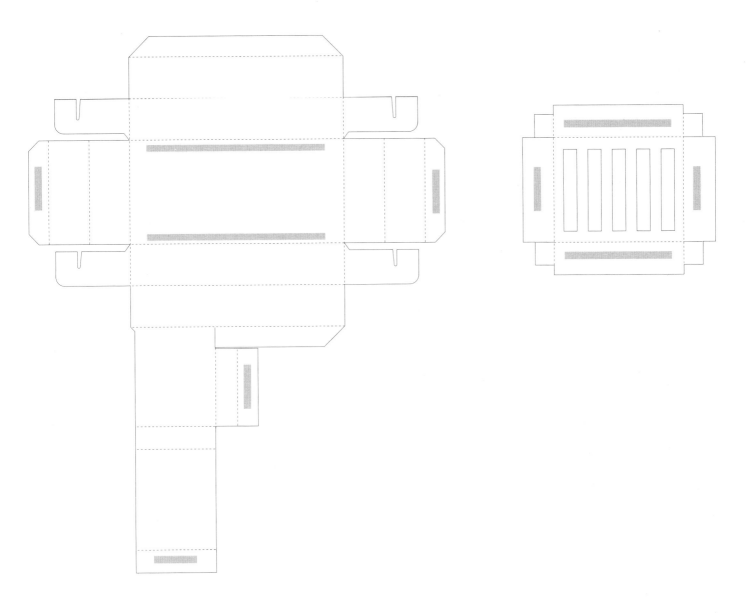

Cigarette box with dividers • Coffret pour fumeur avec intercalaires • Schachtel mit Fächern für Zigaretten • Caja para fumador, con separadores • Scatola per fumatori con divisori • Caixa para fumador com separadores • Doos voor sigaretten, met vakjes

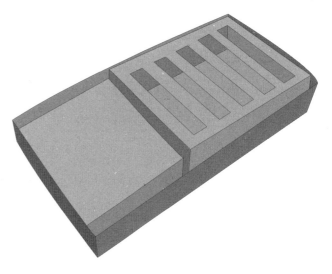

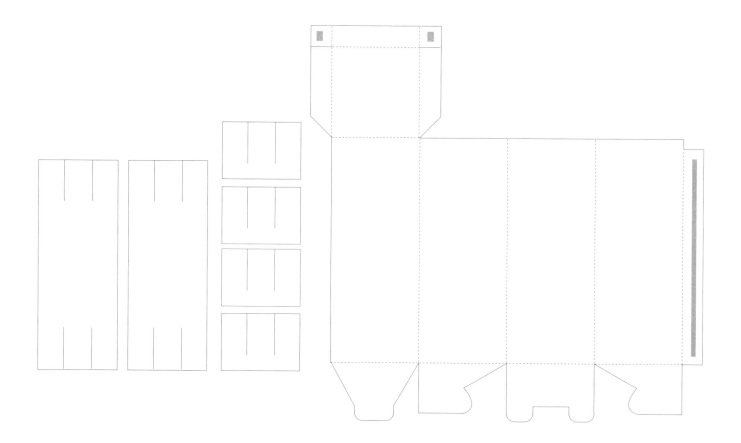

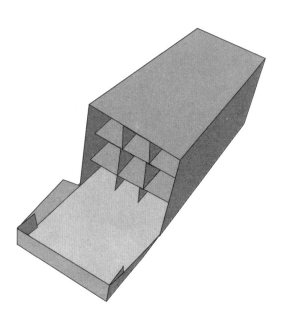

Candle box • Boîte de rangement pour les bougies • Box zum Aufbewahren von Kerzen • Caja para el almacenaje de velas • Scatola portacandele • Caixa para a armazenagem de velas • Bewaardoos voor kaarsen

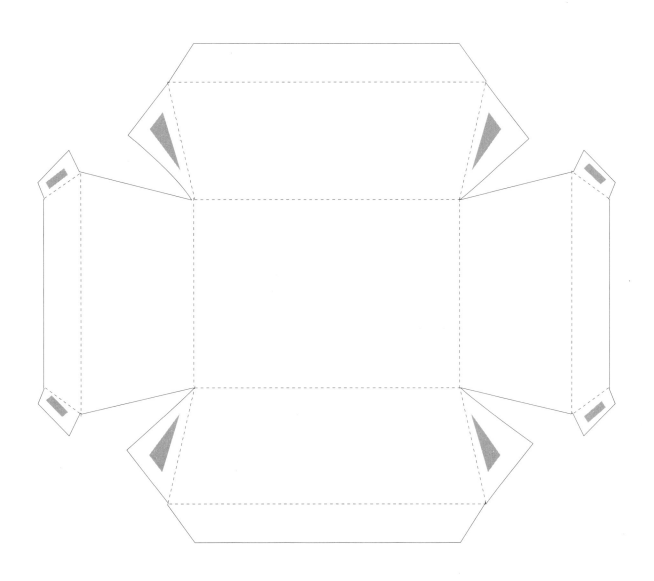

Hold-all basket. Model 1 • Panier range-tout. Modèle 1 •
Korb. Modell 1 • Cesto «guardatodo». Modelo 1 • Cesto portatutto.
Modello 1 • Cesto guarda tudo. Modelo 1 • Verzameldoosje. Model 1

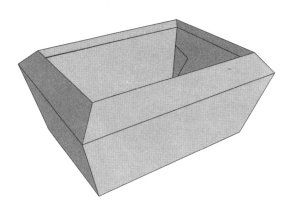

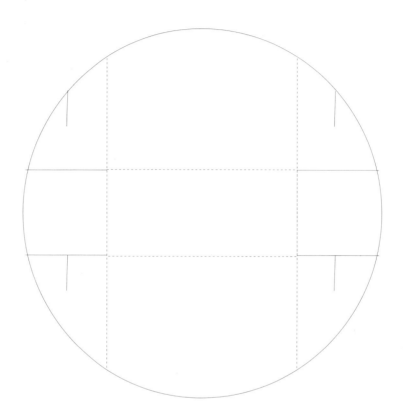

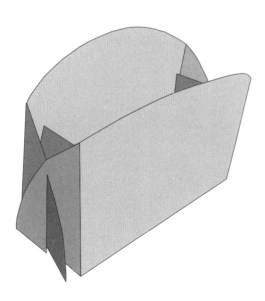

Hold-all basket. Model 2 · Panier range-tout. Modèle 2 ·
Korb. Modell 2 · Cesto «guardatodo». Modelo 2 · Cesto
portatutto. Modello 2 · Cesto guarda tudo. Modelo 2 ·
Verzameldoosje. Model 2

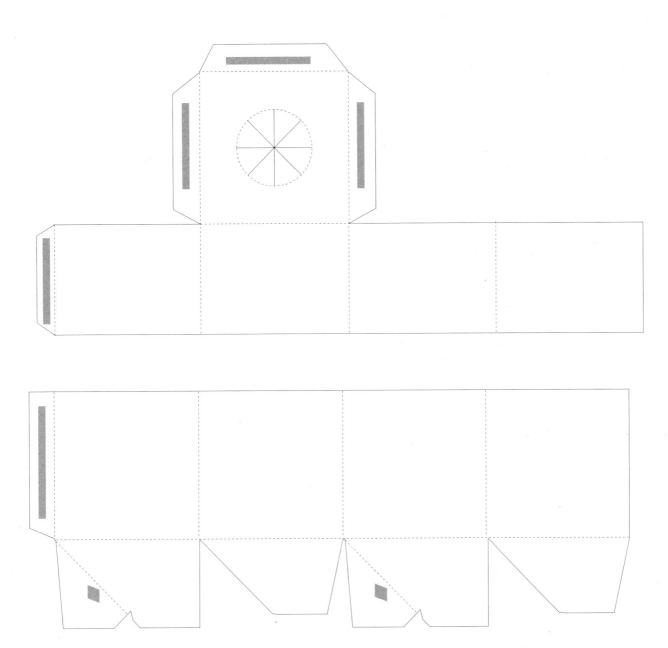

Handkerchief box • Boîte à mouchoirs en papier • Box für
Papiertaschentücher • Caja para pañuelos de papel • Scatola
per fazzolettini di carta • Caixa para toalhetes de papel • Doos
voor papieren zakdoekjes

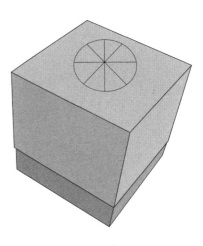

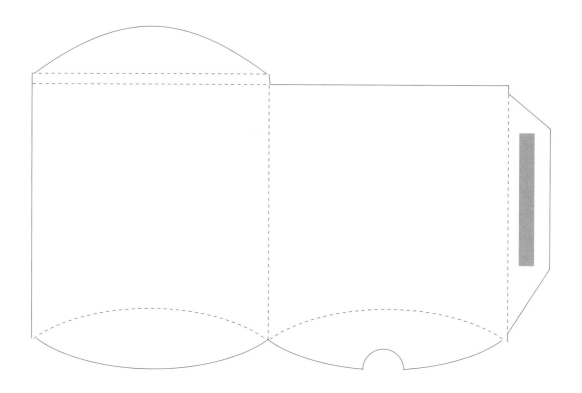

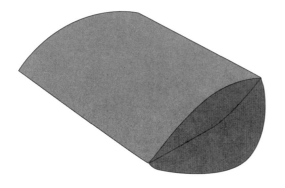

Flip top coin purse • Boîte porte-monnaie avec fermeture à bascule • Geldbörse mit Klappverschluss • Monedero con cierre basculante • Portamonete con chiusura basculante • Porta-moedas com fecho basculante • Portemonnee met sluiting

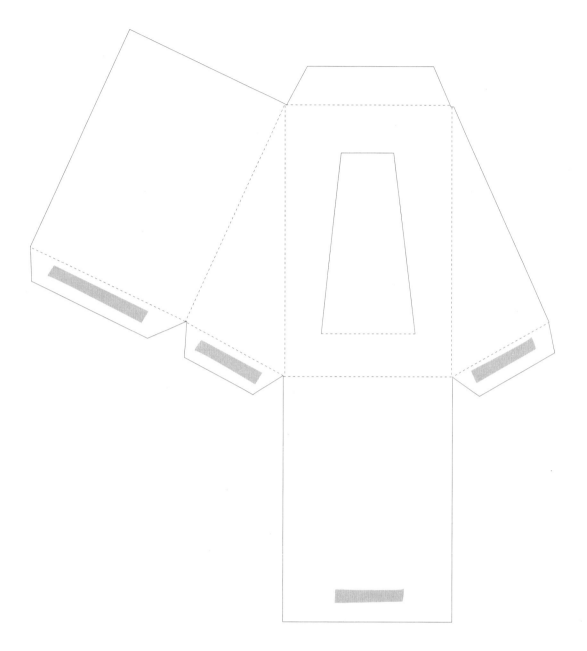

Mobile phone box. Model 1 • Boîtier pour téléphone mobile.
Modèle 1 • Handy-Box. Modell 1 • Caja para teléfono móvil.
Modelo 1 • Scatola per telefono cellulare. Modello 1 • Caixa para
telemóvel. Modelo 1 • Doos voor mobiele telefoon. Model 1

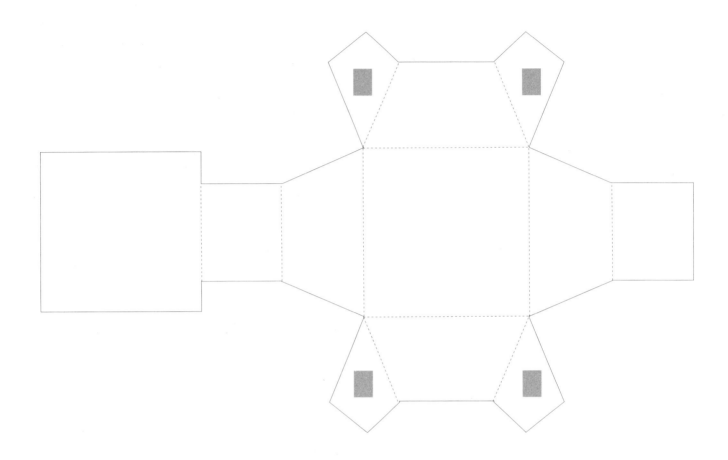

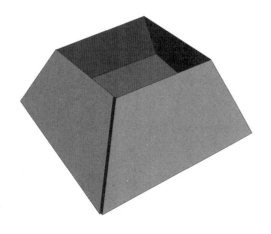

Mobile phone box. Model 2 • Boîtier pour téléphone mobile. Modèle 2 • Handy-Box. Modell 2 • Caja para teléfono móvil. Modelo 2 • Scatola per telefono cellulare. Modello 2 • Caixa para telemóvel. Modelo 2 • Doos voor mobiele telefoon. Model 2

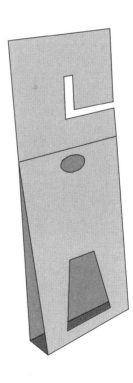

Hanging box for glasses · Boîtier à lunettes à suspendre ·
Hängeschachtel für Brillen · Caja colgante para gafas · Scatola sospesa
per occhiali · Caixa de pendurar para óculos · Hangdoos voor bril

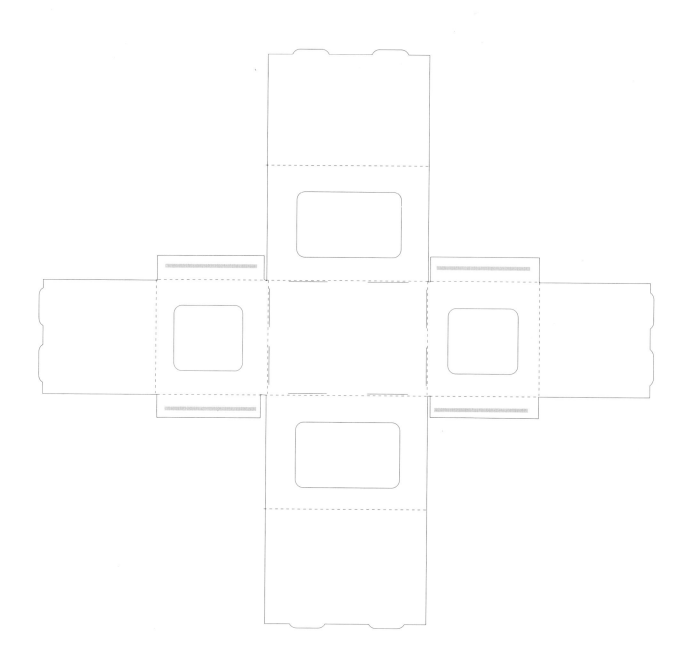

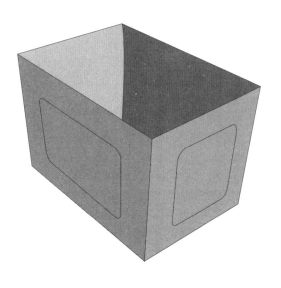

Photo display box • Boîtier porte-photos • Box für Fotos • Caja expositora para fotos • Scatola espositore per foto • Caixa expositora para fotos • Tentoonstellingsdoos voor foto's

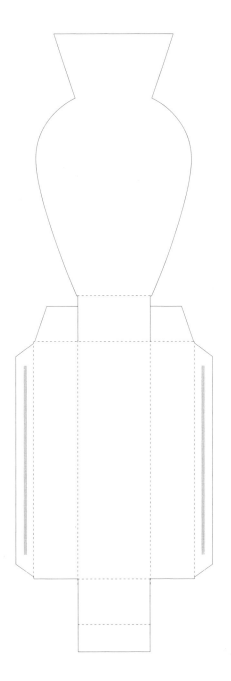

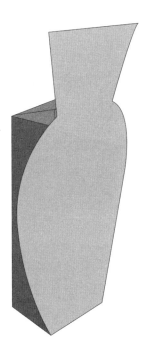

Jug-shaped decorative box • Boîte fantaisie en forme
de jarre • Dekorative Schachtel in Form einer Vase • Caja
decorativa con forma de jarra • Scatola decorativa a forma di
anfora • Caixa decorativa com forma de jarro • Decoratieve
doos in de vorm van een kan

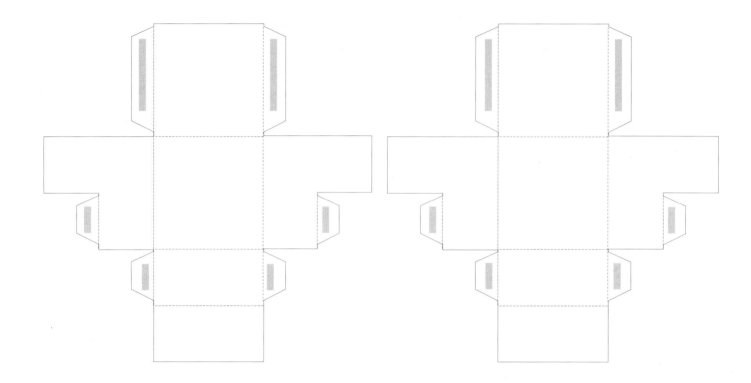

Cube-shaped decorative box with two compartments • Boîte cubique fantaisie à deux volumes • Zweiteilige dekorative Würfelbox • Caja cúbica decorativa de dos cuerpos • Scatola cubica ornamentale a due volumi • Caixa cúbica decorativa de dois corpos • Vierkante tweedelige decoratieve doos

×2

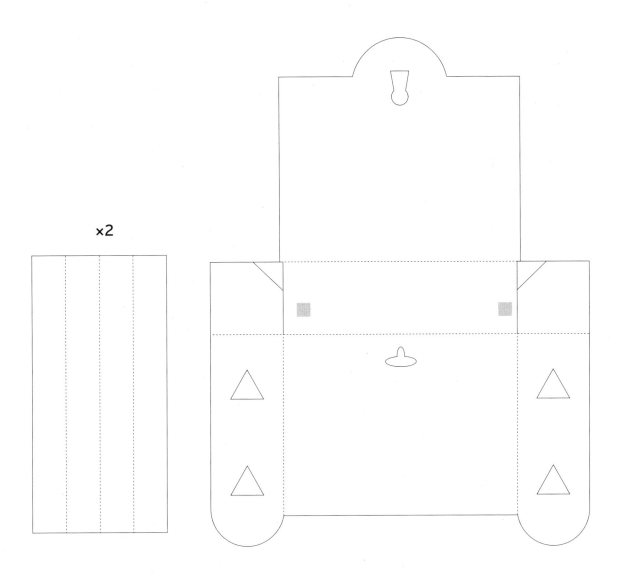

Cupboard for keys with hook • Boîte à clés avec
crochet de suspension • Schlüsselschränkchen mit
Aufhänger • Armario para llaves, con colgador • Armadietto
portachiavi con gancio • Armário para chaves com sistema
de pendurar • Sleutelkastje, met haakje

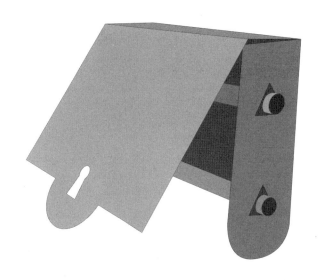

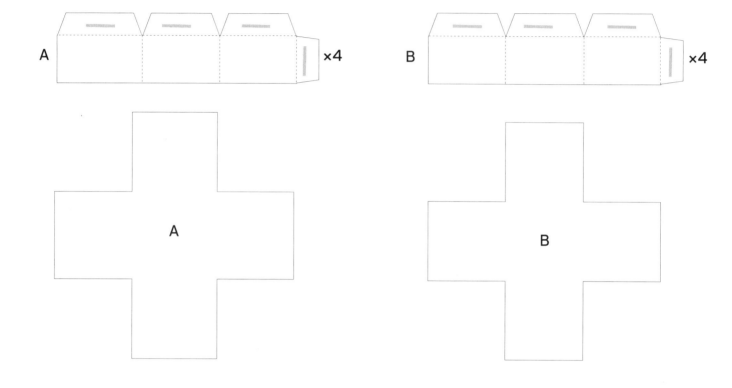

A ×4

B ×4

A

B

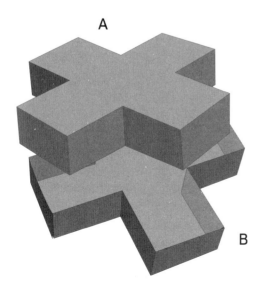

A

B

Cross-shaped medicine box · Armoire à pharmacie en frome de croix · Kreuzförmige Medikamentenbox · Caja para medicinas, con forma de cruz · Scatola per medicinali a forma di croce · Caixa para medicamentos com forma de cruz · Medicijndoos, in de vorm van een kruis

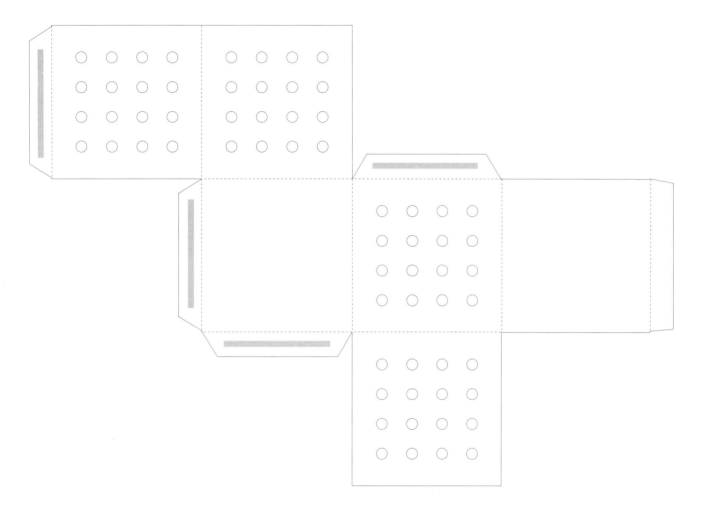

Perforated cube-shaped box for small pet • Boîte cubique perforée pour les petits animaux de compagnie • Transportbox mit Luftlöchern für ein kleines Haustier • Caja cúbica perforada para pequeña mascota • Scatola cubica perforata per piccolo animale domestico • Caixa cúbica perfurada para pequeno animal de estimação • Vierkante geperforeerde doos voor klein huisdier

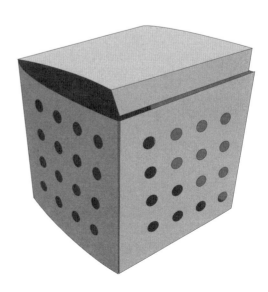

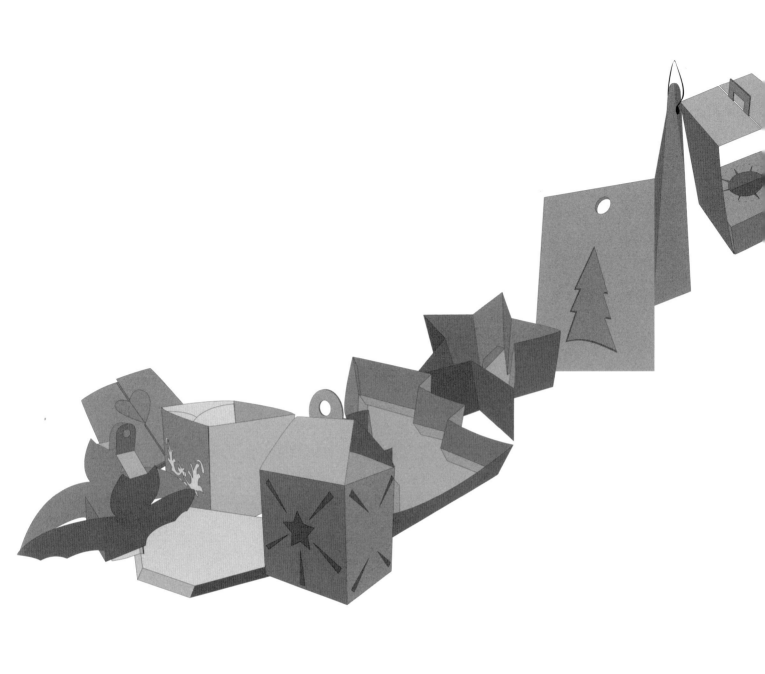

Themed boxes for celebrations

Boîtes thématiques pour différentes occasions

Verpackungen für besondere Anlässe und Feiern

Cajas temáticas y para celebraciones

Scatole tematiche per eventi e ricorrenze

Caixas temáticas e para celebrações

Dozen voor thema's en feesten

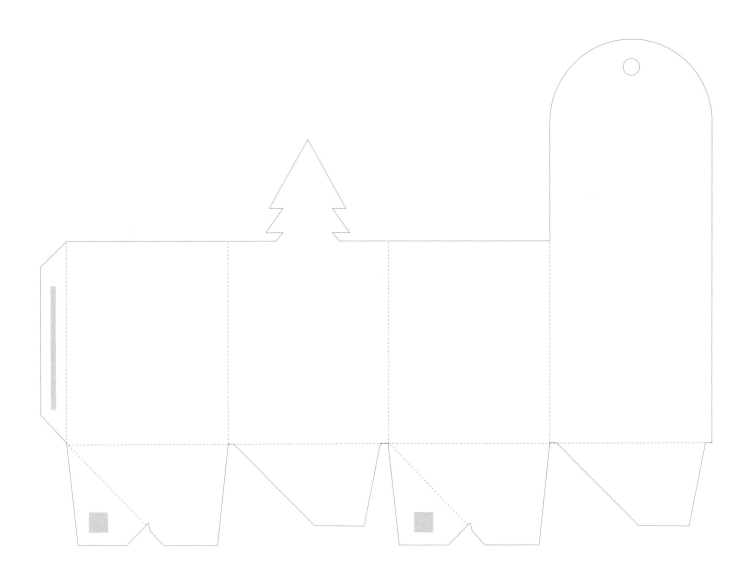

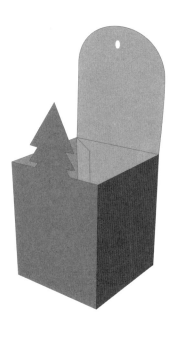

Hanging dispenser with Christmas detail • Distributeur à suspendre avec motif de Noël • Hängende Spenderbox mit Weihnachtsdekoration • Dispensadora colgante con detalle navideño • Dispenser sospeso con decorazione natalizia • Dispensadora de pendurar com motivo natalício • Hangende sorteerdoos met kerstdetail

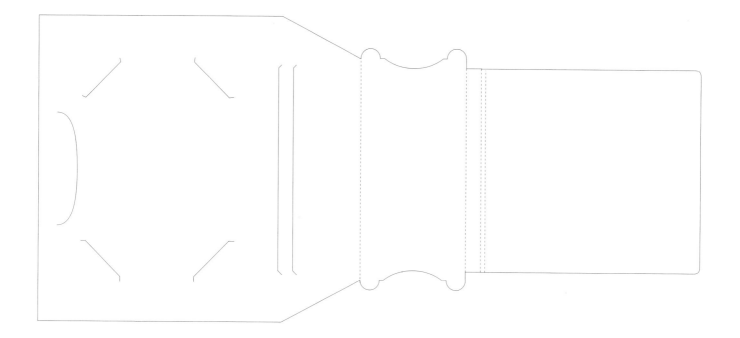

Graduation folder with diploma and photo holder · Dossier de fin d'études avec support pour ranger les diplômes et les photos · Mappe zum Studienabschluss mit Halterung für Diplom und Foto · Carpeta para la graduación con soporte para el diploma y la foto · Cartella per laurea con supporto per il diploma e la foto · Pasta para a graduação com suporte para o diploma e para a foto · Afstudeermap voor het diploma en de foto

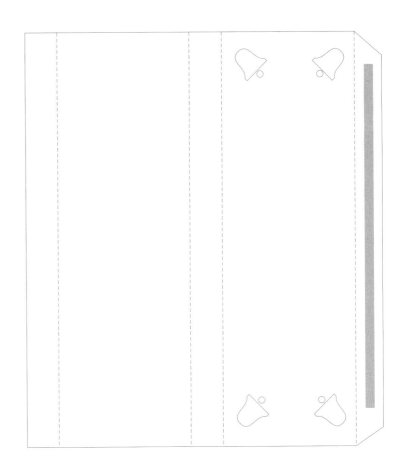

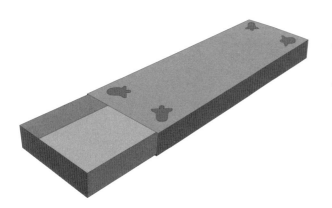

Christmas gift box with sleeve and decorated window • Boîte pour cadeau de Noël avec étui et fenêtre décorée • Weihnachtsgeschenkschachtel mit Schuber und Verzierungen • Caja para regalo de Navidad, con faja y ventana decorada • Scatola per regalo natalizio con fascetta e finestrella decorata • Caixa para presente de Natal com faixa e janela decorada • Doos voor kerstcadeau, met hoes en versierd venster

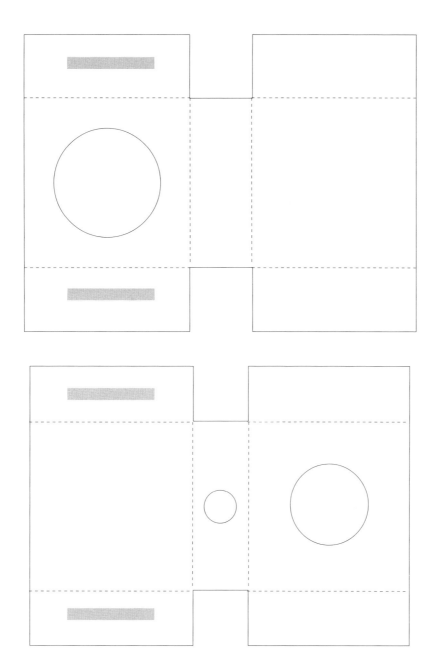

Flat telescopic box with decorated lid · Boîte télescopique plate avec couvercle décoré · Ausziehbare, flache Schachtel mit Deckel · Caja telescópica plana con tapa decorada · Scatola telescopica piana con coperchio decorato · Caixa telescópica plana com tampa decorada · Vlakke telescopische doos met versierd deksel

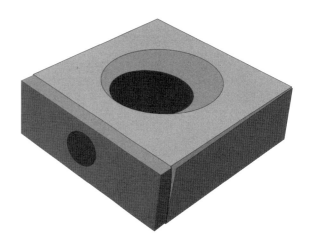

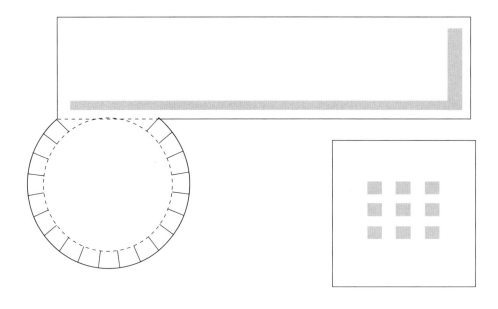

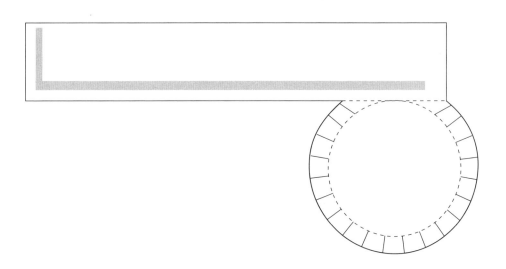

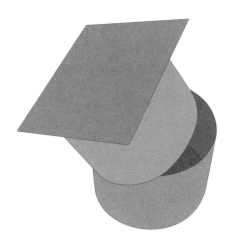

Academic cap box • Boîte en forme de chapeau de cérémonie de fin d'études • Barettschachtel • Caja con forma de birrete de graduación • Scatola a forma di cappello di laurea • Caixa em forma de chapéu de graduação • Doos in de vorm van afstudeerbaret

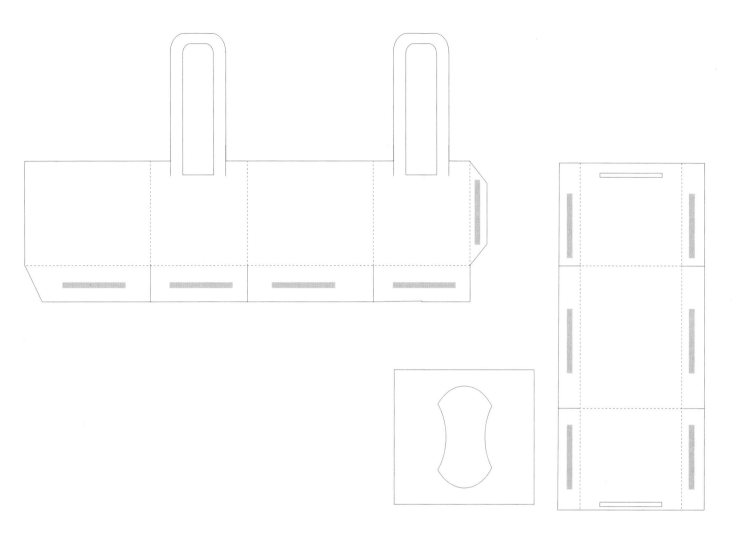

Easter egg box with handle • Boîte pour œufs de Pâques avec anse • Ostereierschachtel mit Henkel • Caja para huevo de Pascua, con asa • Scatola per uovo di Pasqua con maniglia • Caixa para ovo de Páscoa com asa • Doos voor paasei, met hengsel

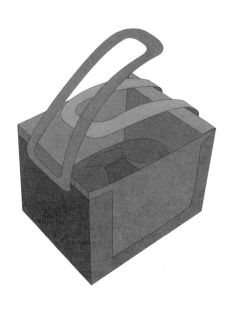

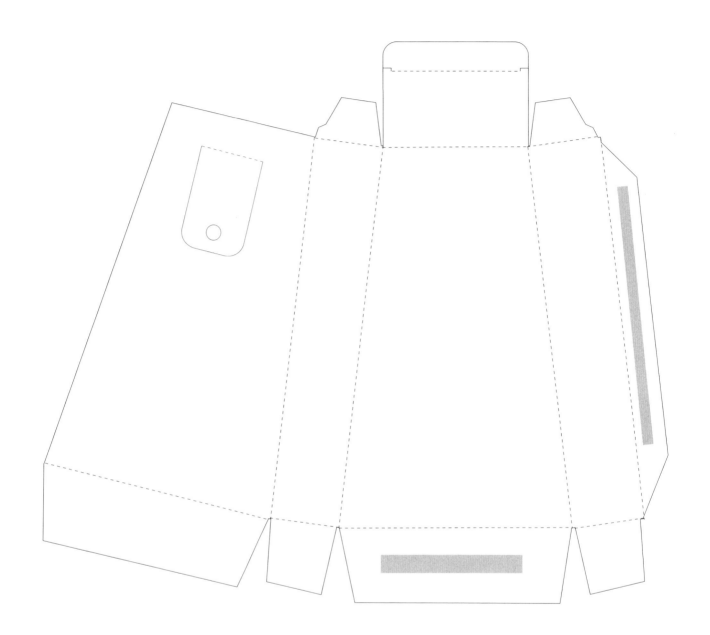

Hanging box for Christmas tree gift. Model 1 • Boîte à cadeau à suspendre au sapin de Noël. Modèle 1 • Hängende Geschenkschachtel für den Weihnachtsbaum. Modell 1 • Caja colgante para regalo de árbol navideño. Modelo 1 • Scatola sospesa da regalo per albero di natale. Modello 1 • Caixa de pendurar para presente de árvore de natal. Modelo 1 • Geschenkdoos voor in de kerstboom. Model 1

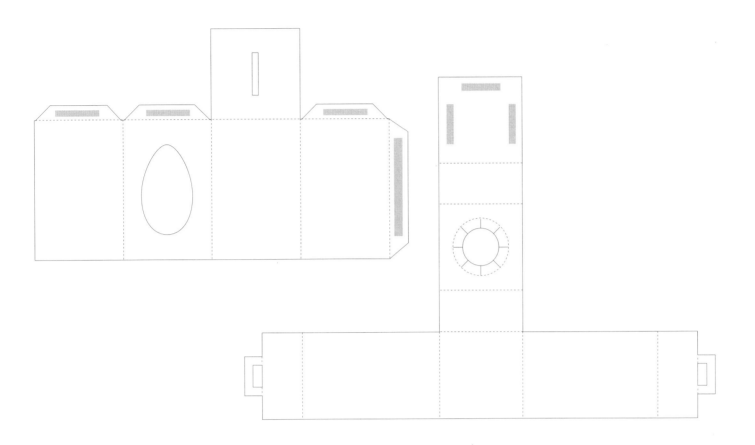

Telescopic box for Easter gift with interior support •
Boîte télescopique pour cadeau de Pâques avec support
intérieur • Geschenkbox für Ostern mit Schuber • Caja
telescópica para regalo de Pascua, con soporte interior • Scatola
telescopica per regalo di Pasqua con supporto interno • Caixa
telescópica para presente de Páscoa com suporte interior •
Telescopische doos voor paascadeau, met binnensteun

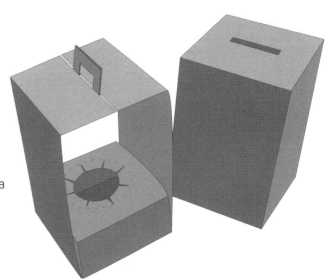

Hanging box for Christmas tree gift. Model 2 • Boîte à cadeau à suspendre au sapin de Noël. Modèle 2 • Hängende Geschenkschachtel für den Weihnachtsbaum. Modell 2 • Caja colgante para regalo de árbol navideño. Modelo 2 • Scatola sospesa da regalo per albero di natale. Modello 2 • Caixa de pendurar para presente de árvore de natal. Modelo 2 • Geschenkdoos voor in de kerstboom. Model 2

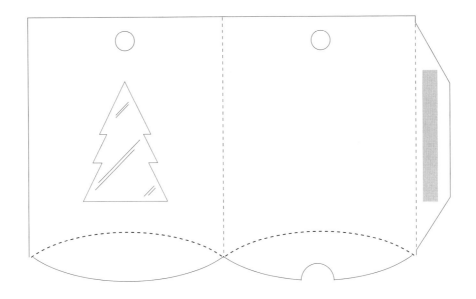

Hanging box for Christmas tree gift. Model 3 · Boîte à cadeau à suspendre au sapin de Noël. Modèle 3 · Hängende Geschenkschachtel für den Weihnachtsbaum. Modell 3 · Caja colgante para regalo de árbol navideño. Modelo 3 · Scatola sospesa da regalo per albero di natale. Modello 3 · Caixa de pendurar para presente de árvore de natal. Modelo 3 · Geschenkdoos voor in de kerstboom. Model 3

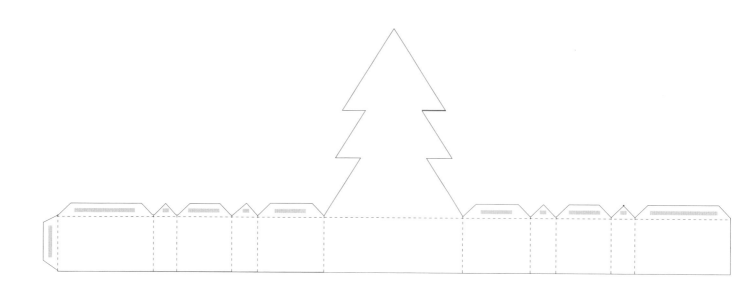

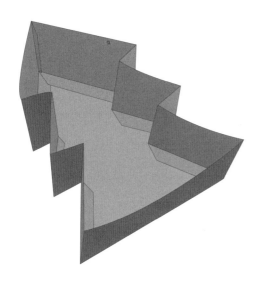

Christmas tree-shaped box • Boîte en forme de sapin de Noël • Schachtel in Form eines Weihnachtsbaums • Caja con forma de árbol de Navidad • Scatola a forma di albero di Natale • Caixa com forma de árvore de natal • Doos in de vorm van een kerstboom

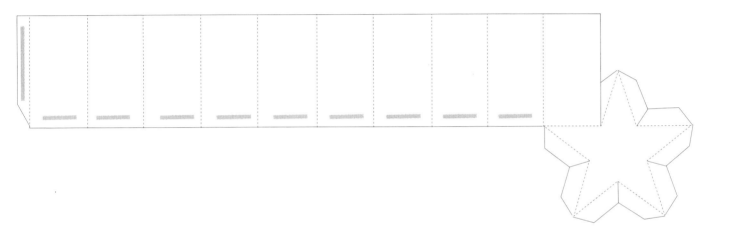

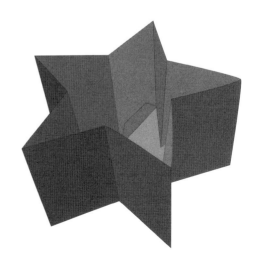

Star-shaped box · Boîte en forme d'étoiles · Sternförmige
Schachtel · Caja con forma de estrella · Scatola a forma di
stella · Caixa com forma de estrela · Doos in de vorm van een ster

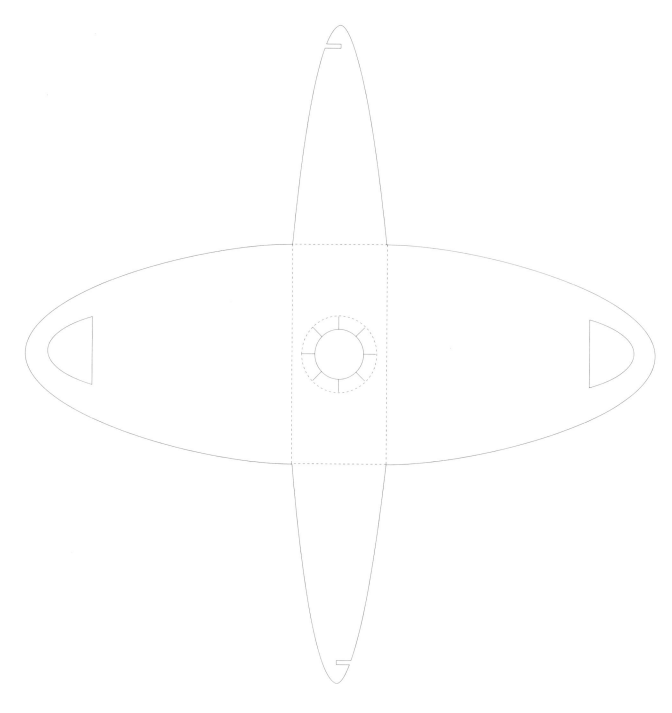

Oval-shaped box for Easter gift with handle, die cut and lid • Boîte ovale pour cadeau de Pâques avec poignée, ouverture et couvercle • Ovale Geschenkbox für Ostern mit Griff und Ausstanzungen • Caja ovalada para regalo de Pascua, con asa, troquel y tapa • Scatola ovale per regalo di Pasqua, con maniglia, fustella e coperchio • Caixa ovalada para presente de Páscoa, com asa, cunha e tampa • Ovale doos voor paasversiering, met handgreep en deksel

Hanging box for Christmas tree gift. Model 4 • Boîte à cadeau à suspendre à l'arbre de Noël. Modèle 4 • Hängende Geschenkschachtel für den Weihnachtsbaum. Modell 4 • Caja colgante para regalo de árbol navideño. Modelo 4 • Scatola sospesa da regalo per albero di Natale. Modello 4 • Caixa de pendurar para presente de árvore de natal. Modelo 4 • Hangdoos voor kerstboomversiering. Model 4

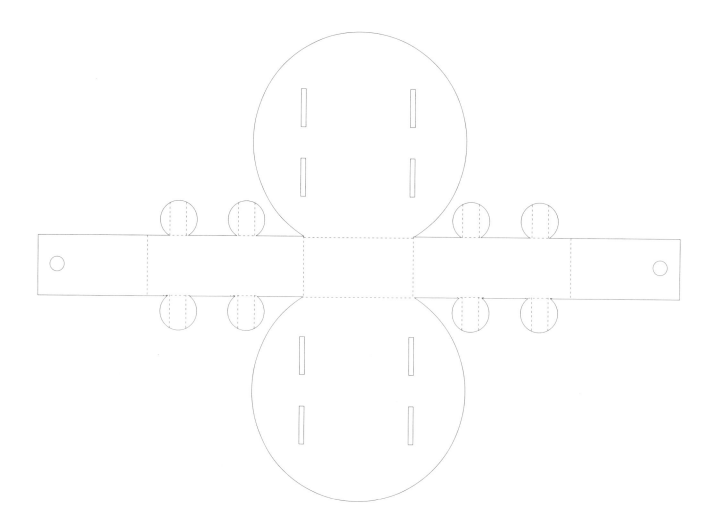

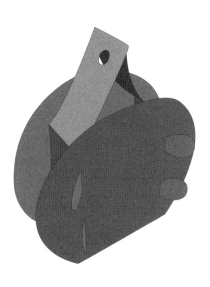

Hanging box for Christmas tree gift. Model 5 • Boîte à cadeau à suspendre à l'arbre de Noël. Modèle 5 • Hängende Geschenkschachtel für den Weihnachtsbaum. Modell 5 • Caja colgante para regalo de árbol navideño. Modelo 5 • Scatola da regalo sospesa per albero di Natale. Modello 5 • Caixa de pendurar para presente de árvore de natal. Modelo 5 • Geschenkdoos voor in de kerstboom. Model 5

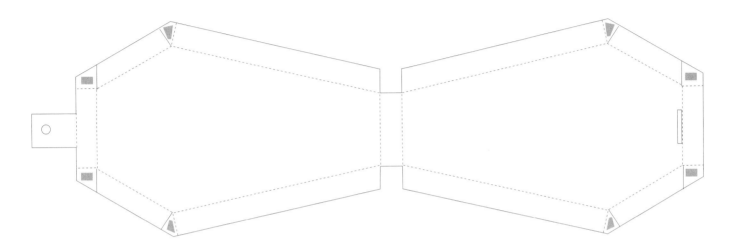

Coffin-shaped hanging box for Halloween • Boîte à suspendre en forme de cercueil pour Halloween • Sargförmige Hängeschachtel für Halloween • Caja colgante en forma de ataúd, para Halloween • Scatola sospesa a forma di bara per Halloween • Caixa de pendurar em forma de ataúde para Halloween • Hangdoos in de vorm van een doodskist, voor Halloween

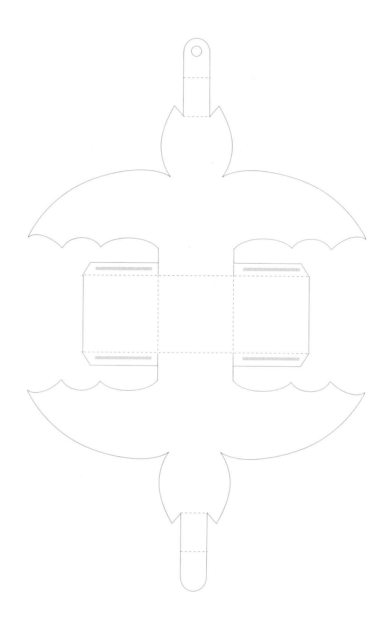

Bat-shaped hanging box for Halloween • Boîte à suspendre en forme de chauve-souris pour Halloween • Fledermausförmige Hängeschachtel für Halloween • Caja colgante en forma de murciélago, para Halloween • Scatola sospesa a forma di pipistrello per Halloween • Caixa de pendurar em forma de morcego para Halloween • Hangdoos in de vorm van een vleermuis, voor Halloween

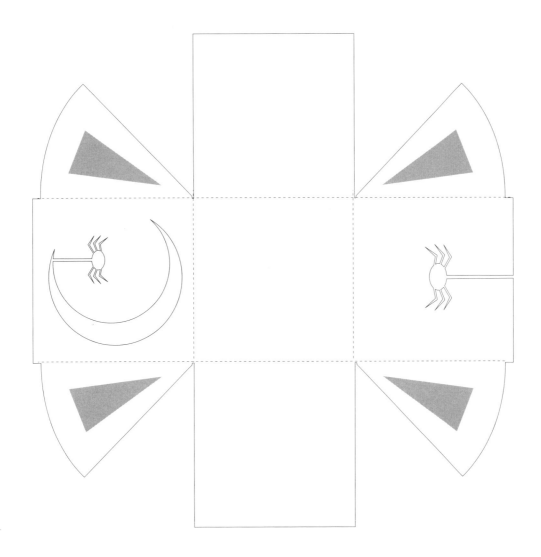

Open candle holder with die cut sides for Halloween •
Photophore avec les bords ajourés pour Halloween • Offene
Kerzenbox mit gestanzten Seitenteilen für Halloween • Caja
abierta para vela, con los lados troquelados, para Halloween •
Scatola aperta per candela, con lati fustellati, per Halloween • Caixa
aberta para vela, com os lados cunhados, para Halloween • Open
doos voor kaars, met twee gestanste kanten, voor Halloween

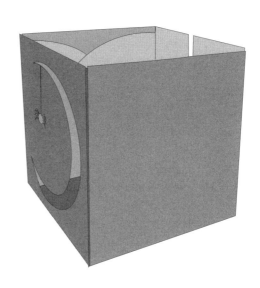

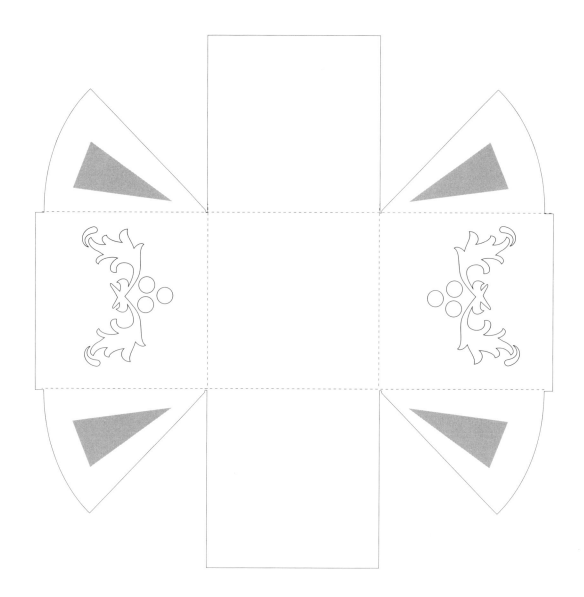

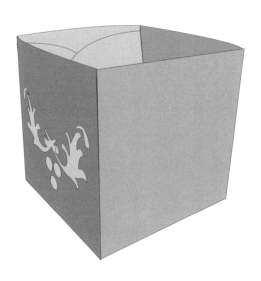

Open candle holder with die cut sides for Christmas •
Photophore avec les bords ajourés pour Noël • Offene
Kerzenbox mit gestanzten Seitenteilen für Weihnachten • Caja
abierta para vela, con los lados troquelados, para Navidad •
Scatola aperta per candela, con lati fustellati, per
Natale • Caixa aberta para vela, com os lados cunhados,
para Natal • Open doos voor kaars, met twee gestanste
kanten, voor Kerstmis

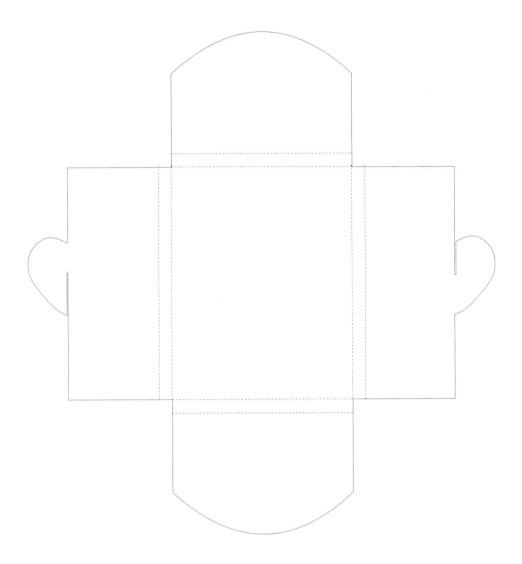

Valentine's Day envelope with interior gusset and heart-shaped tuck-in closure • Enveloppe de Saint-Valentin avec soufflé inférieur et fermeture à rabat en forme de cœur • Umschlag mit herzförmigem Laschenverschluss für den Valentinstag • Sobre de San Valentín con fuelle inferior y cierre de pestaña en forma de corazón • Busta di San Valentino con soffietto inferiore e lembo di chiusura a forma di cuore • Envelope de São Valentim com fole inferior e fecho de língua em forma de coração • Enveloppe voor Valentijn met hartvormige lipsluiting

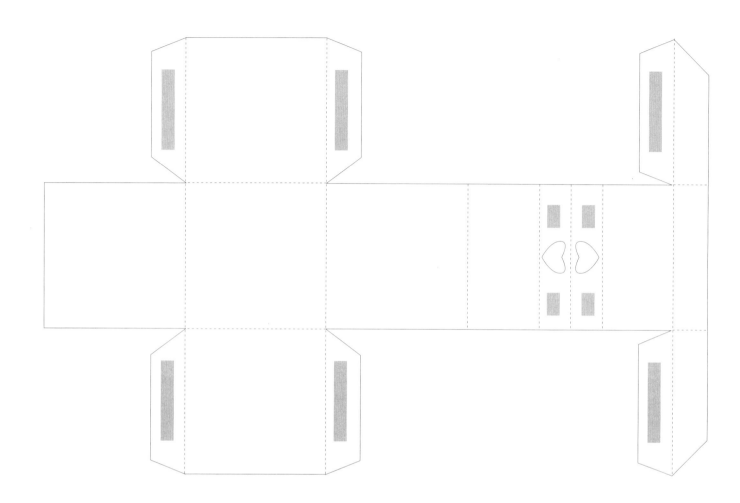

Valentine's Day box with handle and die cut • Boîte pour cadeau de Saint-Valentin avec poignée et ouverture • Geschenkbox mit Griff und Ausstanzung für den Valentinstag • Caja para regalo de San Valentín, con asa y troquel • Scatola per regalo di San Valentino con maniglia e fustella • Caixa para presente de São Valentim com asa e cunha • Doos voor valentijnsgeschenk, met handgreep

Valentine's Day gift box with heart-shaped sides • Boîte pour cadeau de Saint-Valentin avec côtés en forme de cœur • Geschenkbox mit herzförmigen Seitenteilen für den Valentinstag • Caja para regalo de San Valentín con laterales en forma de corazón • Scatola per regalo di San Valentino con lati a forma di cuore • Caixa para presente de São Valentim com laterais em forma de coração • Doos voor valentijnsgeschenk met harten

Boxes for gifts
Boîtes cadeaux

Geschenkverpackungen

Cajas para regalos

Scatole per regali

Caixas para presentes

Geschenkdozen

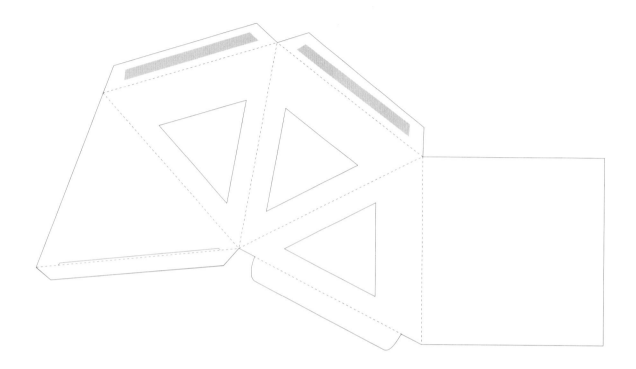

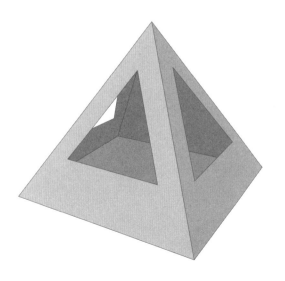

Pyramid-shaped box with three windows • Boîte pyramidale pour cadeau pyramidal avec trois fenêtres • Pyramidenförmige Box mit drei Fenstern • Caja piramidal para regalo piramidal, con tres ventanas • Scatola piramidale per regalo piramidale con tre finestrelle • Caixa piramidal para presente piramidal com três janelas • Piramidedoos voor piramidevormig geschenk, met drie vensters

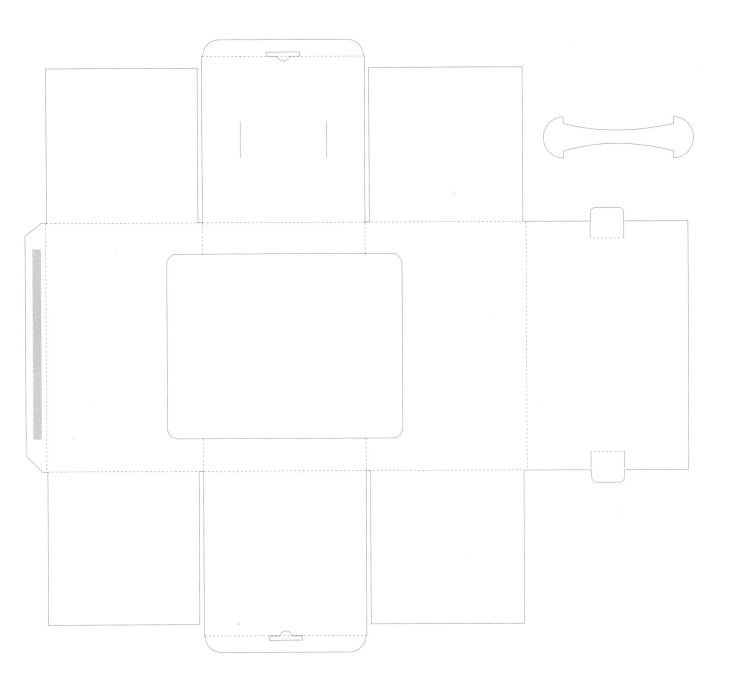

Gift box with three irregular-shaped windows and back closure · Boîte à cadeau avec trois fenêtres irrégulières et fermeture arrière · Geschenkbox mit Fenster und rückseitigem Verschluss · Caja para regalo con tres ventanas irregulares y cierre trasero · Scatola per regalo con tre finestrelle irregolari e chiusura posteriore · Caixa para presente com três janelas irregulares e fecho traseiro · Geschenkdoos met openingen en dichte achterkant

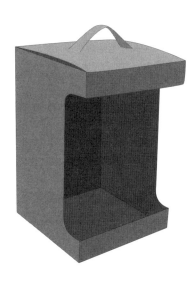

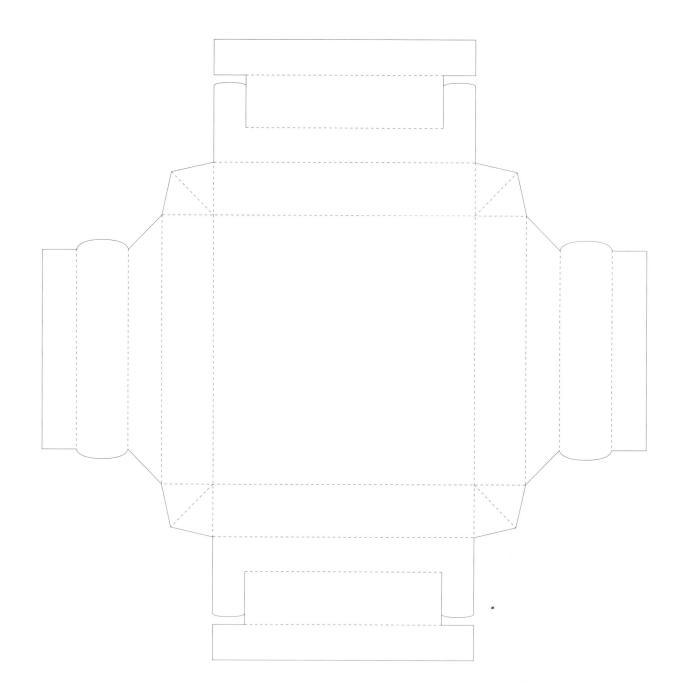

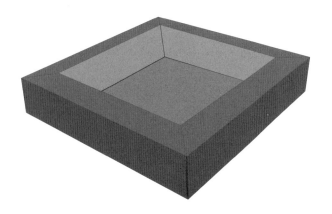

Self-assembly box with frame and sleeve. Part 1 • Boîte avec bords repliables et étui. Partie 1 • Doppelwandige Schachtel mit Schuber. Teil 1 • Caja con marco automontable y faja. Parte 1 • Scatola con cornice automontante e fascia. Parte 1 • Caixa com moldura automontável e faixa. Parte 1 • Zelfbouwdoos met opstaande rand en hoes met opening. Deel 1

Self-assembly box with frame and sleeve. Part 2 • Boîte avec bords repliables et étui. Partie 2 • Doppelwandige Schachtel mit Schuber. Teil 2 • Caja con marco automontable y faja. Parte 2 • Scatola con cornice automontante e fascia. Parte 2 • Caixa com moldura automontável e faixa. Parte 2 • Zelfbouwdoos met opstaande rand en hoes. Deel 2

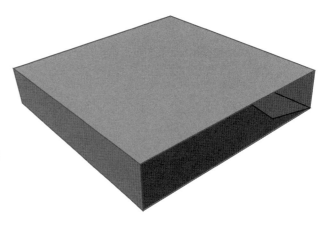

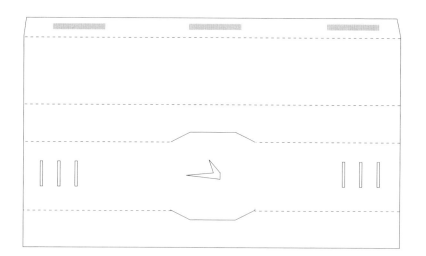

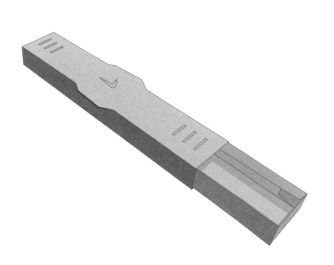

Watch-shaped gift box • Boîte à cadeau en forme de montre • Uhrenförmige Geschenkschachtel • Caja para regalo con forma de reloj • Scatola da regalo a forma di orologio • Caixa para presente com forma de relógio • Geschenkdoos in de vorm van een klok

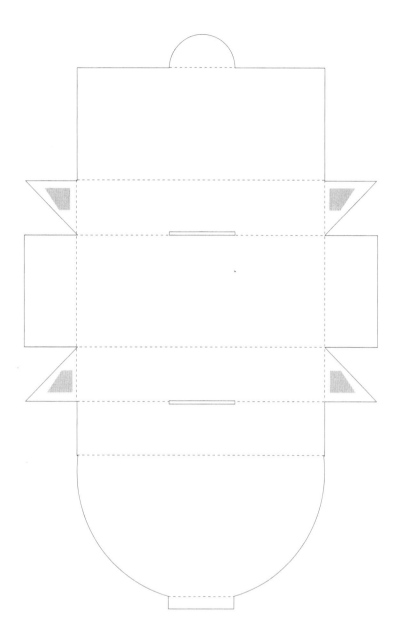

Spectacle case • Étui à lunettes • Brillenetui • Estuche para gafas • Astuccio per occhiali • Estojo para óculos • Kokervormig doosje voor bril

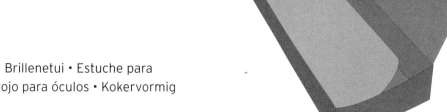

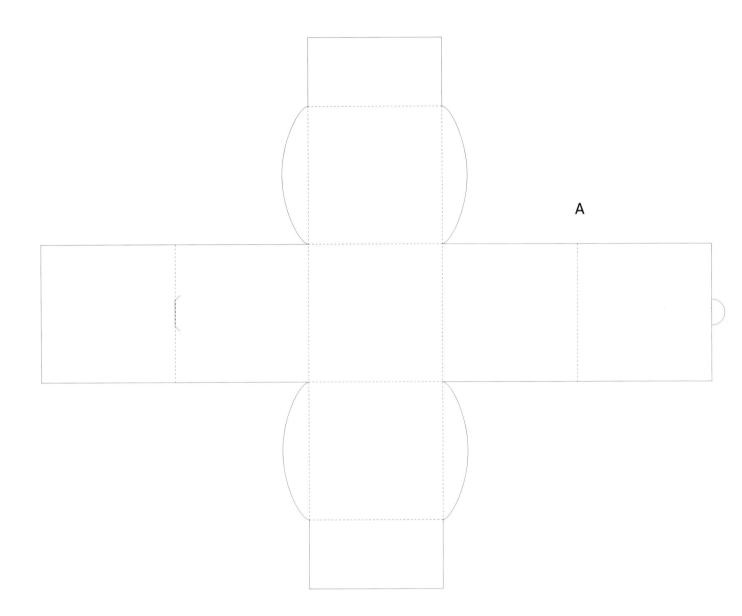

A

Gift box with circular interior support and re-sealable closure. Part 1 • Boîte à cadeau avec support intérieur circulaire et couvercle à fermeture automatique. Partie 1 • Geschenkbox mit runder Halterung innen und Deckel mit Selbstverschluss. Teil 1 • Caja para regalo con soporte interior circular y tapa con autocierre. Parte 1 • Scatola per regalo con supporto interno circolare e coperchio a chiusura automatica. Parte 1 • Caixa para presente com suporte interior circular e tampa com autofecho. Parte 1 • Geschenkdoos met ronde binnensteun en deksel met zelfsluiting. Deel 1

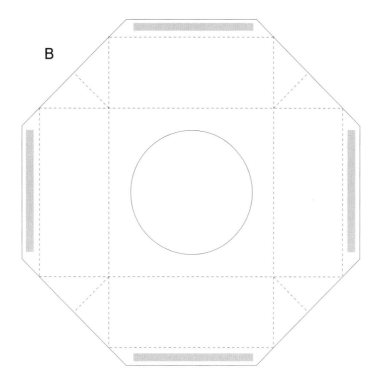

Gift box with circular interior support and re-sealable closure. Part 2 • Boîte à cadeau avec support intérieur circulaire et couvercle à fermeture automatique. Partie 2 • Geschenkbox mit runder Halterung innen und Deckel mit Selbstverschluss. Teil 2 • Caja para regalo con soporte interior circular y tapa con autocierre. Parte 2 • Scatola per regalo con supporto interno circolare e coperchio a chiusura automatica. Parte 2 • Caixa para presente com suporte interior circular e tampa com autofecho. Parte 2 • Geschenkdoos met ronde binnensteun en deksel met zelfsluiting. Deel 2

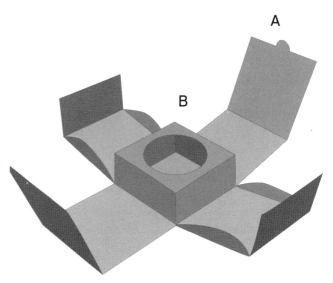

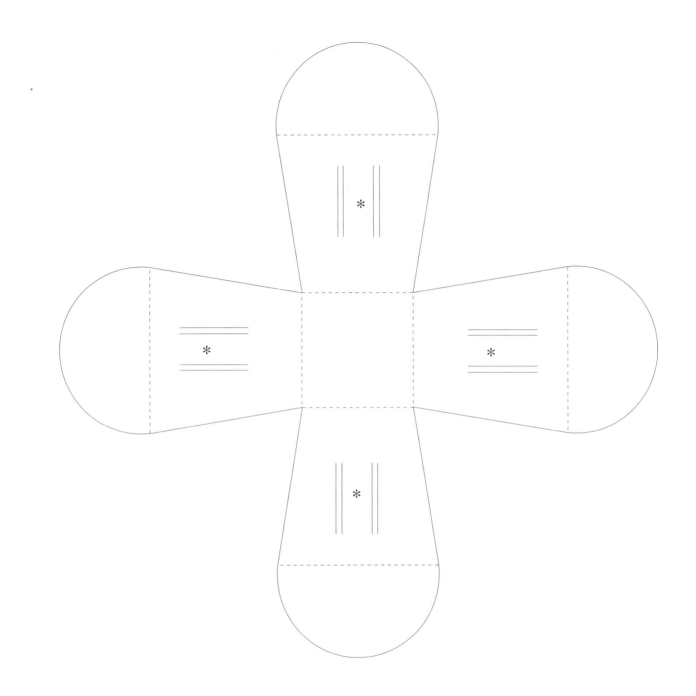

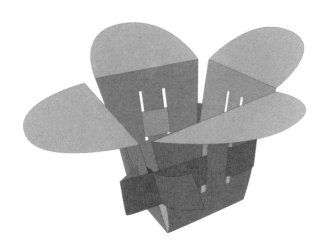

Fold-out basket for gift wrapped with ribbon • Panier dépliable pour cadeau avec ruban • Entfaltbarer Geschenkkorb mit Wickelband • Cesta desplegable para regalo, con cinta envolvente • Cesta richiudibile per regalo con nastro avvolgente • Cesta desdobrável para presente com cinta envolvente • Uitvouwbare geschenkmand met lint

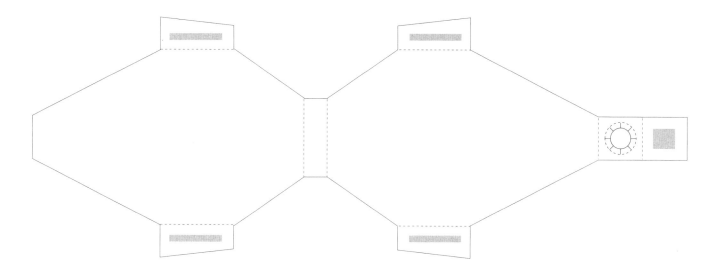

Box for racket • Boîte pour raquette • Box für einen
Tennisschläger • Caja para raqueta • Scatola per
racchetta • Caixa para raqueta • Doos voor racket

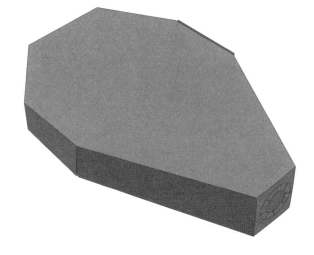

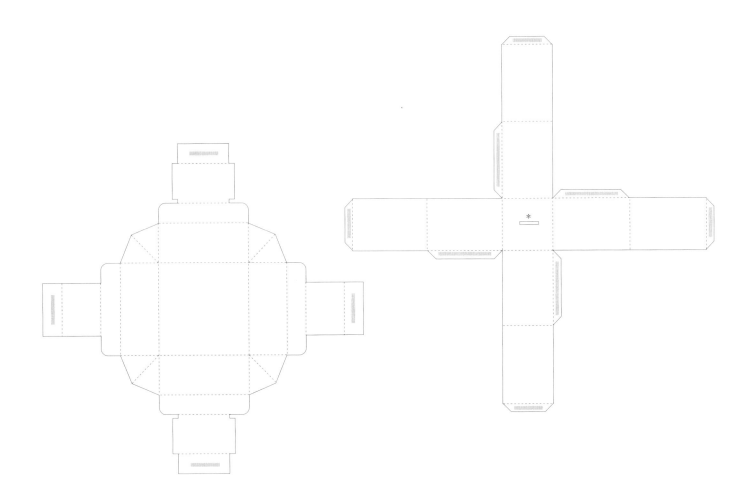

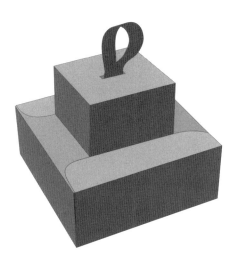

Telescopic gift box with handle • Boîte télescopique pour cadeau avec poignée • Ausziehbare Geschenkbox mit Trageband • Caja telescópica para regalo, con asa • Scatola telescopica per regalo con maniglia • Caixa telescópica para presente com asa • Telescopische geschenkdoos, met hengsel

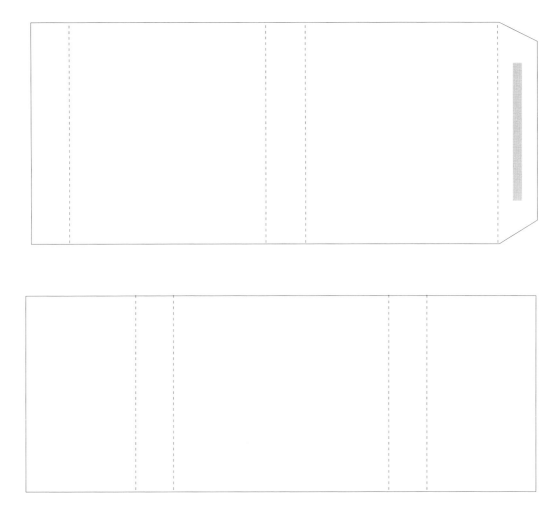

Box for wallet with double sleeve • Boîte a portefeuille avec double étui • Verpackung für Brieftaschen • Caja para cartera, con doble faja • Scatola per portafogli con doppia aletta • Caixa para carteira com dupla faixa • Doos voor schrijfmap, met dubbele hoes

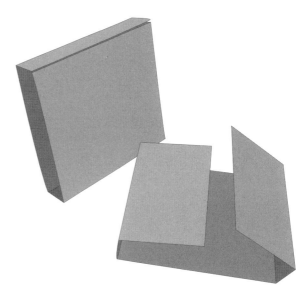

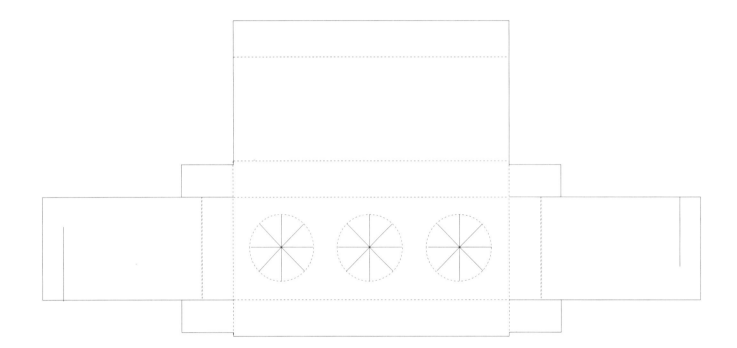

Box for three golf balls with support and corner window.
Part 1 • Coffret pour trois balles de golf avec support et fenêtre dans l'angle. Partie 1 • Box für drei Golfbälle mit Halterung und Sichtfenster. Teil 1 • Caja para tres pelotas de golf, con soporte y ventana esquinera. Parte 1 • Scatola per tre palline da golf con supporto e finestrella angolare. Parte 1 • Caixa para três bolas de golfe com suporte e janela de canto. Parte 1 • Doos voor drie golfballen, met binnensteun en hoekvenster. Deel 1

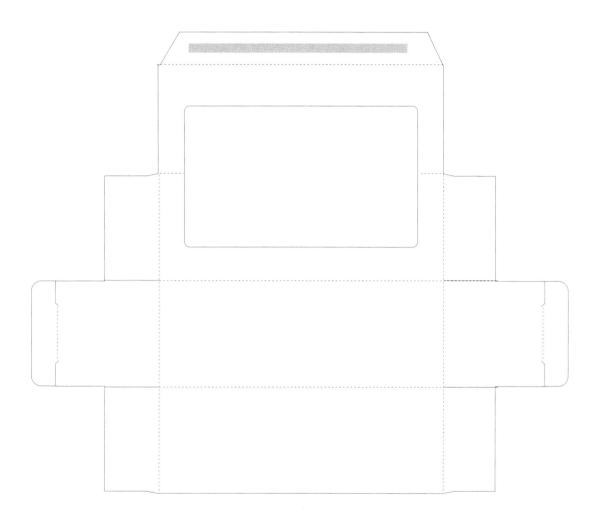

Box for three golf balls with support and corner window.
Part 2 · Coffret pour trois balles de golf avec support et fenêtre
dans l'angle. Partie 2 · Box für drei Golfbälle mit Halterung und
Sichtfenster. Teil 2 · Caja para tres pelotas de golf, con soporte y
ventana esquinera. Parte 2 · Scatola per tre palline da golf con
supporto e finestrella angolare. Parte 2 · Caixa para três bolas
de golfe com suporte e janela de canto. Parte 2 · Doos voor drie
golfballen, met binnensteun en hoekvenster. Deel 2

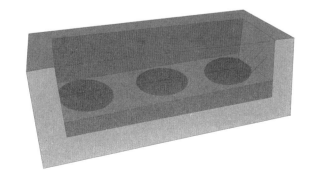

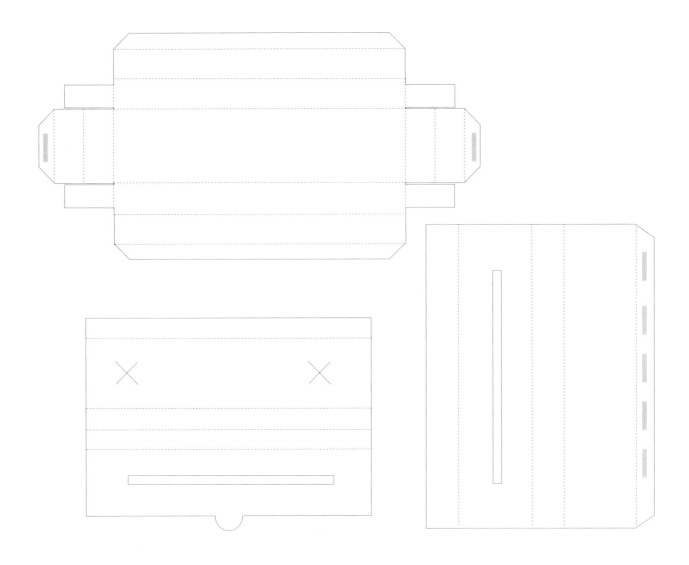

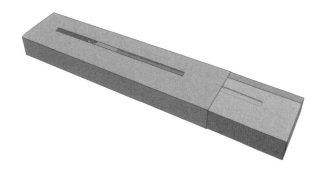

Necklace case with cover and interior support • Coffret pour collier avec étui et support intérieur • Schachtel mit Schuber und Innenhalterung für eine Halskette • Estuche para collar, con faja y soporte interior • Astuccio per collana con fascetta e supporto interno • Estojo para colar com faixa e suporte interior • Doosje voor ketting, met hoes en binnensteun

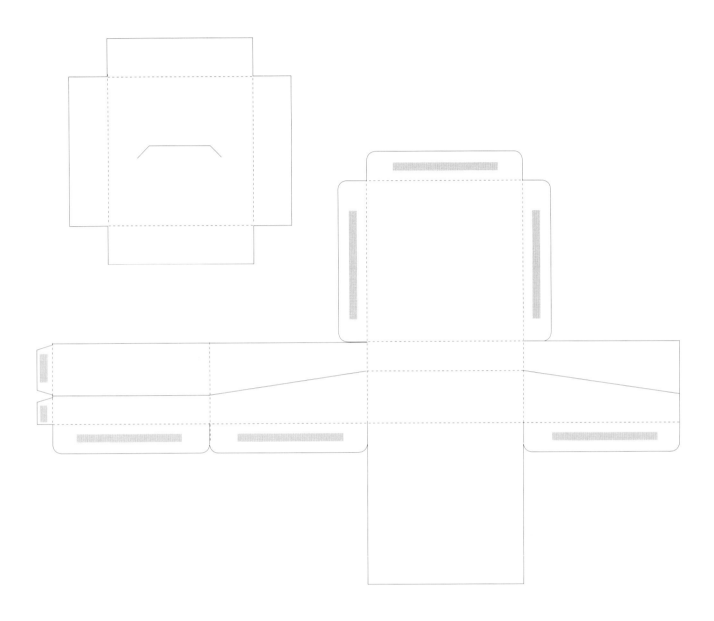

Bracelet Case with interior support • Coffret pour bracelet avec support intérieur • Schatulle mit Innenhalterung für ein Armband • Estuche para pulsera, con soporte interior • Astuccio per bracciale con supporto interno • Estojo para pulseira com suporte interior • Doos voor armband, met binnensteun

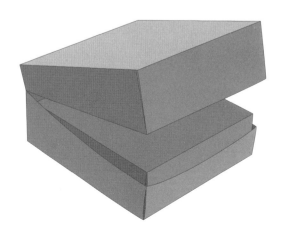

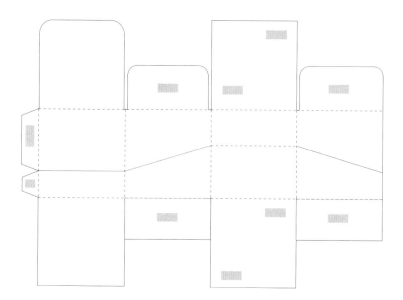

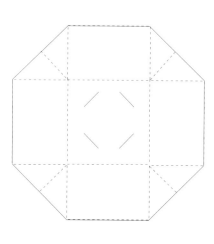

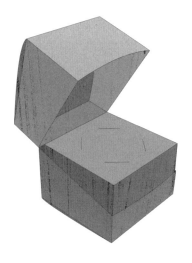

Ring case with cover and interior support · Coffret pour bague avec couvercle et support intérieur · Kästchen mit Deckel und Innenhalterung für Ringe · Estuche para anillo, con tapa y soporte interior · Astuccio per anello con coperchio e supporto interno · Estojo para anel com tampa e suporte interior · Doosje voor ring, met deksel en binnensteun

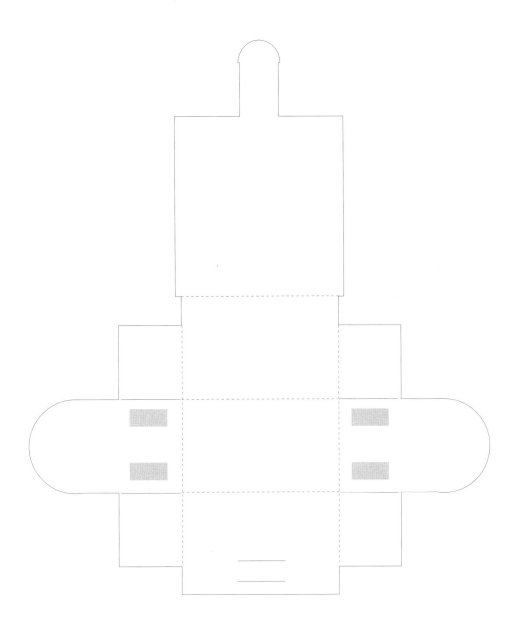

Chest-shaped gift box with flap • Boîte à cadeau en forme de malle et avec rabat • Geschenkbox mit Lasche in Form einer Truhe • Caja para regalo, con forma de baúl y con solapa • Scatola per regalo a forma di baule con aletta • Caixa para presente com forma de baú e com aba • Geschenkdoos in de vorm van een koffer en met flap

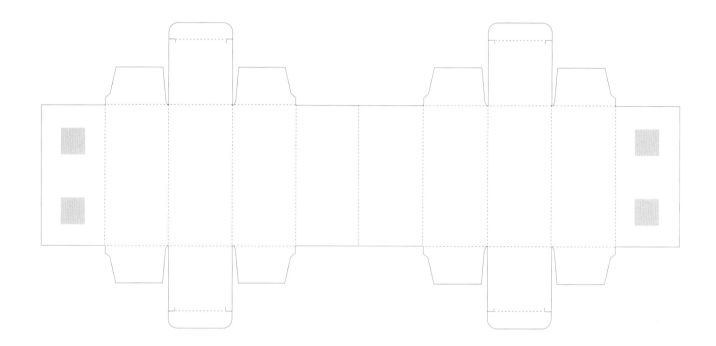

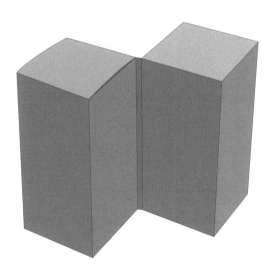

Double gift box (matching pair) • Boîte double (jumelle normale) pour cadeau • Geschenk-Doppelbox (regelmäßige Zwillingsbox) • Caja doble (gemela regular) para regalo • Scatola doppia (gemella regolare) per regalo • Caixa dupla (gémea regular) para presente • Dubbele geschenkdoos (gelijke vorm)

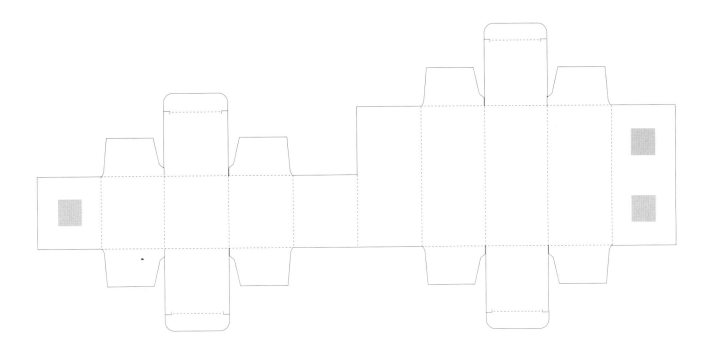

Double gift box (unmatched pair) • Boîte double (jumelle spéciale) pour cadeau • Geschenk-Doppelbox (unregelmäßige Zwillingsbox) • Caja doble (gemela irregular) para regalo • Scatola doppia (gemella irregolare) per regalo • Caixa dupla (gémea irregular) para presente • Dubbele geschenkdoos (ongelijke vorm)

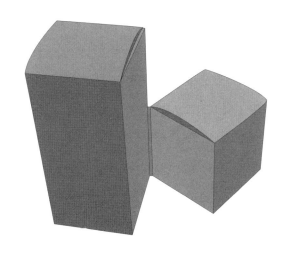

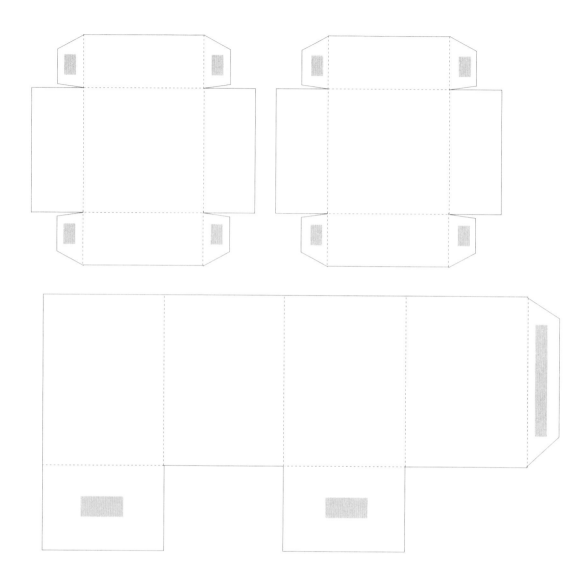

Gift box with sides and double lid • Boîte à cadeau avec cloison et double couvercle • Geschenkbox mit zwei Deckeln • Caja para regalo, con pared y doble tapa • Scatola per regalo con parete e coperchio doppio • Caixa para presente com parede e dupla tampa • Geschenkdoos met dubbel deksel

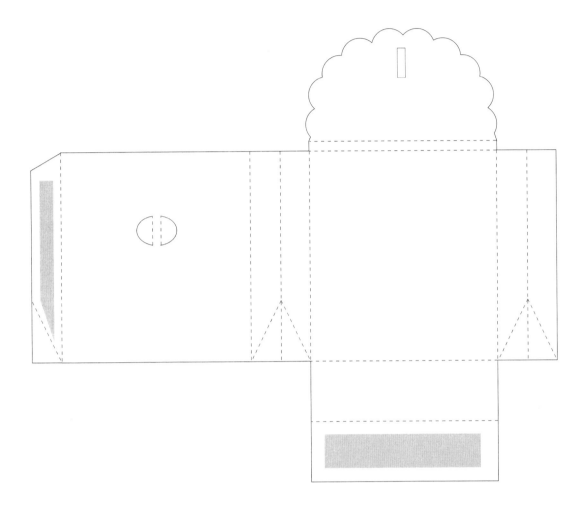

Envelope with lower gusset and cloud-shaped tuck-in closure · Enveloppe avec soufflé inférieur et languette de fermeture en forme de nuage · Umschlag mit balgartig geformtem Unterteil und wolkenförmiger Verschlussklappe · Sobre con fuelle inferior y pestaña de cierre, con forma de nube · Busta con soffietto inferiore e lembo di chiusura a forma di nuvola · Envelope com fole inferior e língua de fecho com forma de nuvem · Omslag met binnenvouw en lipsluiting, in de vorm van een wolk

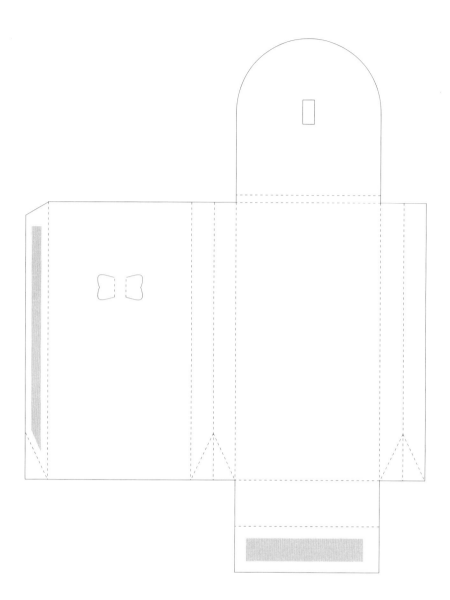

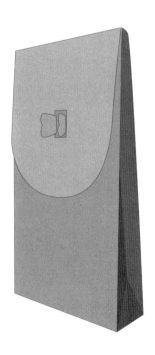

Envelope with lower gusset and tuck-in closure • Enveloppe avec soufflé inférieur et languette de fermeture • Umschlag mit balgartig geformtem Unterteil und Verschlusslasche • Sobre con fuelle inferior y pestaña con cierre • Busta con soffietto inferiore e lembo di chiusura • Envelope com fole inferior e língua de fecho • Omslag met binnenvouw en lipsluiting

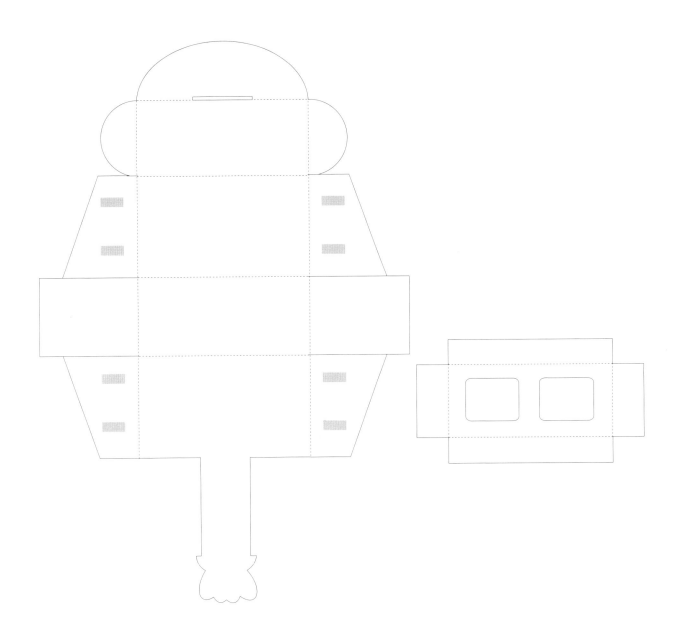

Box for two candles with semicircle lid with holder •
Boîte pour deux bougies avec couvercle semi-circulaire
et support • Box mit Halterung für zwei Kerzen und
halbkreisförmigem Deckel • Caja para dos velas, con tapa
semicircular con soporte • Scatola per due candele con
coperchio semicircolare con supporto • Caixa para duas
velas com tampa semicircular com suporte • Doos voor twee
kaarsen, met halfrond deksel en houder

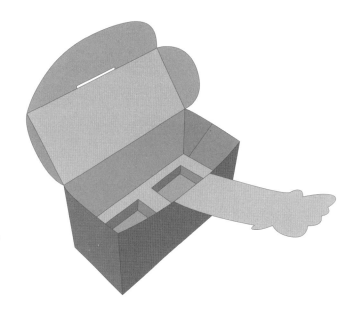

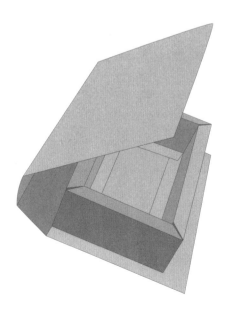

Box for book with oval spine • Boîte à livre avec tranche ovale • Buch-Box mit ovalem Rücken • Caja para libro con lomo ovalado • Scatola per libro con dorso ovale • Caixa para livro com lombada ovalada • Doos voor boek met ovale rug

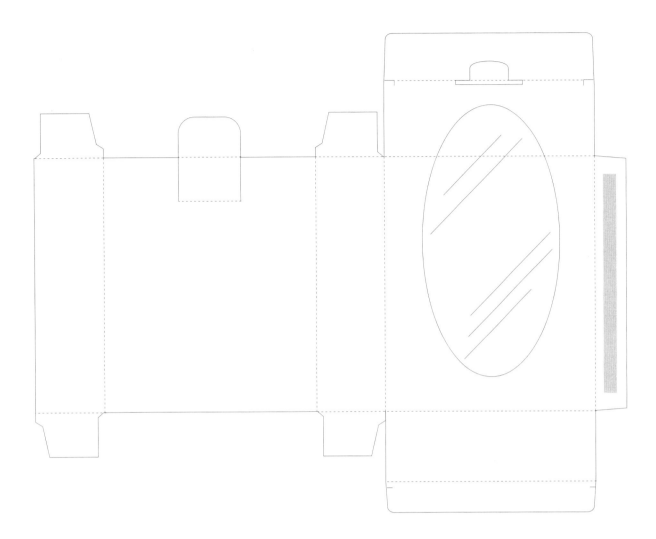

Flat box for scarves with re-sealable closure • Boîte à
écharpes plate avec fermeture automatique • Flache Schachtel
für Schals • Caja plana para bufandas, con autocierre • Scatola
piana per sciarpe con chiusura automatica • Caixa lisa
para cachecol com autofecho • Platte doos voor das, met
hersluitbare sluiting

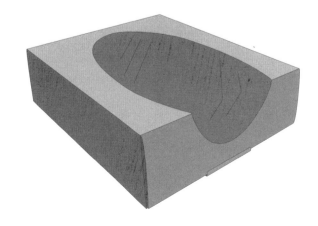

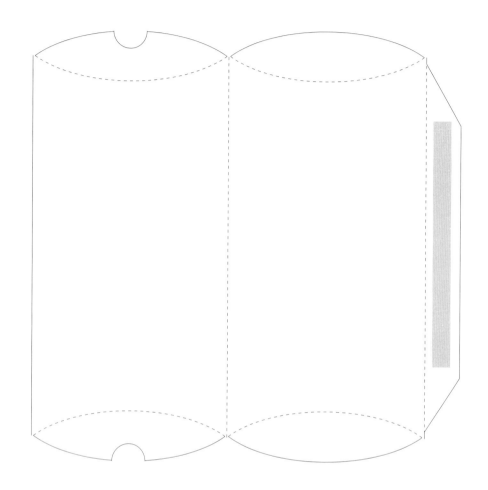

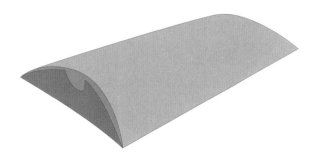

Pillow-shaped gift box • Boîte à cadeau en forme d'oreiller • Kissenförmige Geschenkbox • Caja para regalo con forma de almohada • Scatola da regalo a forma di cuscino • Caixa para presente com forma de almofada • Geschenkdoos in de vorm van een kussen

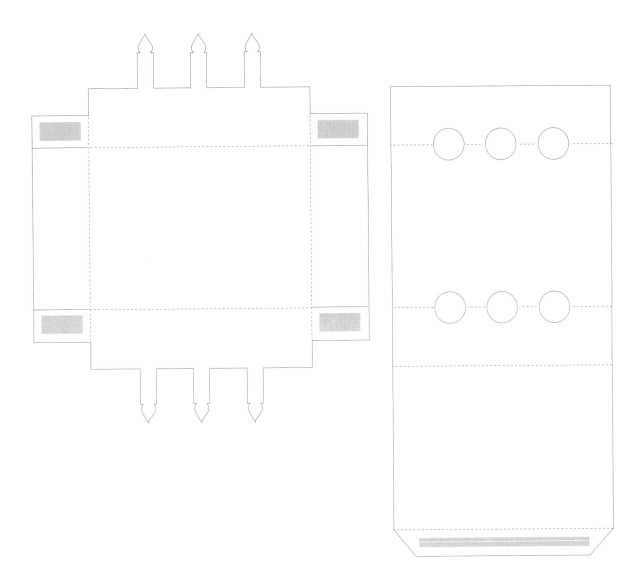

Cake-shaped gift box with sleeve to close • Boîte à cadeau en forme de gâteau et son étui de fermeture • Kuchenförmige Geschenkbox • Caja para regalo con forma de pastel y con faja de cierre • Scatola da regalo a forma di torta con fascia di chiusura • Caixa para presente com forma de bolo e com faixa de fecho • Geschenkdoos in de vorm van een taart en met hoes

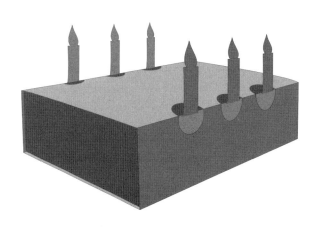

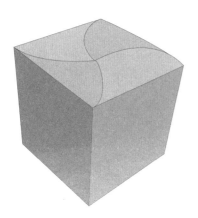

Perfume box with special closure · Boîte à parfum avec fermeture spéciale · Parfümschachtel mit Spezialverschluss · Caja para perfume, con cierre especial · Scatola per profumo con chiusura speciale · Caixa para perfume com fecho especial · Doos voor parfum, met speciale sluiting

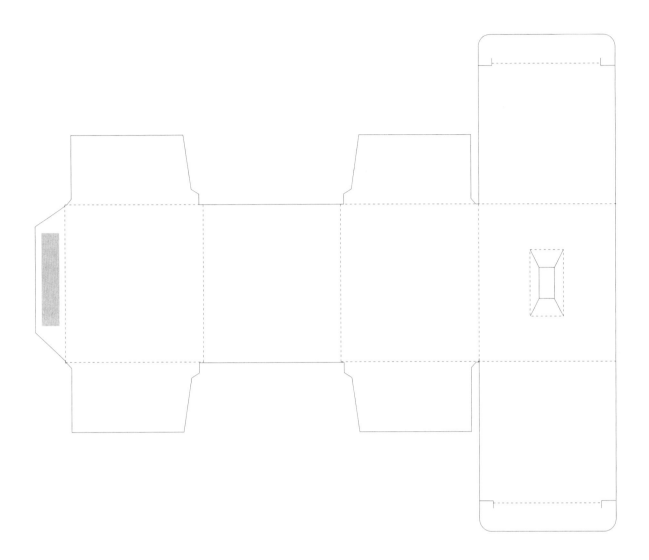

Cup box with handle • Boîte pour tasse avec anse • Box für eine Henkeltasse • Caja para taza, con asa • Scatola per tazza con maniglia • Caixa para chávena com asa • Doos voor kopje met oor

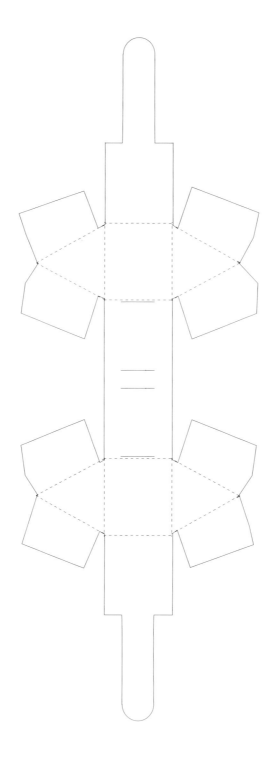

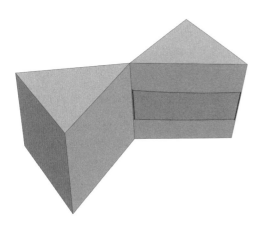

Three-dimensional gift box · Boîte à cadeau polyédrique ·
Polyedrische Geschenkbox · Caja poliédrica para regalo ·
Scatola per regalo poliedrica · Caixa poliédrica para presente ·
Geschenkdoos met veel vlakken

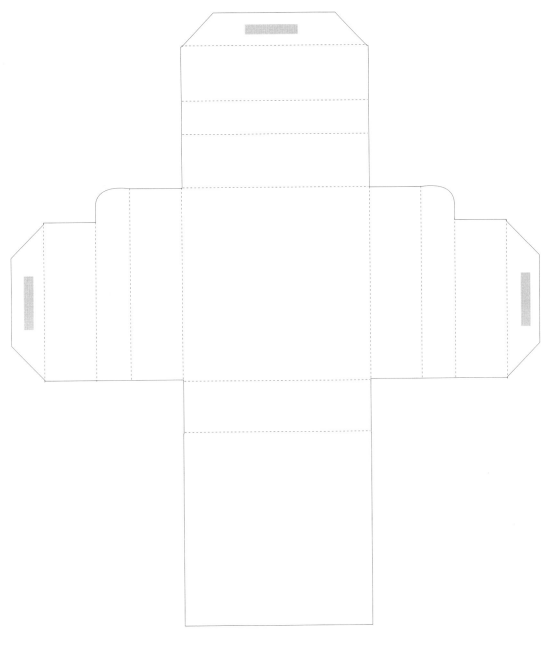

Belt box with wide frame • Boîte à ceinture, avec rebords larges • Doppelwandige Schachtel für einen Gürtel • Caja para cinturón, con marco ancho • Scatola per cintura con cornice larga • Caixa para cinto, com moldura larga • Doos voor riem, met brede rand

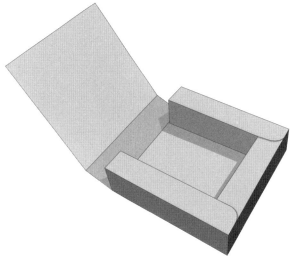

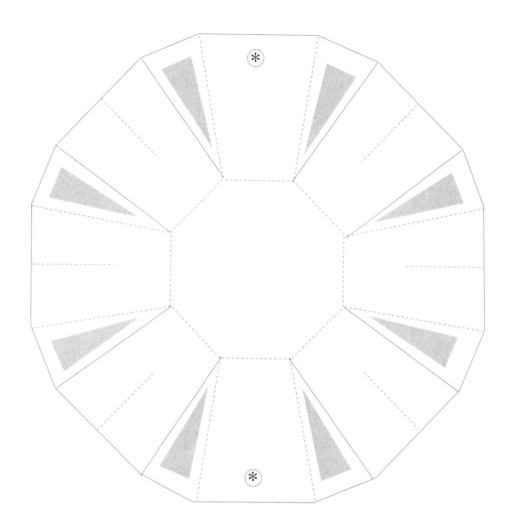

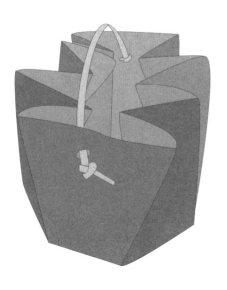

Gift basket with handle and exterior gussets · Panier pour cadeau avec anse et soufflés extérieurs · Geschenkkorb mit Trageband und balgartig geformten Außenteilen · Cesta para regalo, con asa y fuelles exteriores · Cesto da regalo con maniglia e soffietti esterni · Cesta para presente com asa e foles exteriores · Geschenkmand met hengsel en vouwen aan buitenkant

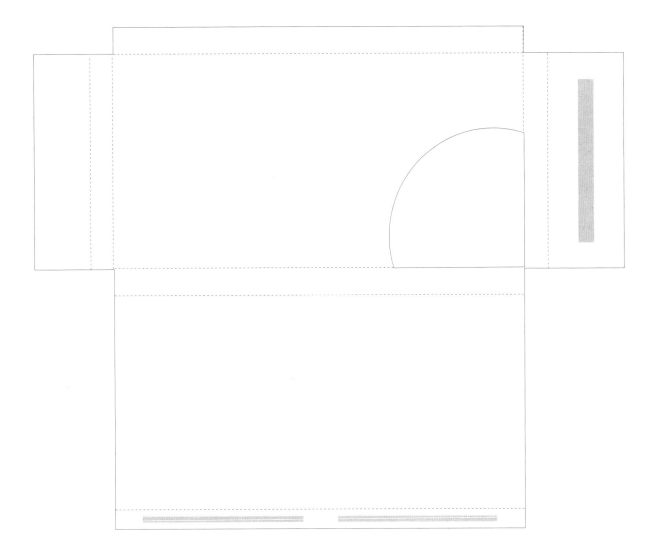

Semi-flat gift box with corner window • Boîte à cadeau
semi-plate avec fenêtre d'angle • Halbflache Geschenkbox
mit Fenster an einer Ecke • Caja semiplana para regalo y con
ventana esquinera • Scatola da regalo semipiana con finestrella
angolare • Caixa semiplana para presente e com janela de
canto • Halfplatte geschenkdoos met hoekvenster

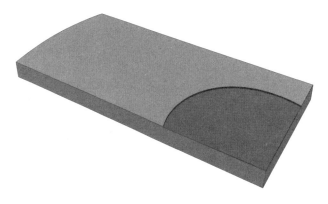

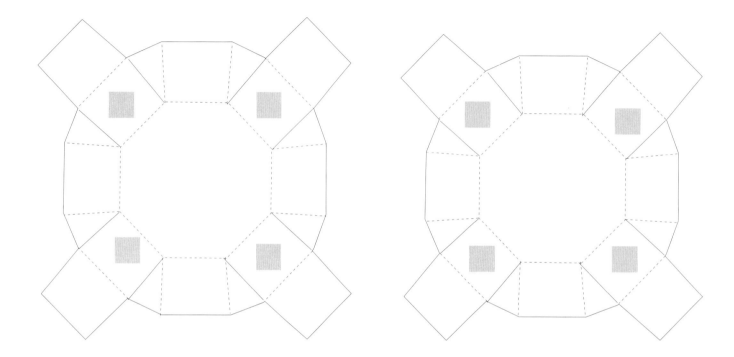

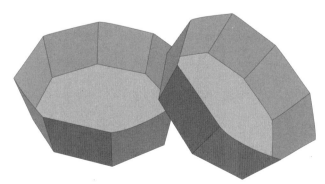

Octagonal gift box • Boîte à cadeau octogonale • Achteckige Geschenkschachtel • Caja octogonal para regalo • Scatola per regalo ottagonale • Caixa octogonal para presente • Achthoekige geschenkdoos

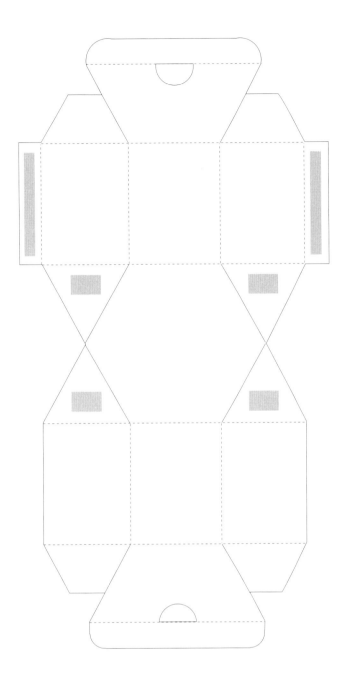

Hexagonal gift box • Boîte à cadeau hexagonale • Sechseckige Geschenkschachtel • Caja hexagonal para regalo • Scatola per regalo esagonale • Caixa hexagonal para presente • Zeshoekige geschenkdoos

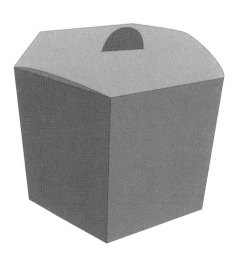

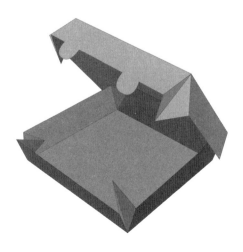

Fold-out box with lid and ear-shaped closure • Boîte dépliable avec couvercle et fermetures à languettes • Entfaltbare Box mit Deckel und Ohrenverschluss • Caja desplegable con tapa y cierre de orejas • Scatola pieghevole con coperchio e chiusura «a orecchie» • Caixa desdobrável com tampa e fecho de orelhas • Uitvouwbare doos met deksel en beugelsluiting

Obelisk-shaped box · Boîte obélisque · Obeliskenbox · Caja
obelisco · Scatola obelisco · Caixa obelisco · Obeliskdoos

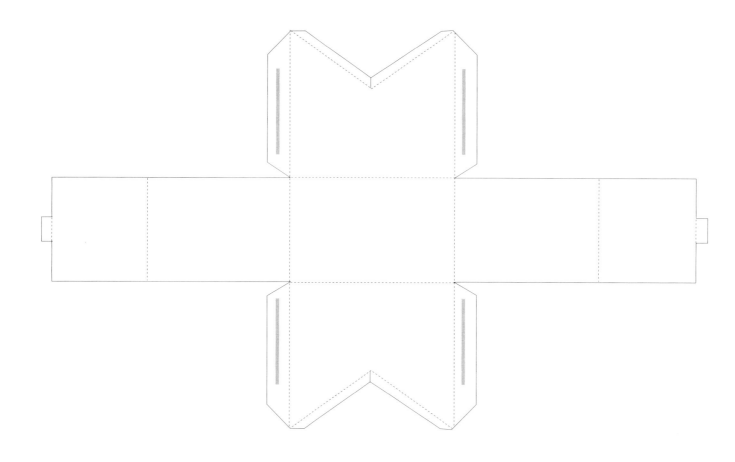

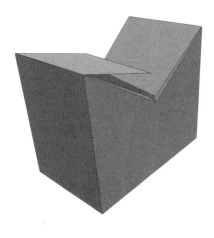

Box with two peaks and interior opening • Boîtes à deux becs et ouvertures intérieures • Box mit zwei Klappen • Caja con dos picos y trampillas interiores • Scatola con due punte e sportellini interni • Caixa com dois picos e escotilhas interiores • Doos met twee punten en binnenklep

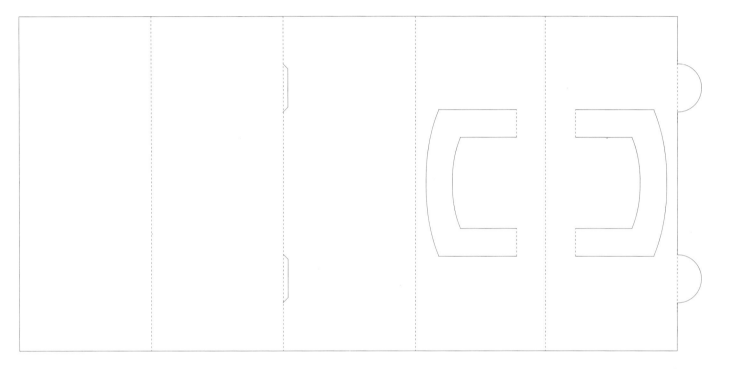

Triangular poster box with handle • Boîte triangulaire pour posters avec poignée • Dreieckige Posterbox mit Griff • Caja triangular para pósters, con asa • Scatola triangolare per poster con maniglia • Caixa triangular para posters com asa • Driehoekige doos voor posters, met hengsel

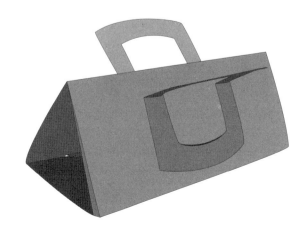

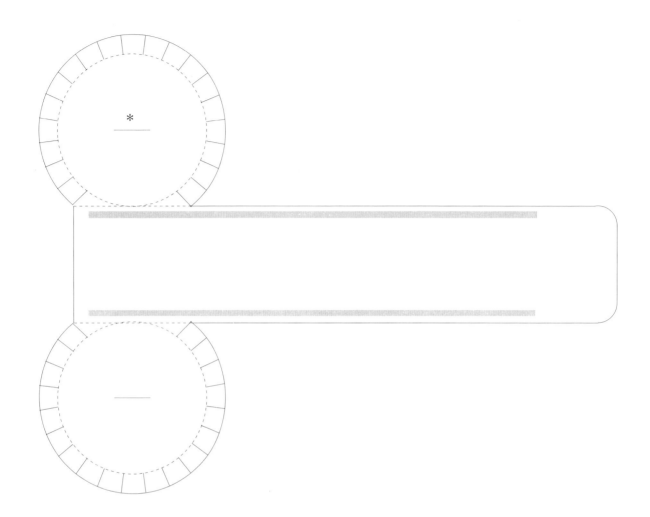

Cylinder-shaped box with lid and handle • Boîte cylindrique avec couvercle et poignée • Zylindrische Box mit Deckel und Trageband • Caja cilíndrica con tapa y asa • Scatola cilindrica con coperchio e maniglia • Caixa cilíndrica com tampa e asa • Ronde doos met deksel en hengsel

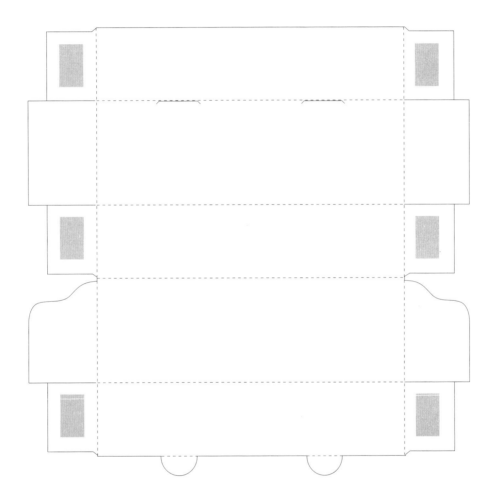

Sectioned chocolate box • Boîte compartimentée pour les chocolats • Pralinenschachtel mit drei Fächern • Caja compartimentada para bombones • Scatola a scomparti per dolciumi • Caixa compartimentada para bombons • Doos met vakjes voor bonbons

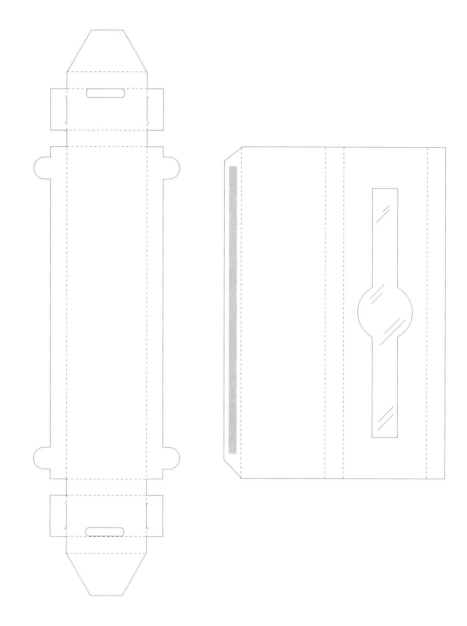

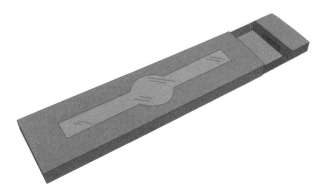

Watch box with removable tray with sleeve with window •
Présentoir amovible pour montre avec étui à fenêtre • Schachtel
mit Fensterschuber für eine Uhr • Caja para reloj con bandeja
extraíble y faja con ventana • Scatola per orologio con vassoio
estraibile e fascia con finestrella • Caixa para relógio com bandeja
extraível e faixa com janela • Uitschuifbakje voor horloge, en
hoes met venster

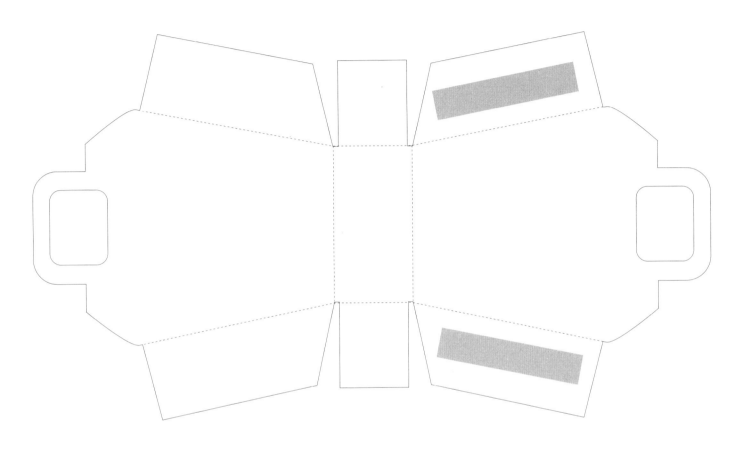

Bag-shaped box. Model 1 • Boîte en forme de sac. Modèle 1 •
Taschenförmige Box. Modell 1 • Caja en forma de bolso.
Modelo 1 • Scatola a forma di borsa. Modello 1 • Caixa em forma
de saco. Modelo 1 • Doos in de vorm van een tas. Model 1

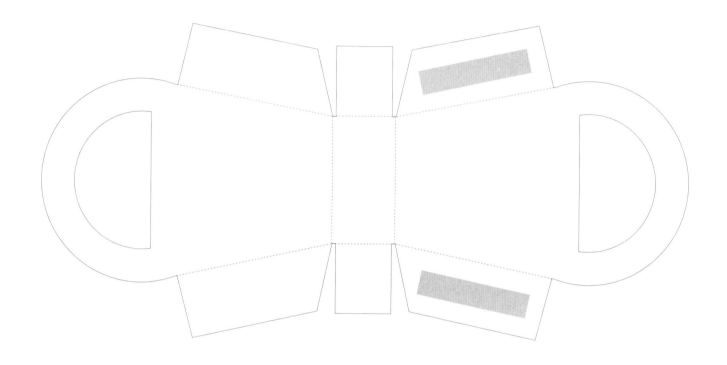

Bag-shaped box. Model 2 • Boîte en forme de sac. Modèle 2 • Taschenförmige Box. Modell 2 • Caja en forma de bolso. Modelo 2 • Scatola a forma di borsa. Modello 2 • Caixa em forma de saco. Modelo 2 • Doos in de vorm van een tas. Model 2

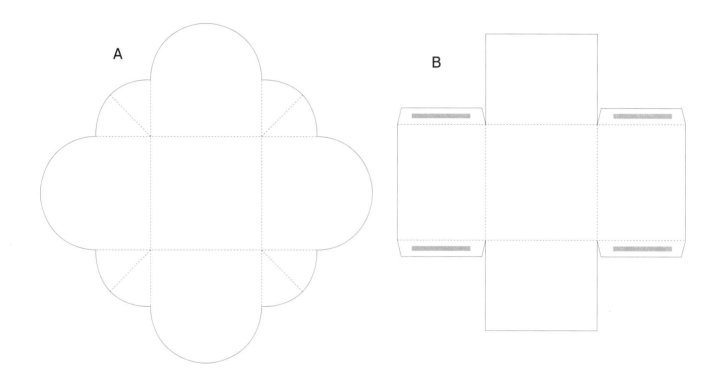

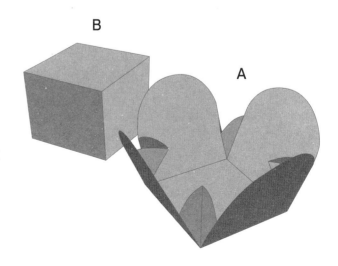

Box with special closure • Boîte avec fermeture spéciale • Box
mit Spezialverschluss • Caja con cierre especial • Scatola
con chiusura speciale • Caixa com fecho especial • Doos met
speciale sluiting

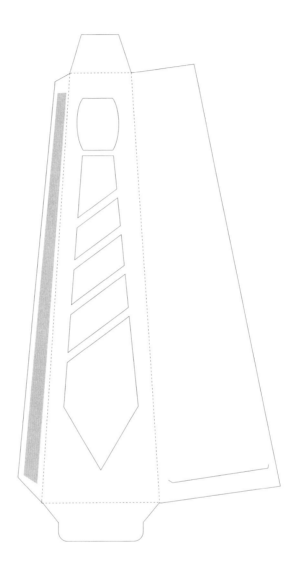

Tie box • Boîte à cravate • Krawattenschachtel • Caja para corbata • Scatola per cravatta • Caixa para gravata • Doos voor stropdas

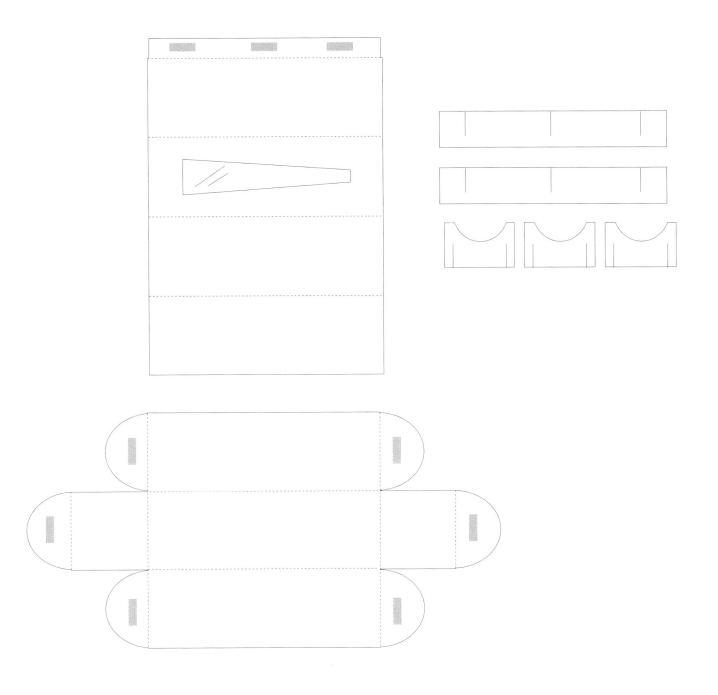

Box for vase with interior support • Boîte pour vase avec support intérieur • Schachtel für eine Vase • Caja para jarrón, con soporte interior • Scatola portavaso con supporto interno • Caixa para jarra com suporte interior • Doos voor vaas, met binnensteun

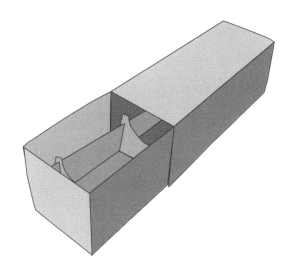

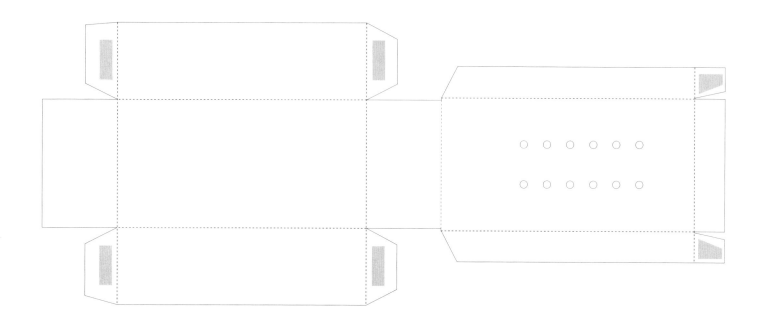

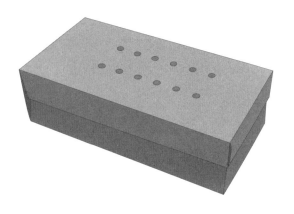

Sport shoe box • Boîte à chaussures de sport • Sportschuhkarton • Caja para zapatillas deportivas • Scatola per scarpe da ginnastica • Caixa para sapatilhas desportivas • Doos voor sportschoenen

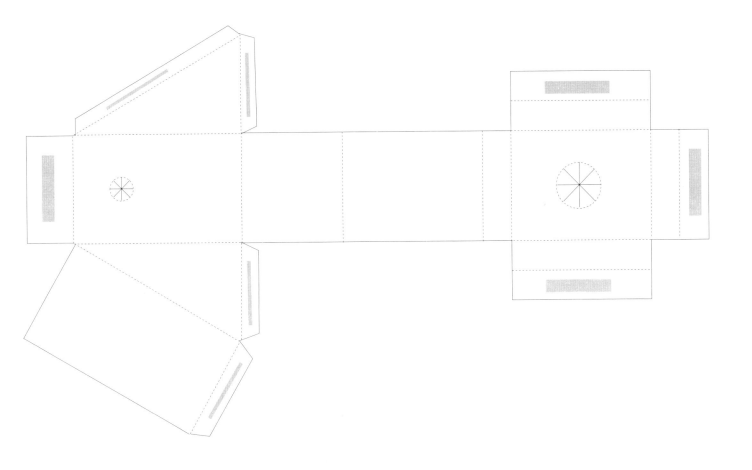

Box for pipe • Boîte à pipe • Pfeifenbox • Caja para
pipa • Scatola per pipa • Caixa para cachimbo • Doos voor pijp

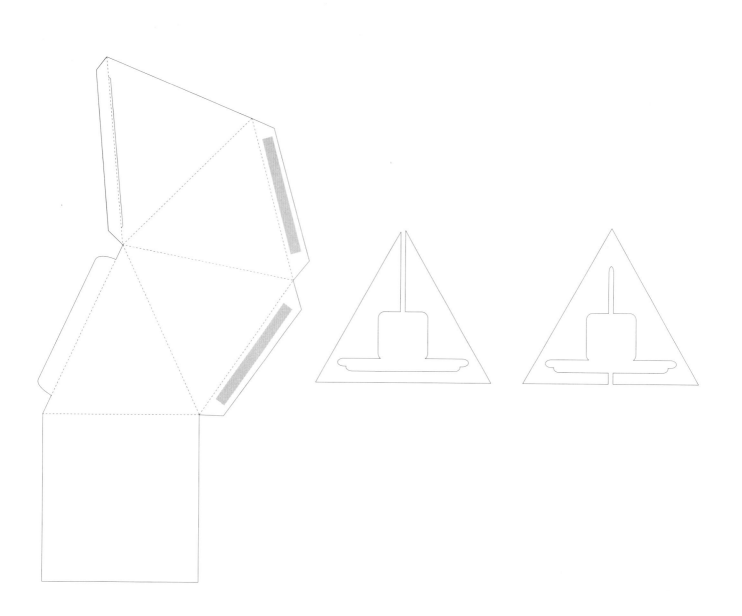

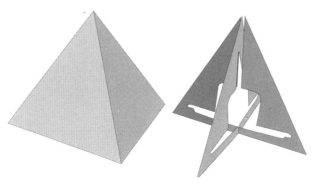

Box for plate and cup • Boîte pour tasse et soucoupe • Box für Tasse und Teller • Caja para taza y plato • Scatola per tazza e piattino • Caixa para chávena e prato • Doos voor kop en schotel

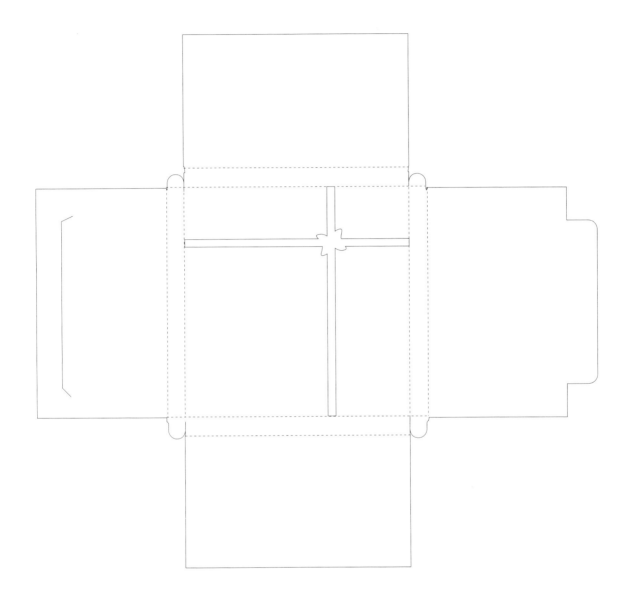

CD box • Boîte pour CD • CD-Hülle • Caja para CD • Scatola per CD • Caixa para CD • Doos voor cd

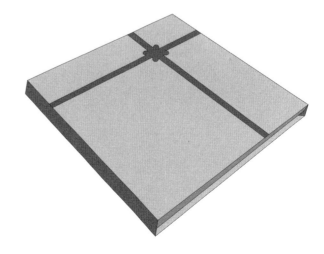

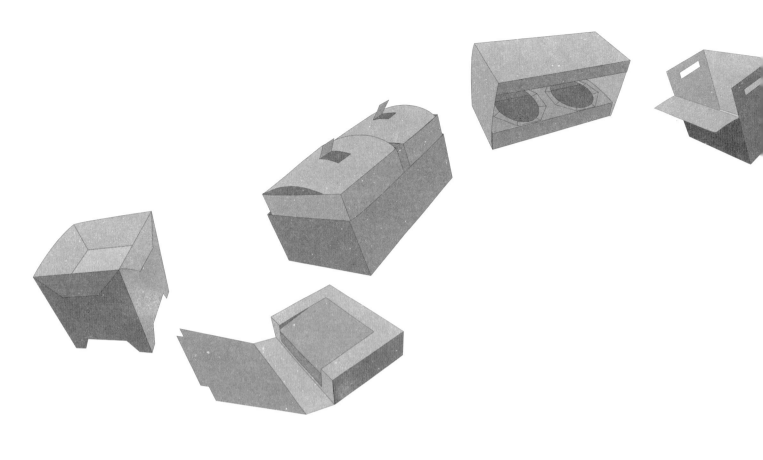

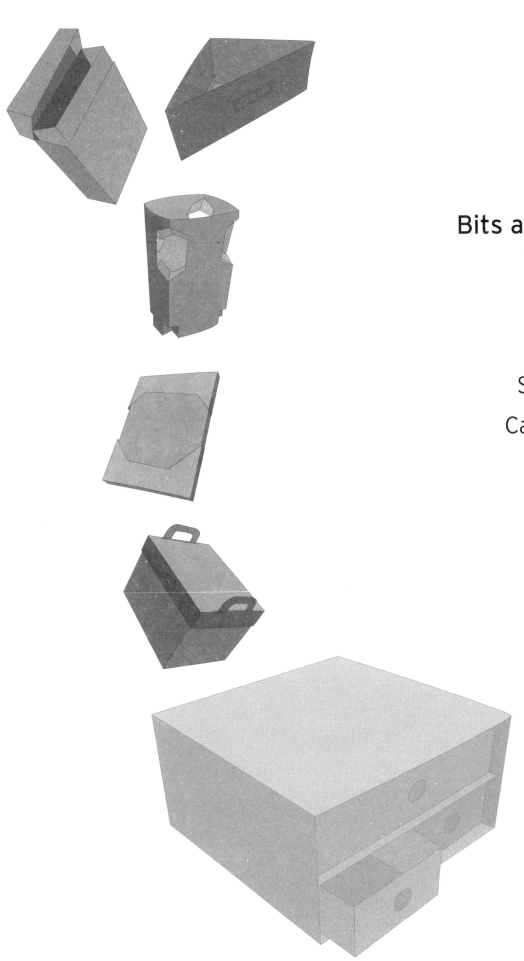

Bits and bobs drawer

Divers

Dies und das

Cajón de sastre

Scatole portatutto

Caixote de arrumos

Rommeldozen

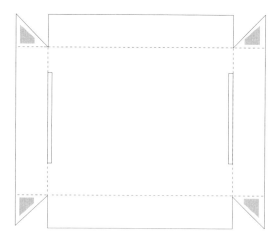

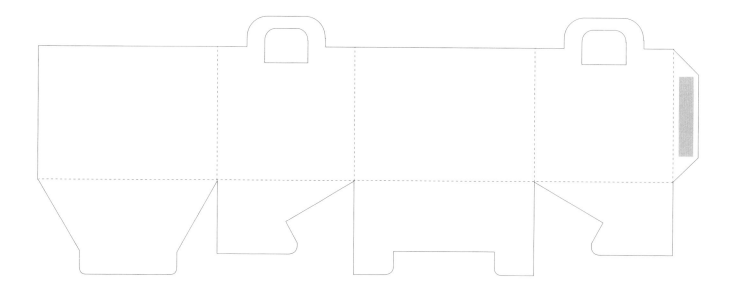

Box handle and die cut lid • Boîte ajourée avec couvercle et poignées • Box mit Deckel und Tragegriffen • Caja con asas y tapa troquelada • Scatola con maniglie e coperchio e fustellato • Caixa com asas e tampa cunhada • Gestanste doos, met deksel en handgrepen

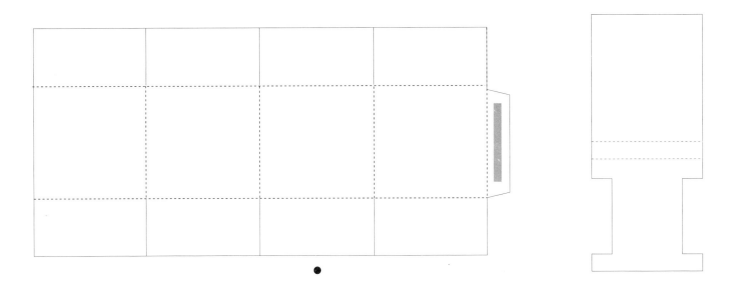

Box for wires with separating panels • Boîte pour câbles avec plaques de séparation • Kabelbox • Caja para cables, con planchas separadoras • Scatola per cavi elettrici con piastre separatrici • Caixa para cabos com placas separadoras • Doos voor snoeren met sorteerschotten

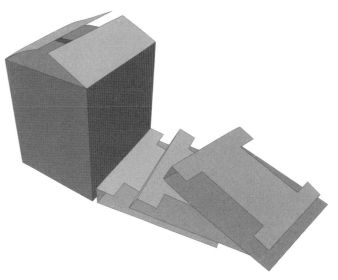

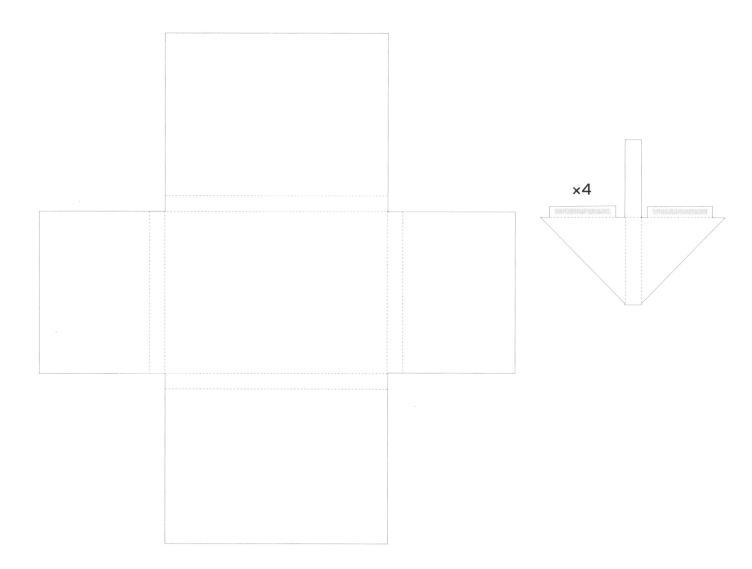

Box for paintings. Model 1 • Boîte à cahiers. Modèle 1 • Box für Bilder. Modell 1 • Caja para cuadros. Modelo 1 • Scatola per quadri. Modello 1 • Caixa para quadros. Modelo 1 • Doos voor schetsen. Model 1

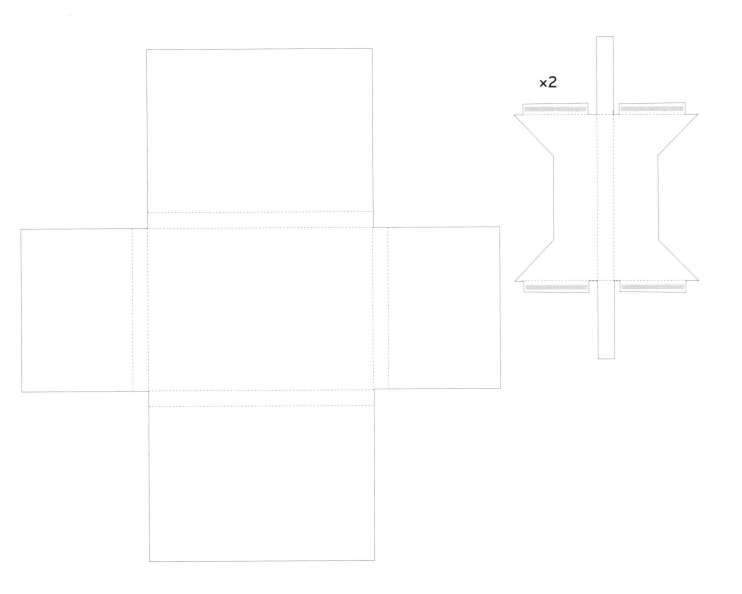

×2

Box for paintings. Model 2 · Boîte à cahiers. Modèle 2 · Box für Bilder. Modell 2 · Caja para cuadros. Modelo 2 · Scatola per quadri. Modello 2 · Caixa para quadros. Modelo 2 · Doos voor schetsen. Model 2

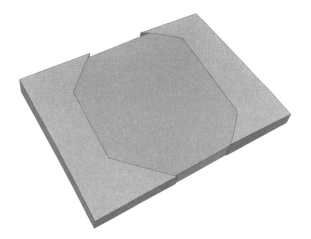

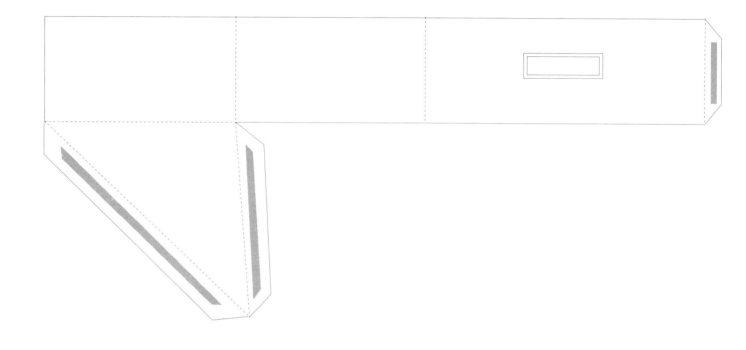

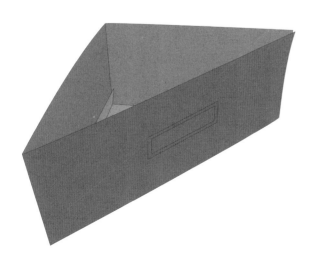

Triangular box for corners • Boîte triangulaire pour coins • Dreieckige Box • Caja triangular para esquinas • Scatola triangolare per angoli • Caixa triangular para cantos • Driehoekige doos voor in de hoek

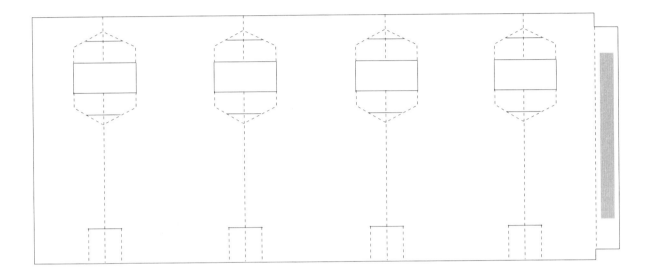

Box for bulbs • Boîte à ampoules • Box für Glühbirnen • Caja para bombillas • Scatola per lampadine • Caixa para lâmpadas • Doos voor gloeilampen

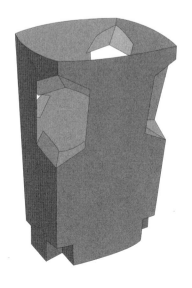

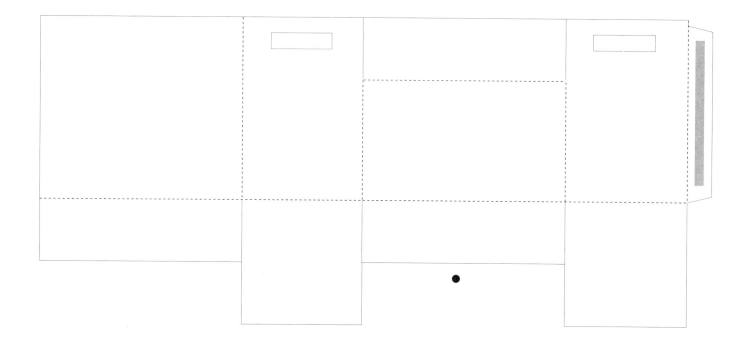

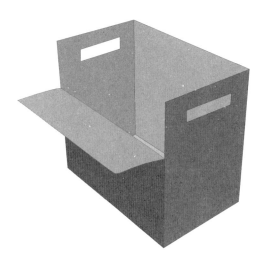

Bow with die cut handle and lift up side • Boîte avec poignée évidée et un côté basculable • Box mit Griffen und einer klappbaren Seite • Caja con asa troquelada y un lado basculante • Scatola fustellata con maniglia e un lato basculante • Caixa com asa cunhada e um lado móvel • Doos met gestanste handgrepen en een kantelzijde

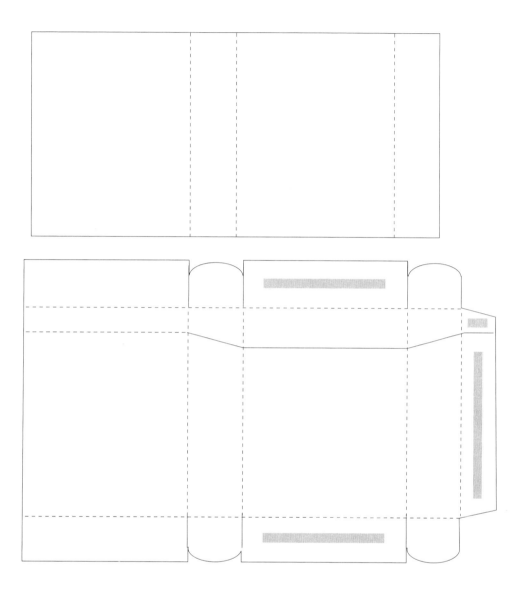

Classic cigarette box • Étui à cigarettes classique • Klassische Zigarettenbox • Caja clásica para cigarrillos • Scatola classica per sigarette • Caixa clássica para cigarros • Klassieke doos voor sigaartjes

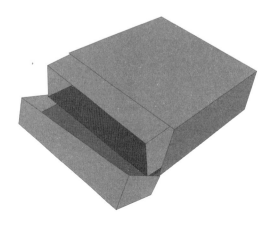

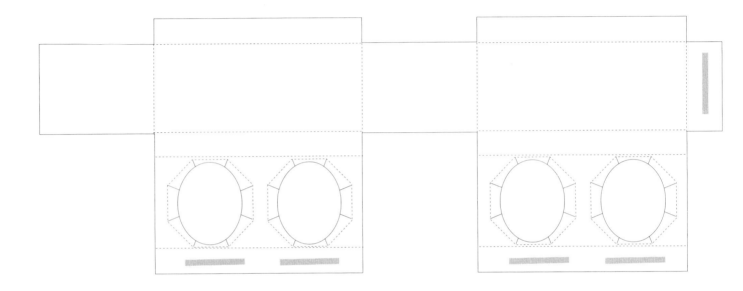

Box for glasses with dividers • Casier pour verres • Schachtel mit Halterungen für Gläser • Caja para vasos, con separadores • Scatola per bicchieri con divisori • Caixa para copos com separadores • Doos voor glazen, met houders

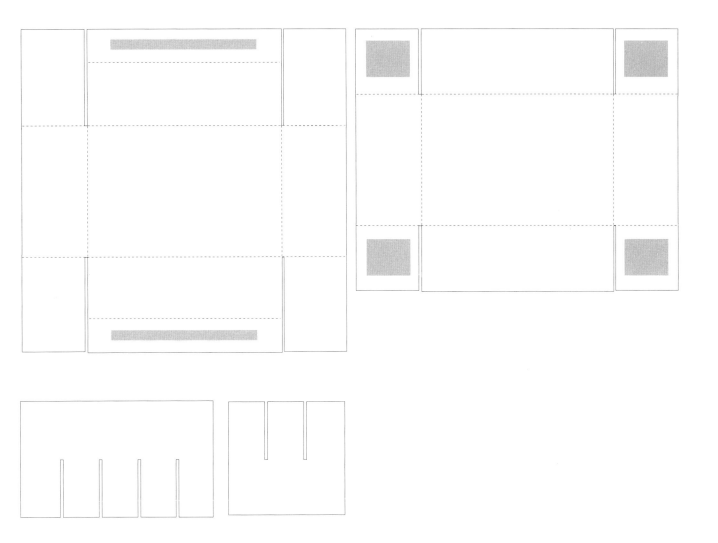

Box for wine glasses with dividers • Casier pour verres à vin • Schachtel mit Einsatz für Weingläser • Caja para copas, con separadores • Scatola per calici con divisori • Caixa para taças com separadores • Doos voor wijnglazen, met verdeelvakjes

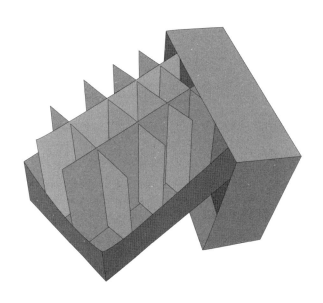

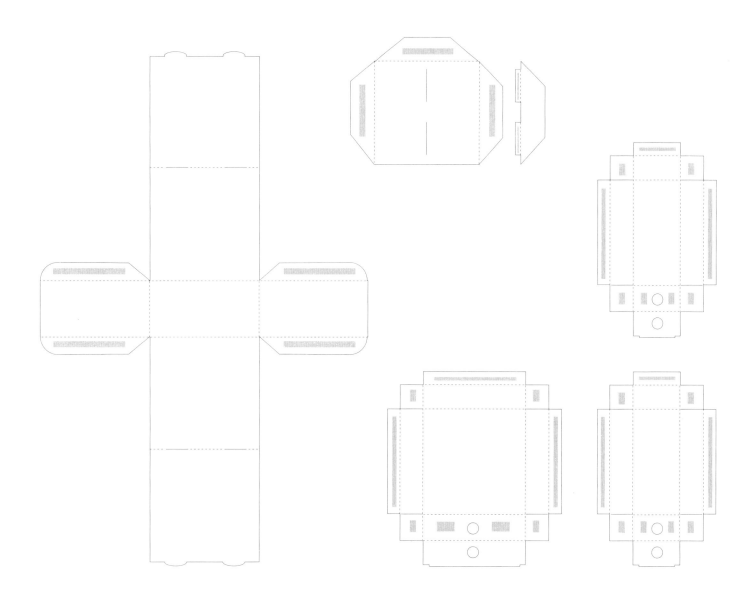

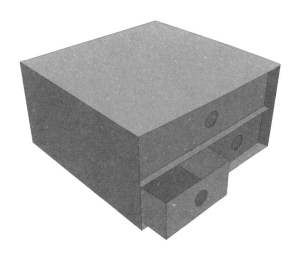

Three drawer box • Boîte avec trois tiroirs • Box mit drei Schubladen • Caja con tres cajones • Scatola con tre cassetti • Caixa com três gavetas • Doos met drie lades

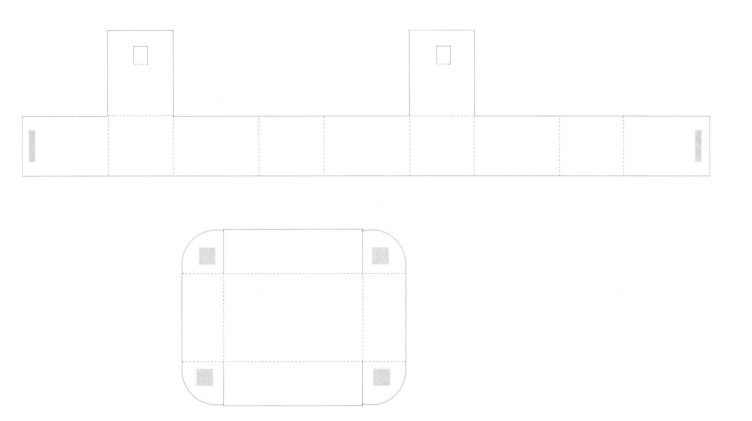

Two drawer box with wing · Boîte avec deux tiroirs et aileron · Box mit zwei Schubladen und Grifflasche · Caja con dos cajones y aleta · Scatola con due cassetti e aletta · Caixa com duas gavetas e asa · Doos met twee lades en flapje

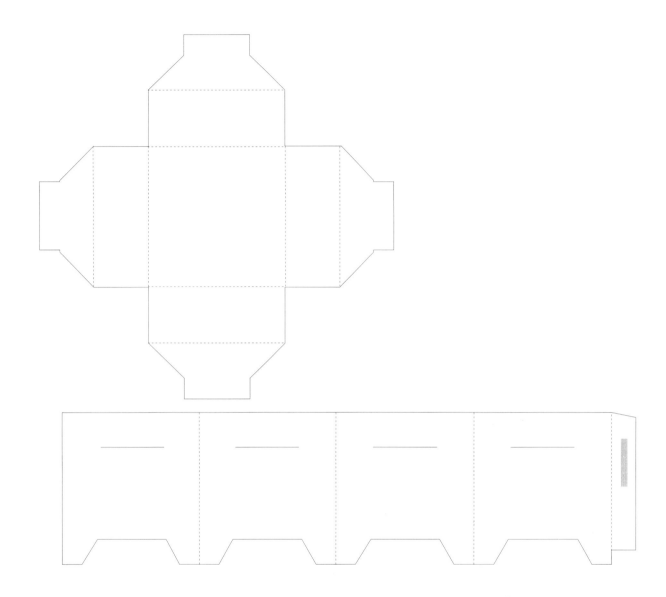

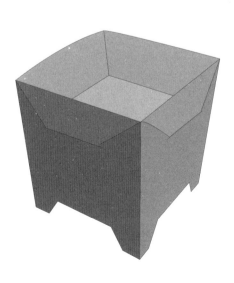

Box with inclined legs • Boîte avec pattes inclinées • Box mit abgeschrägten Füßen • Caja con patas inclinadas • Scatola con piedini inclinati • Caixa com pés inclinados • Doos met pootjes

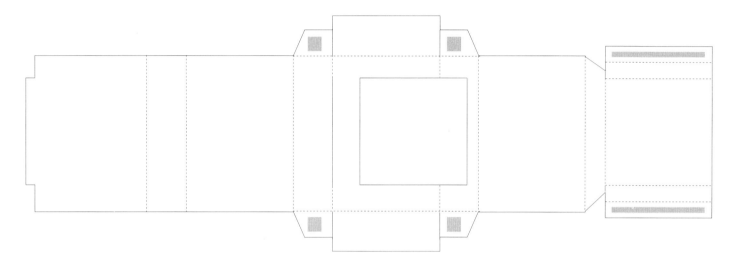

Box with lid and interior separator • Boîte avec couvercle et intercalaire • Box mit Deckel und Innenunterteilung • Caja con tapa y separador interior • Scatola con coperchio e separatore interno • Caixa com tampa e separador interior • Doos met deksel en houder

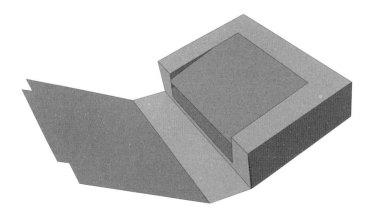